Child Care and Corporate Productivity

Resolving Family/Work Conflicts

John P. Fernandez
American Telephone and
Telegraph Company

Lexington Books
D.C. Heath and Company/Lexington, Massachusetts/Toronto

Library of Congress Cataloging-in-Publication Data

Main entry under title:

Fernandez, John P., 1941–
    Child care and corporate productivity.

    Bibliography: p.
    Includes index.
    1. Work and family—United States. 2. Industrial productivity—United States. 3. Children of working parents—United States. 4. Day care centers and industry—United States. I. Title.
HD4904.25.F47 1986   331.25   85-40022
ISBN 0-669-10335-7 (alk. paper)

Published simultaneously in Canada
Printed in the United States of America
International Standard Book Number: 0-669-10335-7
Library of Congress Catalog Card Number: 85-40022

The paper used in this publication meets the minimum requirements of American National Standard for Information Sciences—Permanence of Paper for Printed Library Materials, ANSI Z39.48–1984.
⊗ ™

The last numbers on the right below indicate the number and date of printing.

10 9 8 7 6 5 4 3 2 1

95 94 93 92 91 90 89 88 87 86 85

This book is dedicated to Maureen T. McGinley, who has greatly influenced my life.

Contents

Figures and Tables

Figures

Tables

Preface

As it becomes increasingly apparent that the United States is losing its world economic dominance, corporations are beginning to look for ways to increase efficiency and productivity. Some of the means being undertaken toward this end are the modernization of plants and better utilization and development of the work force. My previous book, *Racism and Sexism in Corporate Life: Changing Values in American Business,* clearly demonstrated that corporate America has not made great strides in fully utilizing employees who are women and people of color. Comments from the vast majority of the employees surveyed pointed out that racism and sexism are alive and well in corporate America. Once again, in the words of the employees who participated in the survey on which this book is based, we see the evil of sexism manifesting itself in the reluctance of corporate executives to deal constructively with child care problems and family/work conflicts that are literally short-circuiting the productive potential of their companies.

While increasing numbers of men, for a whole host of reasons, are becoming more involved with child care and family responsibilities, these are still seen primarily as women's issues. And, because of this point of view, most corporate executives refuse to believe that their companies should become involved in these areas. Many male executives have never had to deal on a personal level with the everyday problems of child care. Further, many of them cling to the obsolete notion that a woman's place—particularly if she is a mother—is at home, not in the workplace.

Whether women should work and whether men should share in the responsibilities of parenting and household chores are no longer hypothetical issues. The fact is that women, in rapidly increasing numbers, are working, most of them in jobs as stressful and as demanding as those held by men. Another fact is that increasing numbers of men are married to women who are pursuing full-time, permanent careers, and these men are finding that in order to survive, a dual-career marriage *must* involve a sharing of family responsibilities. Finally, as the ranks of single parents—both male and female—expand, men as well as women must engage in the balancing act of working full-time on the job and also at home.

Corporations whose executives ignore the realities of today's work force will pay dearly for their recalcitrance in terms of diminished productivity, competitive disadvantage, and, ultimately, reduced profits. The clock will not turn back (and for all the reasons set forth in *Racism and Sexism in Corporate Life,* it should not be turned back).

Just as modernizing a plant and adopting new technologies are seen as evidences of progressive management, instituting measures such as those suggested in the second part of this book to alleviate employees' child care and family/work problems is a wise investment that pays huge dividends in reduced absenteeism, tardiness, and turnover; lowered stress levels; and increased productivity.

I hope that corporate executives who read this book will find new insights into their own employees' problems through the replies of over 5,000 survey respondents, and at least several appropriate ways to address those problems. This book is also directed toward helping government officials and students of business and the family to better understand child care problems and family/work conflicts.

Finally, I hope that readers who are wrestling with the burdens of single parenthood or of balancing dual careers will come to see themselves as part of a much larger problem that can be resolved through a partnership between management and employees—a partnership that can be mutually profitable and rewarding.

Acknowledgments

Sincerity needs no embellishment.

I am, quite simply, enormously grateful to a number of individuals who made this book better than it would have been without their involvement.

Foremost among these are the company coordinators and advisors at the corporations that participated in the survey which made this book possible. In order to preserve the anonymity of the companies, these individuals must, unfortunately, also remain nameless, but I would be remiss if I did not mention that all of them went beyond their normal duties to make the survey and this book a success.

Peggy Albert, who combined her professional editing talent with newly acquired word-processing skills to keep the manuscript on track through its many revisions, greatly influenced the analyses of all data and the basic direction of the book.

Dr. David Nasatir, Noelle Beerman, and Ellen Galinsky not only assisted me in using and avoiding the misuse of statistics but also contributed significantly to the content of the book.

Clark Kerr, Ann Nelson, Sara Abraham, Barbi Kelly, Vicky Banach, Mary Callery, and Maureen Locke, among many others, provided very helpful editorial suggestions as well as substantial changes throughout the stages of manuscript preparation.

Again I am grateful to Philip Hallen, president of the Maurice Falk Medical Fund, who supported my previous book, *Racism and Sexism in Corporate Life,* and who contributed financial assistance in the preparation of this manuscript.

Finally, my special thanks to Michele, Eleni, and Sevgi, who, for the third time, patiently tolerated their father's ups and downs while he was writing a book.

Part I
Child Care and Family/Work Problems

1
Overview

The Problems: Vignettes

A 39-year-old, white, female upper–middle-level manager who had a 3-year-old child and a husband employed as an upper-level executive in an insurance company commented:

> I waited quite a while to have a baby, because I did not want the child to interfere with my career. However, I have found the balancing of my work and family responsibilities somewhat difficult even though we have a maid and child care sitter five days a week. I feel guilty that I don't spend enough time with my child, especially when she is sick. I also don't feel my husband does his share.

A single, 33-year-old, black craftswoman who had three children, aged 13, 9, and 5, said:

> I don't know if I could still be working if it were not for my mother and grandmother. They have always been there to watch the kids after school and when they are sick. I still have to come home, cook, clean house, and do all of those things. I think I am perpetually tired, both at work and at home.

A 50-year-old, white, male upper-level executive with three children, aged 22, 19, and 16, stated:

> I have never had any child care or parenting problems. My wife has never worked. Her role was to raise the kids and take care of the home. My role was to earn the money.

A 30-year-old, Hispanic, male lower-level manager with four children—10, 7, and 4-year-old twins—said:

> My wife stayed home when we had our first two kids, but after our twins were born, we both recognized that my income would not sustain our life-style unless she worked. Not only were four kids expensive, but inflation was killing us. We are fortunate that we found an excellent and reasonably priced day care center run at our church. My wife's parents live nearby and help out when we run into problems like a sick child or overtime.

A 29-year-old, white, female lower-level manager whose husband was a craftsman in the same company she works in said:

My husband is a male chauvinist pig. He expects me to work all day, cook, clean, shop, etc., and all he does when he comes home is sit down in front of the TV. I really feel guilty about leaving my 2-year-old with the woman who watches him and three other young children, but I have no alternative. My boss has been mad at me because I have missed work three times in the past six months in order to watch my child when he was sick. The sitter would not take him. I tried to get my husband to alternate with me, but he will have none of it. He has been especially hard to deal with since I got promoted into management. At times the stress makes me want to quit.

A 38-year-old black male in middle management with children aged 10, 17, and 18 described his situation in this way:

My wife is a schoolteacher, so we have it somewhat easier than other folks with kids. In the summers she is always home during their vacations. When the 10-year-old gets sick, either my wife or I will stay home with him. When the other kids were young, we also shared in this task.

A 34-year-old, white, male middle-level manager wrote:

My wife and I try to share everything—the household chores, the child-raising, the stress at work and at home. Our two children (7 and 9) are very responsible and try to help out at home. After school they go to a community center two days a week, and the other three days they are watched by our next-door neighbor, who doesn't work.

A single, white, female lower–middle-level manager with an 8-year-old boy commented:

I have problems with my child care provider when it comes to working overtime. She also is reluctant to watch my child when I must travel overnight. My ex-husband helps out sometimes, but he is not dependable.

A single, white, male lower–middle-level manager who had two children, aged 10 and 13, expressed concerns shared by many parents, both single and with partners:

I have a difficult time balancing the scheduling of my work and family responsibilities. This corporation is more sensitive to women's problems in balancing dual roles than to men's—especially single men. My kids get on me a lot about not making school events. Sometimes they have to see the doctor on their own. He is near our home, but they don't like doctors. Fortunately, my present boss understands that I might be late or leave early because of family responsibilities, but that hasn't always been the case.

A married, white, female lower–middle-level manager who had three teenagers, aged 15, 17, and 19, in addition to a 23-year-old, wrote:

I have always worked. When my children were young, I was made to feel guilty by my family (not my husband) for abandoning my children. They all went to our church day care center, which was excellent. However, I was guilt-ridden about not being a good mother. Sometimes I believe it affected my career, because most of my bosses were men and they felt women should be home with their kids like their wives were. I used to miss work on occasion because of my children's needs.

Finally, a white, female middle-level manager who had no children vividly described the circumstances of most working women with or without children under 18:

I have no children, but I can sympathize with my peers who do. My job is extremely demanding—long hours, tight time frames, increasing spans of control, tremendous pressure. My husband has a similar high-pressure job, but he expects me to do everything at home. He has one full-time job. I have two!

These comments illustrate the child care and family/work problems facing employees in today's heterogeneous work force. With the possible exception of those men, chiefly at the management level, whose wives stay at home and assume full responsibility for the children, the picture bears little resemblance to the blissful middle-America life-style one sees in old Dagwood and Blondie comic strips. Today's Dagwood, for the most part, has much more on his mind than satisfying Mr. Dithers, and in 1985, Blondie herself is dashing out the door to catch the bus to work with at least one child in tow, to be dropped at a sitter's before she punches in for a full day's work.

Indeed, many of the families whose lives were observed in a survey of 5,000 workers in five major corporations differ significantly from the Bumstead household. In terms of the demography of America in 1985, however, they are representative. Nearly half of the respondents were women. Of those employees with children 18 and under, 22 percent of the women, compared to only 3 percent of the men, were single parents. Among two-parent households with children 18 and under, nearly 90 percent of the women and nearly 60 percent of the men had working spouses.

Although some dual-career families had developed sharing roles that eased, to some extent, the stress of balancing home and work responsibilities, most of the women (married or single), as well as the single men, were shouldering the primary responsibility for family life and child care. Their responses reflect both the stress placed on family relationships as a result of this balancing act and the toll it takes in terms of productivity in the workplace—a hidden cost that represents a steadily growing drain on the corporate "battery." As the data gathered in our survey indicate, wise managers may find that a relatively small investment in supporting employees' child care, directly or indirectly, will pay large dividends in increased productivity.

A Brief History of Women's Participation in the Work Force

While it is true that women have been joining the active work force in increasing numbers over the past two decades, the vast majority of women have always worked; only the location and conditions of their labor have varied.

A brief review of women's participation in the work force will demonstrate that they have played a crucial role in the economy and that they are, indeed, capable of performing far more than menial tasks within the home. Prior to the industrial revolution, little differentiation existed between men's work and women's work. Most jobs were performed by both men and women, and members of the family *had* to work. "No work was too hard, no labor too strenuous to exclude women. Among the masses of people emerging from serfdom and existing in terrible poverty, the family was an economic unit in which men, women, and children worked in order to survive."[1]

The industrial revolution rang the death knell for the cottage industries that had provided a preferred work location for women, who were expected both to raise children and produce marketable products.[2] It concentrated labor in urban work centers and led to working circumstances not much different from those of serfdom. Women and children as young as age 6 were forced to work fourteen-hour days, seven days a week, in factories, sweatshops, and mines, for less than subsistence wages. Heating, lighting, and ventilation were inadequate, if not totally lacking. Anyone who missed a day's work for illness or any other reason was automatically fired.[3]

In his 1906 revelation of the inhuman working conditions imposed on women in Chicago's meat-packing industry, Upton Sinclair described the women standing all day long, ankle-deep in briny water, freezing in the winter and sweltering in the summer.[4] At this time women were needed in the factories, and no one suggested that women's working had a detrimental effect on their children. In fact, some experts claimed that a mother who was *too* available and *too* caring could actually harm her children's development. For an excellent review of the pros and cons of child care in general, see S. Scarr's *Mothers Care, Others Care.*

The emergence of a middle class in which men could support their families single-handedly was a by-product of the industrial revolution, and along with the middle class came some notions that to some extent remain with us today. These notions, legitimized by the experts of the day, included the beliefs that the role of a man, if he was a "real" man, was to work and support his family, and that the proper role for a woman was to stay home and nurture, feed, and care for that family. Most devastating of all the theories that emerged along with the middle class was the newly held conviction that women who chose to work were doing so at the expense of their children's development and psyches. Those women who defied society's rules and insisted on working were considered, at best, to be out of step with the mainstream of American thinking and, at worst, to be psychologically unbalanced.

In homes where the need for a second wage earner no longer existed and where new technology was reducing housekeeping chores to a minimum, women found themselves able to pursue other, albeit closely circumscribed, endeavors. Volunteer work for charities and the church was acceptable only because it supported and reinforced a woman's "natural" role as the nurturing force.

At the same time the industrial revolution was creating a middle class, it was also creating a multitude of jobs for women in offices and factories—jobs that were held, for the most part, by minority and immigrant women. These were considered jobs, not careers, because for the middle class and an increasing number of blue-collar wives, the work was assumed to be temporary—a short-term effort to meet an emergency need for funds or to establish a nest egg for the future. Despite the reality that working would not be temporary for the vast majority of these women, and particularly for the immigrants and minorities, women were discouraged from thinking about careers. Considered temporary or part-time workers, they were made to understand that they were not to press for advancement, equal pay, or men's jobs.

Throughout history, indeed, men have called the shots in the workplace. They have determined when women could work and what work they could do, and they have defined women's work as largely those positions that men, owing to social class, education, or a national priority such as war, were either unwilling or unable to fill.[5] Dramatic evidence of this pattern occurred during the Great Depression and later during World War II.

When unemployment hit record peaks during the depression of 1932, female workers, along with racial minorities, were the first to be fired or laid off. Strenuous efforts were made to circumscribe the work of women, who appeared to be depriving the male heads of household of their livelihoods. Women were still welcome to work in specified, low-paying fields, but any woman presuming to compete for a man's job was met with hostility and resentment. Government policy during the depression was to "get the *man* [italics mine] back to work." In 1932, a "married persons" clause for federal and civil service workers specified that the first employees dismissed during personnel reductions were to be those who had spouses holding another federal position. Three-quarters of employees dismissed under this act were women, even though the law did not specify that it was the husband who was to retain his job. Under the New Deal, men received preference for Works Progress Administration (WPA) jobs, and single women, some lacking all other resources, were consigned to the bottom of the list.[6]

World War II forced a complete reversal of this attitude with Rosie the Riveter emerging as a patriotic folk heroine. Women poured into the labor force and proved themselves competent laborers in many areas heretofore restricted to men. The nation had little choice; women were needed to fill both women's and men's jobs. In steel mills, women were found pounding typewriters in the offices *and* rolling steel next to the furnaces. These jobs were clearly only temporary, having been brought about because of an emergency, but women were encouraged by the government to take them.

At the war's end, the tune changed. Women were urged to go back home in order to make room in the labor force for the returning veterans. Employers were surprised to find that many women preferred to retain their jobs, even though they were often demoted from their wartime positions. Women were developing a new ethic, a new self-worth, and a new independence.[7]

In 1940, only 9 percent of the women with school-age children were working. By 1948, that figure had more than doubled to 20 percent, and by 1972, the figure was 50 percent. In 1982, 65 percent of women with children under age 18 were working. The most dramatic rise was among working women with preschool children: In 1948, 10 percent of these women were working. By 1960, the figure had risen to 19 percent; by 1971, to 30 percent;[8] and by 1982, to 50 percent.

In the work history of the United States, a larger proportion of immigrant women and women of color than of white American-born women has been employed, primarily out of financial necessity. As early as 1890, 36 percent of black women, compared to 14 percent of white women, worked outside the home. In 1930, the figures were 39 percent for blacks and 20 percent for whites. By 1948, the numbers had jumped to 46 percent and 31 percent, respectively;[9] and figures for 1983 showed that 71 percent of black women were working, compared to 64 percent of white women, and that employed black mothers were more likely than their white counterparts to work full-time.[10]

There is no indication that the number of working women will subside. On the contrary, for many reasons, these numbers, particularly for those who hold full-time jobs, will continue to grow at a rapid rate in the coming decades. The increasing independence of women is creating the desire to work for personal satisfaction rather than because of financial necessity alone. Men and women surveyed in the 1981 *General Mills American Family Report* supported this notion. Asked what reasons were important to their working, 90 percent of the men and 87 percent of the women listed a "personal sense of accomplishment." The second most often cited reason both for men and women was "helping to make ends meet," followed by "improving the family's standard of living."[11] The rising divorce rate, along with the liberalization of divorce laws and reduction in alimony and child support awards, is causing more women who are single parents to enter the work force. Further, the small but growing number of employers who are willing to offer flexible work options (such as permanent part-time work and job-sharing) are making it easier for many women, and a growing number of men, to balance their personal and work lives.

The ever-increasing number of working women will have a significant impact not only on public attitudes toward themselves but also on their own children, particularly their daughters, who will comprise an even larger portion of tomorrow's work force. Social scientists agree that a daughter's occupational location is affected by whether her mother works outside the home and by her mother's choice of occupation.[12] Since a majority of the undergraduate college enrollment is women and since increasingly large numbers of women are attending graduate schools in business, law, and other professions, the next decades will show an accelerated increase of daughters entering similar occupations. Regardless of what impels women to work, they are a major component of today's work force, and they will continue to be so, particularly as the baby boom moves through the occupational structure, leaving more vacancies for younger entrants than there will be individuals to fill them.

Whether women in a family work also affects the attitudes of the men in the household, but the male perspective on women in the workplace has changed much more slowly than have women's attitudes toward work and careers. Slowest to change are those men whose wives and/or daughters do not work outside the home. These men find it difficult to adjust to the presence of female managers, especially high-level female managers; they can conceptualize and accept women only in subservient roles. Any other perspective creates tremendous conflicts for them. Because they believe that their wives, mothers, and daughters are happy in subordinate roles, these men do not understand the growing number of women who refuse to be subservient and who want to move up the corporate ladder, often into nontraditional jobs.[13]

America's executives, on the whole, are representatives of this psychological profile. The implications of this are profound, considering the need for corporations to move decisively and constructively toward dealing with child care problems and family/work conflicts. It has been estimated that only about 2,000 out of more than 6 million employers currently offer any type of child care assistance to their employees. This reality notwithstanding, the increasingly permanent participation of women in the U.S. work force has endowed child care and parenting issues with a seriousness not previously accorded them in societal, governmental, and corporate discussions. The question of woman's role in society (and, by extension, child care and family/work issues) is far from resolved. The United States—unlike Sweden, West Germany, France, China, and Hungary, among others—has made no clear, formal, national commitment to assist employers in dealing with these concerns. Scarr has observed that the conflicts and guilt most American women deal with today are societal problems, not individual problems. She has argued that the dilemmas facing American women are the result of "a mismatch between the current realities of family life and ideas about mothers and children that suited [earlier decades]." She writes further that child care issues "are hostage to the active but indirect battles between the sexes over woman's proper role in society."[14]

Even as these battles rage, more and more corporate executives are beginning to see that women are important, vital, and integral members of their organizations. They are starting to realize that productivity and organizational efficiency could be greatly increased if their companies were to help employees deal with their child care and family/work problems. They believe these issues are costing their companies a great deal of money because of the amount of productive work time that is lost to high turnover, absenteeism, tardiness, family stress, and work stress.

These corporate executives are not changing on their own. The federal government and some states have decided that child care and family/work conflicts related to the changing make-up of the work force are important societal issues that should at least be discussed in a serious manner. There is also an incipient recognition that if this country is to remain a dominant force in the competitive world market, the full participation of women in the work force will be essential.

In the fall of 1984, Representative George Miller, liberal Democrat from California and chairperson of the Select Committee on Children, Youth, and Families, and Dan Marriott, conservative Mormon Republican from Utah, joined forces to urge the U.S. House of Representatives to boost federal tax breaks for child care significantly as an incentive for schools and employees to assist working parents in providing proper child care. The committee's recommendation came about not because all committee members believed that women should work but because all of them agreed on the inescapable conclusion that women are and will remain an ever-increasing part of the work force; and having thus agreed, they recognized that good child care for working parents is absolutely necessary to our nation's economic survival. Whether this recommendation will pass the Congress is still in question.

Arizona's Governor Bruce E. Babbitt devoted his 1984 State of the State address to children's issues. Among his recommendations were the creation of incentives for school districts to establish before- and after-school programs for children of working parents; increased spending on prenatal and postpartum care programs; child immunization and dental health care; encouragement of school districts to extend the kindergarten day; and additional spending to improve educational programs from kindergarten through third grade.

In the state of New Jersey, numerous bills have been introduced to deal with child care issues. One such bill would provide a tax credit against the Corporation Business Tax Act of 1945 for employers who have established child care centers for the children of their employees. Another bill would exempt property used in the operation of certain child care centers from the assessment of real estate taxes.

Whether the state legislatures or the U.S. Congress will pass any of these proposals is unclear. The important point is that the issues are at least being given serious consideration. Such data as those contained in these pages should provide convincing evidence to corporate and governmental leaders that helping employees deal with family/work conflicts and child care issues is a win/win proposition for all concerned: employees, children, employers, the economy, the government, and society as a whole.

The Study

Participants

Five large, technically oriented companies participated in the study. All of them have recognized the need to address the issues of child care/parenting and family/work problems. A total of 7,000 management and crafts employees were mailed questionnaires in March of 1984. A census was taken of middle- and upper-level managers, and random samples of lower-level managers and crafts employees.

Race, Gender, and Occupational Level. Of about 5,000 employees who returned the questionnaires, 4,971 provided all the information requested on race, gender, and occupational level. Crafts employees represented 41 percent of the survey participants. Women comprised 63 percent of the total craft sample and 40 percent of the management sample. People of color represented only 9 percent of the total sample. Table 1-1 gives the race, gender, and

Table 1-1
Study Participants

	Blacks		Others[a]		Whites		
	Women	Men	Women	Men	Women	Men	Total
Craftsworkers	118	41	77	47	1,094	684	2,061
Lower-level managers	39	22	18	22	740	975	1,816
Lower–middle-level managers	11	12	6	2	258	556	845
Middle-level managers	3	3	0	0	14	146	166
Upper–middle-level managers	0	1	0	0	7	48	56
Upper-level managers	0	1	0	0	1	25	27
Total	171	80	101	71	2,114	2,434	4,971

[a]Others include those who indicated they are Hispanic, native American, or Asian.

occupational level breakdown of those who returned the questionnaire and supplied all requested information.

Age. As tables 1-2 and 1-3 show, white female respondents were generally older than women of color, while white male managers represented by far the oldest overall race/gender group. Blacks and other people of color were quite similar in age, and we will see in forthcoming chapters that age had a great influence on employees' responses to the survey.

Family Characteristics. Out of the total sample, a substantial proportion of the employees were single, particularly among the women and among blacks of both sexes. More than half (52 percent) of the black women, 38 percent of the other women of color, and 33 percent of the white women were single. Of the men, 28 percent of the blacks, 23 percent of the other men of color, and 11 percent of the whites were single.

Eighty-five to 90 percent of the mates of *all* participating women were employed, compared to lower percentages for the mates of black men (72 percent), white men (60 percent), and other men of color (52 percent). Note that although 91 to 100 percent of the women's mates (depending on race) were employed full-time, only 60 percent of the white men, 71 percent of the other

Table 1-2
Age of Female Participants
(percentages)

Years	Blacks		Others		Whites	
	Craftsworkers (N = 123)	Managers (N = 53)	Craftsworkers (N = 80)	Managers (N = 24)	Craftsworkers (N = 1,114)	Managers (N = 1,020)
30 and under	26	11	31	17	26	11
31 to 40	46	64	39	58	36	54
41 to 50	20	21	23	21	21	25
Over 50	8	4	8	4	16	10

Table 1-3
Age of Male Participants
(percentages)

Years	Blacks		Others		Whites	
	Craftsworkers (N = 42)	Managers (N = 39)	Craftsworkers (N = 49)	Managers (N = 24)	Craftsworkers (N = 697)	Managers (N = 1,748)
30 and under	17	15	20	13	17	4
31 to 40	57	46	61	54	45	35
41 to 50	5	31	14	25	19	38
Over 50	21	8	4	8	19	23

Table 1-4
Number of Children—Female Participants
(percentages)

Number of Children	Blacks		Others		Whites	
	Craftsworkers (N = 116)	Managers (N = 51)	Craftsworkers (N = 79)	Managers (N = 24)	Craftsworkers (N = 1,097)	Managers (N = 1,012)
0	31	35	29	29	47	53
1 to 3	66	65	66	70	53	47
4 to 6	3	0	4	0	1	0
Over 6	0	0	1	0	0	0

Table 1-5
Number of Children—Male Participants
(percentages)

Number of Children	Blacks		Others		Whites	
	Craftsworkers (N = 39)	Managers (N = 38)	Craftsworkers (N = 48)	Managers (N = 24)	Craftsworkers (N = 676)	Managers (N = 1,734)
0	49	34	17	33	38	37
1 to 3	49	63	69	54	59	59
4 to 6	2	2	13	12	4	4
Over 6	0	0	0	0	0	0

men of color, and 81 percent of the black men had spouses who were employed full-time. Ninety-two percent of the women and 59 percent of the men with children 18 and under had both partners working. Finally, 96 percent of the women, regardless of parenthood status, had husbands who were employed full-time; but 70 percent of the men with *no* children under 18, compared to 56 percent with children 18 and under, had both partners working full-time.

The higher percentage of black wives who work full-time compared to white wives who work full-time supports previous comments that black women have a much higher full-time work participation rate than do white women. H. Hayghe noted that historically black wives have a higher employment participation rate than wives in other racial groups. He wrote that in 1980 55 percent of black married couples (compared to about 50 percent of white and Hispanic couples) were dual-career families. He also noted, and census data confirm, that the gap between the figures for full-time work for black and white wives has closed rapidly in the past twenty years.[15]

With regard to the participants' children, white female workers were much less likely to have children 18 and under than were women of color. For example, 50 percent of the white women, compared to 29 percent of the other women of color, excluding blacks, had no children 18 and under. Black craftsmen were least likely to have children 18 and under, and other men of color in crafts positions were most likely to have children 18 and under. Tables 1-4 and 1-5 show number of children of participants.

Research Instrument

The data were collected through a self-administered, mailed questionnaire that had both multiple-choice questions and open-ended questions to which participants were able to give their own responses. Thus, both quantitative statistical data and qualitative individual comments were solicited to achieve a better understanding of employees' feelings, beliefs, and attitudes. All questionnaires were reviewed in order to eliminate improper responses (such as replying to questions one should have skipped or giving more than one response to a question that required only one). As noted earlier, the response rate was approximately 71 percent, or 5,000 out of 7,000 employees.

The content of the questionnaire was determined from several sources, including the following: reports requested by the five companies from groups of employees, in which the employees listed issues they believed were crucial for their corporations to face in the next five years; extensive open-ended interviews conducted with the employees of the companies and with working people from other companies; comments on the questionnaire from child care and parenting consultants; and the literature on child care and family/work issues. The questionnaire included these ten major sections:

Perceptions of the effects of child care on children

Child care and corporate productivity issues

What companies should do to assist employees with family/work conflicts and child care problems

You and your work

Training for working parents

Biographical information

Child care problems of parents with children 18 and under

Most important form of child care employees use

Second most important form of child care employees use

Summary of Major Findings

A significant majority of the employees (67 percent) agreed that child care problems exact a high price in unproductive use of employees' minds and time. Some of the data that emerged in support of this perception were as follows:

Among employees with children 18 and under, 77 percent of the women and 73 percent of the men had dealt with family issues during working hours.

Forty-eight percent of the women and 25 percent of the men had spent unproductive time at work because of child care issues.

Instances of missed days at work, tardiness, leaving work early, and dealing with family issues during working hours were highly positively correlated with employees' difficulties in coping with child care and handling dual family/work roles.

Another major finding in the survey was that women shouldered a much greater burden with regard to child care problems than men did. The following data pertaining to parents with children 18 and under illustrate this point:

Forty-five percent of the women, compared to 17 percent of the men, indicated that providing care for a sick child was at least somewhat of a problem.

Thirty-nine percent of the women and 24 percent of the men said that attending a school conference or program during working hours was at least somewhat of a problem.

Overall, with regard to fifteen family/work and child care issues, only 27 percent of the women, compared to 58 percent of the men, had *no* problem.

The questionnaires also documented the fact that women dealt with more family responsibilities than men, with the result that women experienced greater stress both at home and at work (which ultimately reduces productivity). For those employees with children 18 and under:

Thirty-nine percent of the women, compared to 13 percent of the men, believed that handling dual family/work roles was more than a minimal problem.

Thirty-seven percent of the women, compared to 16 percent of the men, felt that handling dual roles created stress on the job at least to some extent.

Forty-three percent of the women, compared to only 22 percent of the men, said that balancing work and family roles created stress at home.

A fourth important finding is that a very high percentage of employees, regardless of background, believed that corporations should be involved in financially assisting employees with child care problems, providing flexible work options, supplying child care resource assistance, and providing training to deal with child care, dual family/work roles, and child development problems.

A brief review of key controlling variables shows that female and male craftsworkers were more likely than their management counterparts to have child care problems, to believe that companies should assist with child care, and to perceive a greater need for corporate training to help with child care problems and family/work roles.

Race had a decided impact on employees' views. Blacks, for example, were less likely than other people of color or than whites to believe that nonparental child care has a negative impact on children. Blacks were *more* likely than others of color—and the latter were much more likely than whites—to report child care problems and to believe that companies should provide resources and financial support for child care. Finally, blacks were least satisfied with their child care arrangements.

In general, black men and women responded more similarly than did other men and women of color, and the latter agreed more with each other than did white men and women on child care and family/work issues. Put another way, the most significant gender gap in responses to child care and family/work issues occurred between white men and women.

Age played a considerable role in employees' views. Older employees were less likely to have child care problems and thus were less likely to feel a need for training or to believe that companies should assist parents with child care and family/work issues.

Marital status in most cases had very little effect on female employees' responses. However, it significantly affected male responses. Single men responded very similarly to women. Most married men were operating in a world of their own, without child care responsibilities, whereas most married women were functioning as single parents.

Having children under 18 did significantly influence employees' views. Employees with younger children were more likely than those with older children to experience child care problems and stress and to express a need for corporate training, and were more likely to believe that companies should provide various forms of child care and assistance with family/work conflicts.

Attitudes about child care and parenting issues were greatly influenced by employees' sexism and stereotyping; the more sexist employees were, the more likely they were to have negative views regarding the effects of child care on children, to believe that companies should do little or nothing to assist employees with child care and family/work problems, and to feel that they required little training in child-care related issues.

The first part of this book will demonstrate that corporations are losing a great deal of money in terms of lost time due to employees' child care problems and the difficulties involved in handling the dual roles of work and family. The second part of the book will set forth the roles that employees believe corporations can play in solving these problems and the solutions with which they believe companies should become involved. Each of these latter chapters includes a critical analysis of various solutions along with recommendations to help corporations deal effectively with these crucial problems.

2
Child Care Arrangements

I f child care and family/work problems are factors in productivity, it is
important to know how working parents cope with their dual family/work
roles, what kinds of arrangements they make for the care of their children
during the workday, and how satisfied they are with those arrangements. First, a
brief review of the history of U.S. policy regarding child care is in order.

History of Child Care Policy in the United States

Industrialization, urbanization, and mandatory public schooling have had tremendous impacts on child care. As we saw in chapter 1, prior to the industrial revolution the entire family, including children, worked as an economic unit to provide
food, clothing, and basic necessities for itself. The industrial revolution changed
all that. For the first time, a single member of the family could support the entire
unit, and children—boys, in particular—freed of the responsibility to work, were
encouraged to acquire an education in order to prepare themselves for the new
industrial jobs that would allow them, in turn, to support their own families.

The industrial revolution also played a key role in the urbanization of
America. Industry required large numbers of readily available workers concentrated in relatively small areas close to the factories, and this clustering of
workers in urban centers also created a demand for service industries around
the manufacturing industries, which created a further demand for workers. The
labor shortage led to the direct recruitment not only of immigrants, blacks, and
Hispanics, which resulted in the massive migration first from abroad and then
from the plantations of the rural South and Mexico, but also of women. This, in
turn, raised a question: If mothers go to work, who will care for the children?

The seeds of nonparental child care sprouted during the industrial revolution,
but they had been planted some years earlier, in the aftermath of the Civil War.

R.F. Baxandall noted that the first non-Utopian child care centers were
developed during the period between 1840 and 1887. They were both nurseries
and kindergartens. The nurseries were basically philanthropic institutions

established first to assist the children of Civil War widows and later to serve immigrant children whose mothers worked. This type of care, Baxandall pointed out, was custodial, and wealthy women performed it. "The purpose," she continued, "was described as being to 'feed the starving, clothe the naked, enlighten the soul.'"[1]

In contrast to nurseries, the kindergarten was brought to this country by liberal Germans who believed that children should be protected from the harsh world and developed through "creative play, nature study, art and music." Many of the early kindergartens were part of settlement houses that cared for the needy. Thus, kindergarten stressed the education of children rather than the care and protection of underprivileged children, which was the focus of day nurseries.[2]

During the latter part of the nineteenth century, these nurseries and kindergartens, as well as public schools, extended their hours and purposes to address the problems of caring for children after school hours. In 1899, for example, the Cleveland Day Nursery Association began a summer program for young school-age children. During the 1920s and 1930s, the concept of play school programs, which took place after regular school hours and during summer vacations, became popular, especially in New York City. These programs focused on arts and crafts, recreational activities, and creative play, especially during times of war or economic depression.[3]

The concept of providing child care as a support for working mothers was not widespread. It was a notion embraced by only a few of the most enlightened individuals and by the most practical businessmen, who needed large numbers of women workers. These businessmen realized that child care was necessary to attract and retain women on a permanent basis. Indeed, the United States historically has been interested in child care only during periods of war or depression, and the basis for concern has nothing to do with women's liberation or with women's career goals but rather with the need, during wartime, for women to take over men's jobs in defense plants, and, during depressions, for child care centers to provide a source of jobs in a sagging economy.

It was during the Great Depression of the 1930s that federal funds were first used to finance nursery schools under the Works Progress Administration (WPA). Again, the provision of quality child care was a secondary concern; the program's primary purpose was to provide employment for teachers, professional child development experts, artists, laborers, clerical workers, nutritionists, and a host of other unemployed persons, most of them, of course, men. The result, nonetheless, was an excellent child care program that would serve as a model for future generations, and the precedent of public funding for child care provided the foundation for the Lanham Act and for the inclusion of child care services in the social services block grant program today.[4]

The Lanham Act, passed by Congress in 1941, provided 50 percent matching federal grants to states that were willing to provide day care facilities for the children of tens of thousands of women "drafted" to work in defense plants during World War II. Its implementation, under the guidance of the U.S. Children's Bureau, was carried out with less than a total commitment. Bureau officials, along with many child care professionals of that era, were at best ambivalent about the idea of women working outside the home, even on behalf of the war effort, and they certainly had no intention of encouraging the employment of women on a permanent basis; they were fearful about the message such programs might communicate to women. The government, they warned, certainly did not want to suggest that it approved of women working.[5] Still, the immediate requirements of the war effort overshadowed such concerns, and by 1945 more than 3,000 day care centers were serving over 100,000 children of working mothers.

When the war ended, popular support for the day care centers rapidly disintegrated. The men were back, and it was declared time for women to return to their domestic chores. Immediately after the war, federal funding for day care centers was withdrawn, and 95 percent of the centers were closed owing to lack of financial support. Nine years later, in 1954, a revision of the tax law allowed some working parents a small deduction for employment-related child care expenses. It was not until 1962 that the government again invested, albeit minimally, in day care centers, but even these centers were not established directly for the benefit of working mothers: they were, in essence, shelters for children whose parents were not providing proper care for them.

Two years later, Project Head Start was created under the Economic Opportunity Act—again as a remedial effort, this time to provide an educational head start to economically deprived children. At the same time, income thresholds for child care tax deductions were raised.[6]

As the Civil Rights Act of 1964 began slowly to expand employment opportunities for women, and as the women's movement began to pick up steam, increased pressure was put on Congress to develop a systematic policy for dealing with the child care/child development issue. After considerable effort and lobbying on the part of pro-child care forces, Congress did attempt in 1971 to pass the Comprehensive Development Act in order to move the country toward a more uniform policy. Created to provide services for welfare recipients, upgrade physical facilities for child care programs, broaden eligibility for tax deductions, and enrich the program content, this act would have appropriated $2 billion in fiscal 1973, $4 billion in fiscal 1974, and $7 billion in fiscal 1975. Of the first year's total appropriation, $700 million would have funded child care services for welfare recipients, $50 million was earmarked for construction of new child care facilities, and $100 million would have gone into planning and technical assistance. In addition, the income threshold for eligibility to claim child care deductions would have been doubled (from $6,000 to $12,000 annually), and plans were made to expand the Head Start program and to develop health care, nutrition, and education enrichment programs for children

Despite tremendous popular support for the bill, President Nixon vetoed it because of pressure from the Moral Majority and other conservative organizations that believed a woman's proper place is in the home.[7]

By 1975, despite years of lobbying by women's groups and their allies, this country had been able to reach a consensus only on the need to provide limited resources for the care of a relatively few poor children and to make available very limited tax deductions only for those whom the Reagan Administration would label "the truly needy." As Scarr put it, "Before 1975, some limited tax deductions were permitted to women who, the Congress believed, really needed to work. Some widows, divorcees, and mothers of handicapped children were permitted to deduct a small portion of their child care costs from their taxable earnings. For a family with an able-bodied male wage earner, however, child care costs were paid from full taxable income."[8]

In 1976, after more than fifty years of battling, Congress replaced the tax deduction with a tax credit for child care expenses and eliminated eligibility requirements based on income or marital status. It was a step in the right direction, but the credits were very low: families could claim only 20 percent of child care expenses, up to a maximum of $200 per child or $400 for two or more children. Gradually this threshold increased, first through the Economic Recovery Tax Act of 1981, which raised the amount of credit and instituted a sliding scale in order to provide greater relief for those in low-income brackets. The act allowed a maximum credit of 30 percent for families whose incomes were under $10,000 and a maximum of 20 percent for families with incomes over $28,000, and it raised the ceiling on allowable expenses to $2,000 for one child and $4,000 for two or more children. (Currently the ceiling is $2,400 and $4,800, respectively.) Exemption from taxable income for any child care subsidy provided by an employer was another feature of the act. Current tax law also provides tax benefits to employers who offer child care assistance instituted to address the problems of turnover and absenteeism.[9]

The Reagan Administration has aimed at replacing government funding of child care with support from the private sector in the form of employer-sponsored assistance. The first phase of this effort was a series of forums in cities throughout the United States targeted to stimulating corporate involvement and attended by senior executives, government officials, and community organizations. Although progress has been slow, the project is still under way and is receiving a positive response.

In 1982 both houses of Congress formed committees to look at family and child care issues, and in his 1984 State of the Union address, President Ronald Reagan briefly mentioned that the U.S. government should pass legislation encouraging corporate America to begin to deal constructively with its employees' child care problems. The president does not, however, support any substantial commitment of federal funds for the provision of child care services, and the cuts in block grants to states has negatively affected state efforts to address the issue. Despite renewed interest, therefore, the money simply is not there to provide adequate, quality child care for working parents. On 3 September 1984, the *New York Times* noted that there is considerable evidence indicating a worsening of the child care situation as more and more women, owing partly to the economic recovery, are entering the work force:

> The Children's Defense Fund recently surveyed 46 states to determine the effects of Reagan Administration cuts in child care. The study found that 33 states were serving fewer children in 1983 than in 1981; that most states had not made up for Federal budget cuts, and 32 states were spending less for child care in 1983 than in 1981, and that 25 states had made changes diminishing the quality of care. The result...is that "families are putting children in less satisfactory child-care arrangements, and too many children are being left by themselves, including some children under the age of 5.[10]

At the urging primarily of women's groups, some states are attempting to take up the slack resulting from the diminution in federal monies. In Pennsylvania, for example, the Women's Agenda, a nonpartisan organization to promote the interests of women and children, has urged the governor and state legislators to spend an additional $90 million to provide day care services for thousands of children. Currently, the state spends $60.3 million for subsidized day care for 20,000 children.[11]

In addition to those states where there is a move to subsidize day care centers directly, several states are developing tax incentives. For instance, California allows employers to take accelerated depreciation for investments in child care facilities that are built and operated according to state standards. In Connecticut, certain corporations are allowed an income tax credit equal to 25 percent of total expenditures for planning, site preparation, construction, and renovation of facilities that will be used primarily for the child care needs of their employees.[12]

We will now consider ways in which the survey participants, in a climate that is somewhat hostile to single parents and two-career families, are coping with the reality of today's family structure.

Participants' Children Aged 18 and Under

Understandably, the ages of employees children have a significant impact on the degree to which they find child care and family/work issues problematical. Before we examine how the survey participants are dealing with the problems of child care, let's look at their children's ages. Tables 2-1 (by raw numbers) and 2-2 (by percentages) show the ages of the children correlated to the gender and marital status of the parents.

Single women (26 percent) and single men (29 percent) were least likely, and married women (54 percent) were most likely, to have preschool children. A much higher overall percentage of single and married men than of single and married women had children in the 12- to 18-year-old categories, the ages at which children are less likely to cause child care problems and family/work conflicts.

Types of Child Care Arrangements

Survey participants with children 18 and under were asked what types of child care arrangements they had used for child(ren) living at home during the previous two years. Table 2-3 shows the raw numbers of employees who selected various types. (Participants were allowed to select more than one type.)

Table 2-1
Age Range of Participants' Children

Years	Single Women (N = 275)	Married Women (N = 958)	Single Men (N = 48)	Married Men (N = 1,564)
Under 2	17	185	4	215
2 to 5	55	336	10	441
6 to 11	132	385	21	721
12 to 14	87	281	23	589
15 to 18	86	271	15	639

Table 2-2
Age Range of Participants' Children by Percentages

Years	Single Women (N = 275)	Married Women (N = 958)	Single Men (N = 48)	Married Men (N = 1,564)
Under 2	6	19	8	14
2 to 5	20	35	21	28
6 to 11	48	40	44	46
12 to 14	32	29	48	38
15 to 18	31	28	31	41

Note: Percentages are higher than 100 percent because of multiple children in families.

Table 2–3 demonstrates that women, both married and single, most frequently left their children in the home of a caretaker or left the children to care for themselves. Single men also relied on these two means of child care, but in addition they frequently used an older sibling to watch the younger children. By far the most commonly selected type of child care by married men was an adult over 18 in the same household, although they, too, relied on the three types just described.

The adult over 18 who looked after the married man's children was, in most cases, his wife. As we will see throughout this book, the fact that 95 percent of the women (compared to 61 percent of the men) had mates who were employed full-time also influenced the responses.

In general, the most frequently used types of child care and the ones most important in allowing employees to work were almost identical. Table 2–4 shows which forms of child care were the most important in terms of allowing employees to work.

Note that the percentage of married men who relied on an adult over 18 in the home for child care was more than three times that of the group which used this type of child care with the second greatest frequency. Also note that single men were more likely than other groups to have children look after themselves. Given controls for occupation and gender, women in mangement were most likely to use day care centers (15 percent, compared to 2 to 5 percent of craftsmen, craftswomen, and management men), in part because they were better able to afford day care centers than women craftsworkers and in part because many of the men had wives who stayed at home.

Table 2–3
Child Care Arrangements

	Single Women (N = 275)	Married Women (N = 958)	Single Men (N = 48)	Married Men (N = 1,564)
Adult (over 18) member of your household	44	219	6	714
Older brother/sister	61	198	14	314
Children look after themselves	119	347	20	483
Someone who comes to your home	45	166	6	213
Someone in whose home you leave your children	123	518	15	415
Day care center	51	180	7	114
Other	35	99	3	87

Table 2–4

Most Important Child Care Arrangements in Allowing Parents to Work

(percentages)

	Single Women (N = 275)	Married Women (N = 958)	Single Men (N = 48)	Married Men (N = 1,563)
Adult (over 18) member of your household	8	11	14	47
Older brother/sister	5	6	8	5
Children look after themselves	29	20	35	19
Someone who comes to your home	9	9	8	4
Someone in whose home you leave your children	29	37	8	15
Day care center	15	14	24	6
Other	5	3	3	3

How do these overall findings compare to other survey findings? Very similarly, as a study in *Working Mothers—"Who's Minding the Children?"*—shows. Forty percent of the children were cared for in someone else's home, 31 percent in their own home, 15 percent in group centers, and 9 percent by the parent while working either at home or in a workplace.[13]

Because this study's data focus on children 18 and under and not just on very young children, and because of the age of the survey participants, it is not surprising that a significant minority of children looked after themselves. In general, employees were likely to begin leaving both boys and girls alone at home at about the same age. Ten years seems to be the age at which increasing numbers of children were left alone. Before the age of 10, 5 percent or less were left alone. At age 10, the percentage jumped to about 14. By age 12, about 33 percent of children were staying alone.

When the age groups of children and the types of child care arrangements employees used were examined, some predictable patterns emerged. Regardless of the age of the child, at least two out of five of the men, compared to less than one out of ten of the women, had an adult over 18 at home watching the children. Almost 25 percent of the women with preschoolers (children under 6), compared to 11 percent of the men, put their children in day care centers. The data also show that through the age of 11, approximately equal percentages of men and women left their children without adult supervision. Over the age of 11, however, a much higher percentage of women than men left the children by themselves.

An article in *Newsweek* titled "What Price Day Care?" noted that about 5 million children under the age of 10 return home from school to an empty house. In addition, about half a million (7 percent) of preschool children are left at home on their own for at least part of the day while their parents are working. Despite the risks apparent in this situation from the adult perspective, it is not always an unhappy one, particularly for older children.[14] *Working Mothers* noted in a survey that one-third of the 8-year-olds and more than half of the 9-year-olds took care of themselves after school. Most of these children, the survey reported, "said they were happy with their situation, [that] in fact they liked being independent and enjoyed having time to themselves. As for the remaining children in this age group, many expressed eagerness to be on their own—free of their babysitters."[15]

To some, however, this situation constitutes "a national scandal." Indeed, a recent survey indicated that 24 percent of all fires started in the home were caused by children left alone at home, many of them left to care for themselves while their parents worked. Whether the situation constitutes a scandal or an opportunity for independence, children taking care of themselves at an early age is a simple fact of life in many families. A Hispanic, female lower-level manager with two sons commented:

My children have been staying by themselves since they were 10 years old. Due to my husband's being in the military and my working nights, the children have had to accept responsibility of caring for themselves when a parent isn't available.

However, a Hispanic craftswoman with a grade-schooler expressed concern about leaving her child by herself:

My child stays alone and I worry about [her] safety and her ability to handle an unusual situation.

A white craftswoman echoed this anxiety by stating that owing to the same situation, she frequently put in unproductive time at work:

Many times my daughter [age 10] is not home from school when I call on my break. That situation causes concern.

As we shall see in chapters 3 and 4, a source of some stress for a number of parents is inadequate child care arrangements before and after school and during vacations.

Characteristics of Various Child Care Arrangements

The vast majority of employees—90 percent—who used child care arrangements used them Monday through Friday, and most of those employees (about 55 percent) required more than 35 hours of service each week. The next most common frequency of use, reported by 25 percent of the respondents, was one to ten hours weekly.

More than 57 percent of the employees had been using their current child care arrangements for more than eighteen months, but the next highest figure in this category (15 percent) pertained to those employees who had maintained their current arrangements for two months or less. Assuming that to alter child care arrangements is, in some degree, a measure of dissatisfaction and/or increased responsibility for managing this aspect of family life, the data show that women and single men reported the least stability. Only slightly more than half (55 percent) of the women, married or single, and 65 percent of the single men (compared to 81 percent of the married men) had made no alterations in child care arrangements within the previous two years. Women, as in earlier comparisons, were primarily responsible for child care, and the responses of married men were strongly influenced by those whose wives were full-time homemakers.

Overall Satisfaction with Current Child Care Arrangements

Having elicited this basic information about the current child care arrangements of the survey participants, we can review the participants' degree of satisfaction with such arrangements and what types of concerns and problems their current arrangements are causing. Table 2–5 gives the responses (in percentages) of the participants by gender to the question "With regard to the child care arrangement which you indicated previously, how satisfied are you with the following: (a) cost, (b) hours available for child care, (c) location of child care with respect to home, (d) location of child care with respect to work, (e) physical appearance of child care environment, (f) center's curriculum (if applicable), and (g) quality of child care given."

In brief, the range of responses (42 to 51 percent) of women who were very satisfied with various aspects of child care was narrow. Forty-two percent were very satisfied with available hours and with the proximity of child care to their workplace. Fifty-one percent were very satisfied with the quality of the care. The range of responses for men (55 to 59 percent) was also narrow.

Other variables having been controlled, age and race had a predictable impact: younger employees and blacks were least satisfied; older employees and

Table 2–5
Satisfaction with Current Child Care Arrangements
(percentages)

	Very Satisfied		Satisfied		Not Very Satisfied		Not At All Satisfied	
	Women	*Men*	*Women*	*Men*	*Women*	*Men*	*Women*	*Men*
Cost	43	55	43	37	11	5	3	3
Hours	42	55	45	39	11	5	2	1
Proximity to home	50	59	41	37	7	3	2	1
Proximity to work	42	55	41	38	13	6	5	2
Appearance	49	59	47	38	4	3	1	1
Curriculum	46	55	45	40	7	4	2	1
Quality	51	59	44	36	5	4	1	1

whites were most satisfied. Also, men and women in management were slightly more satisfied than their counterparts in crafts.

The only significant difference between single and married women in this series of responses was in the area of cost: 21 percent of the single women (compared to 13 percent of the married women) were not very satisfied with the cost of their child care arrangements. In contrast, except with respect to the center's curriculum and quality of care, single men exhibited significantly less satisfaction than did married men with their current child care arrangements. For example, 22 percent of the single men (compared to 7 percent of the married men) were not very satisfied with the proximity of child care services to their workplace. Also, 19 percent of the single men and 7 percent of the married men were not very satisfied with the cost. Men who were single parents responded very similarly to married and single women on questions relating to child care problems. Married men were in a class by themselves, primarily because their wives (regardless of whether they worked outside the home) took all of the responsibility for child care, or the greatest share of it. Indeed, many married women, even those who work full-time function as single parents when it comes to handling child care.

Analysis of satisfaction by the type of child care arrangements and gender of respondents clearly showed that overall employees were most dissatisfied with day care centers and that men and women responded almost identically regarding most of these characteristics.

A single, white female lower-level manager with two preschoolers noted a variety of concerns about the day care centers to which she was sending her children:

Cost is prohibitive: $476 paid for one month even if kids are sick and can't go; no evening hours; $10 fine for every fifteen minutes past 6 p.m.; no early hours before 6:30 a.m.; I must provide all the food; no sick child care; so far from work and home; child care center schedules parent meetings when my time is already overburdened. I like my work but the day care center assumes there are two parents. This is not realistic.

After day care centers, the arrangement that created the most dissatisfaction among both men and women was a caretaker coming to the home of the child, although men registered comparable dissatisfaction with caretakers who looked after the children in their own homes. A white craftswoman with a toddler and a preschooler wrote about some general problems parents have with home care by providers other than their families:

Sitters, private ones at least, are not dependable. They get sick, they have appointments, etc., and you are left up in the air with no sitter for that day or however long. They also call you at the last minute to tell you they won't be able to babysit that day.

Table 2–6 shows the participants' responses to questions about satisfaction with child care arrangements by gender and type of care.

We will now look more closely at some of the individual factors involved in the broad area of satisfaction with child care arrangements.

Specific Aspects of Child Care Arrangements: Finances, Quality, and Convenience

The financing of child care has been cited frequently as a major concern on the part of large numbers of working parents. In the Pittsburgh Child Care Network study (1984), 30 percent of all respondents ranked affordable child care as the major issue or concern in child care today; 60 percent ranked affordable care among the three most important issues. Of the ninety-six centers responding to the network's survey, 65 percent reported clients who could not be served because they were both ineligible for subsidies and unable to afford the private rates.[16] One of the Pittsburgh providers, the Urban League, has seen its Department of Public Welfare–funded day care program dwindle from twenty centers in 1980 to four in 1985 as a result, in large measure, of narrowing eligibility standards for subsidized care, along with the inability of low-income working parents to pay its private rate of $45 a week, one of the lowest rates in the area. The number of families who are too affluent to qualify for subsidies but too poor to pay for care is huge, according to the Urban League.

Forty-five dollars a week is a bargain in comparison to the prevailing rates in many other large cities. D. Friedman reported that while the majority of parents pay $3,000 per year for child care services, costs vary from $1,500 to $10,000 a year. More specifically, in Boston, costs range from $30.00 to $400.00

Table 2-6
Participants Who Are Not Very Satisfied with Various Characteristics of Child Care Arrangements
(*percentages*)

Arrangement	Cost		Hours		Proximity to Home		Proximity to Work		Appearance		Curriculum		Quality	
	Women	Men	Women	Men	Women	Men	Women	Men	Women	Men	Women	Men	Women	Men
Adult (over 18) member of your household	6	5	13	2	8	1	11	2	2	2	11	2	2	2
Sibling	0	0	2	7	0	2	0	0	0	2	0	7	3	4
Children look after themselves	3	1	3	3	1	1	10	4	2	1	4	4	9	5
Someone who comes to your home	23	6	25	10	8	4	14	13	4	5	17	5	13	8
Someone in whose home you leave your children	14	13	11	8	10	10	18	17	4	6	11	7	4	4
Day care center	35	35	24	25	20	19	32	25	8	13	8	14	4	15
Other	9	6	6	6	9	3	18	6	6	6	11	0	0	0

per week depending on type of care and the age of the child. In Dallas the cost range is $25.00 to $200.00 per week. The most costly care is a caregiver who lives in the home and the least costly care is for school-age children.[17]

Considering that the gross weekly pay at minimum wage is only $134, it is clear that center day care is priced out of the market for many families. In this study, more than three-fourths (76 percent) of the participants, regardless of parenthood status, believed that the lack of quality, affordable care was a problem. Gender, race, and parenthood status played important roles in influencing managers' responses to this question. Women, especially of color, and employees with children 18 and under were most likely to say this was a problem.

Despite strong concerns about finding affordable child care on the part of employees with children 18 and under, the percentage of those who considered the financing of child care to be more than a minor problem was small, relatively speaking. Thirty-two percent of the single women, compared to only 17 percent of the married women, found that financing posed at least some degree of difficulty. Financing was not a problem to 57 percent of the single women (compared to 67 percent of the married women). Twenty-three percent of single men (almost four times the 6 percent rate for married men) found the financing of child care at least somewhat of a problem. Fifty-four percent of the single men and 84 percent of the married men said that the financing of child care presented no problem at all. Predictably, employees with young children were much more likely than those with older children to experience difficulty with the financing of child care. Only 43 percent of the women with preschool children, compared to 79 percent with children over 11, said finances were no problem at all. For men in the same categories, the percentages were 67 and 91, respectively.

In light of the comments from Friedman and from the surveys cited, the degree of concern among this study's respondents with regard to the cost of their children's care was remarkably low. There are several reasons for this. One is that a high percentage of those in the sample were not paying for child care, most often because they were married men with wives at home or because the children were old enough to care for themselves.

Table 2–7 shows the amount of money the participants paid for child care arrangements. Married men, as one would expect, were most likely (63 percent) to pay nothing for child care. The table also shows that married women overall were paying the highest price for child care.

When the costs of child care were analyzed by race, white women (31 percent) proved more likely than black women (24 percent) and other women of color (20 percent) to pay over $50 a week for child care. Black men (23 percent), white men (14 percent), and other men of color (10 percent) responded similarly.

Table 2-7
Cost of Child Care
(percentages)

Amount Paid per Week	Single Women (N = 275)	Married Women (N = 958)	Single Men (N = 42)	Married Men (N = 1,565)
$0	35	31	45	63
$1 to $25	15	9	17	13
$26 to $50	28	28	25	11
$51 to $75	17	18	11	5
$76 to $100	3	8	3	1
Over $100	2	6	0	5

Another explanation for the relatively small percentage of participants who experienced problems with child care finances is that wages in the five companies used in the study are near the top of the industry, especially for craftspersons and lower-level managers. For example, the top wage for the lowest crafts title is more than $15,000 a year, and the top title in crafts earns more than $25,000. Top pay for lowest-level management is about $37,000.

Some comments from the participants will supply the reader with further insight into the large percentage differences between married men, on the one hand, and single men and all women, on the other hand. The comments of three white women—two lower-level managers and one craftsworker—were revealing:

My child care is very expensive: $240 per month and $5 for each five minutes after 6 p.m. As a management person, I can't always walk right out the door at 5 p.m. So, I'm often late when it's my turn to pick up my daughter.

The best child care center around is three blocks from our home. But it's $95 plus $90 a week for our two children, and we can't swing that much for child care.

My day care cost is very high, but I have an exceptionally good day care situation now. Only a few months ago I paid much less—but I got what I paid for.

A black male craftsworker and a Hispanic, female lower-level manager were even less positive in their comments:

For the things I want for my children, the expense is quite great.

We save money in our budget by having the children stay by themselves when my husband is not available.

Contrast these comments with those of two married white males, the first at the upper level and the second at the lower level of management, and a male lower-level Hispanic manager:

I'm very happy that my children are home with my spouse while I work. We feel very fortunate.

There is no substitute for a loving, caring mother to take care of a child.

My wife is very cheap and does the best job possible.

Many single women who paid nothing for child care had some member of their extended family looking after the children at no cost. A black married craftswoman who paid nothing said, "My mother watches the kids for nothing. Without her we could not afford anybody to watch them."

Every parent wants the best available care for his or her child. Quality child care, as forthcoming comments of parents will show, encompasses not only the environment and the skills and integrity of the care giver (if there is one), but also such factors as curriculum, care giver/child ratio, hourly cost, location, and philosophy. In the Pittsburgh Child Care Network study, more than half of the respondents (54 percent) ranked quality as one of the three most important criteria in evaluating child care services, and a quarter of them (25 percent) ranked it as their major concern.[18] Finding quality care that was very satisfactory rather than merely adequate, especially for single parents and dual-career families, often presented a major difficulty. Barriers to finding quality care included the high cost of such care and, in some instances, its unavailability, owing to the gap between supply and demand. Securing quality child care, as later chapters will demonstrate, was one of the biggest factors affecting an employee's ability or inability to cope with dual roles in a productive manner. Employees who were concerned or worried about the quality of care their children were receiving were impaired in their capacity to function on the job.

As Table 2-5 showed, 51 percent of the women and 59 percent of the men surveyed were very satisfied with the quality of care their children were receiving. Only 6 and 5 percent, respectively, registered even some degree of dissatisfaction.

Parents of younger children were much more likely than those with older ones to see this as a problem. For example, five times the percentage of women and twelve times the percentage of men with children under 2, compared to those with children between 15 and 18, said that finding quality child care was at least somewhat of a problem. Table 2-8 dramatically illustrates this point.

Finding quality child care influenced employees' productivity in different ways. Although it did not significantly affect women in terms of time lost on account of absence and tardiness, it did affect them in the area of dealing with

Table 2–8
Parents Who Have Had At Least Some
Problems Finding Quality Child Care
(percentages)

Age of Child	Women (N = 1,239)	Men (N = 1,602)
Under 2	46	24
2 to 5	34	17
6 to 11	28	10
12 to 14	18	5
15 to 18	9	2

family issues during working hours. For men, problems in finding quality child care did have a significant impact on productivity in terms of missed work, tardiness, and dealing with family issues during working hours, but not in terms of leaving work early. Using the issue of tardiness to illustrate the point, 43 percent of the men who said finding quality child care was a big problem had been late for work, whereas 67 percent who said it was no problem had no record of tardiness.

There was a wide range of factors which in parents' opinions helped determine the quality of child care. Two factors that were examined in this study were appearance and curriculum. The correlation was high between perception of quality of child care and satisfaction with the appearance of the environment and facilities. A very strong relationship also existed between satisfaction with curriculum and high marks for child care quality. Eighty-four percent of the employees who were satisfied with curriculum did not view quality of child care as a problem, as opposed to 59 percent who were not satisfied with curriculum and who did perceive quality child care as a problem.

The respondents' own words convey what they meant by quality of care:

The day care center is fair to good; too many children, not as clean as I'd like; sometimes too rowdy.

—Hispanic, female craftsworker

My child care sitter has seven children ranging in age from 3 months to 5 years. I worry about the attention my little 2-year-old boy gets.

—white, female lower-level manager

Cost, time available, and location are fine, but philosophy of child-rearing is very different from mine and has caused some resentment from my son regarding the manner in which he is treated. He dislikes the arrangement very much and wants to stay home alone, but he is too young.

—white, female lower-level manager

I've personally seen, with my job, twenty children at one home, a sort of day care. The children seemed disoriented, lost, and of course they weren't getting proper care because of the size.

—native American, male craftsworker

I don't like the situation because I have only limited control over the events occurring with my child during the day and I have yet to find a provider I feel comfortable with and trust, outside of family.

—white, female craftsworker

In contrast to the preceding extracts, the following comments of participants clearly illustrate why many respondents were pleased with the quality of their child care services. Notice the wide variety of reasons, including children's age, spouse's care, family care, and dependable child care providers:

My children have the most caring, brightest teacher that cares and gives them individual attention—their mother.

—white, male middle-level manager

I am a very grateful individual. My sitter's rates are reasonable, and she creates a real family atmosphere. Located close to grade school where I special-transferred my child. Extremely dependable and I always know when I need to make other arrangements, for example, when the sitter goes on her annual vacation.

—white, female middle-level manager

I've had the same babysitter since I returned to work four years ago. I depend upon that woman more than I've ever depended upon anyone. If I'm even partially successful in my job, it's because my babysitter is more mother to my child than sitter. My heart goes out to women who aren't as lucky.

—white, female lower–middle-level manager

My sons are all teenagers, ages 15 to 17. They are in junior high and high school. If there is ever a problem with them, my husband is available during the day hours to care for them. Seldom do I have to leave work because of a home problem. Thanks to God.

—black, female lower–middle-level manager

My arrangement for the present works out pretty well because my husband is out of a job. He takes care of the children beautifully, but he doesn't instill any worthwhile skills into them.

—black, female lower-level manager

I know that I could never find a better arrangement than I have by having my parents. If it came to leaving my child with a stranger or private day care, I would seriously consider quitting my job.

—black, female craftsworker

Overall I am satisfied, but I wish my sitter's home was larger for the kids to roam and had better nap-time arrangements. I am satisfied with the care and love given.

—*white, female lower-level manager*

My son goes to a tutor after school. There are responsible adults there to greet him. If he's late, they call. My daughter is picked up from the sitter by her father and is brought home. He usually waits for my son and for me to arrive before leaving. I pick up my son.

—*black, female craftsworker*

I am very happy with the care my child receives. The sitter also has a toddler about my child's age, and they are great friends. My daughter loves this family, and I can see it. She didn't like the previous care she was receiving, and it showed.

—*white, female lower-level manager*

K. McCartney et al. made some relevant observations about the importance of quality in a child care program. They wrote that children who attended child care centers with good facilities, teachers, programs and high adult verbal interaction scored better on standardized language tests than those who did not attend such centers. Children in these good centers also were rated more sociable than other children.[19]

No matter how good a child care provider is, if the location of the provider is not convenient for the employee and if the hours are not flexible, additional stress will be added onto an already stressful day.

Thirteen percent of single men, along with women regardless of marital status, said that the transporting of children between the care provider and home pose at least somewhat of a problem; only 5 percent of the married men concurred. Although the percentages were low, the added burden of transporting a child is an additional stress. The following comments about location of child care are typical of the participants.

A family member babysits. I didn't feel comfortable with a stranger. The only problem is that we have to drive a long way to their home, just another added pressure.

—*white, female lower-level manager*

I am very fortunate to have a dependable babysitter, but she cannot sit when school is in session. She lives some distance from me—across the state line, in fact, so geography presents something of a problem.

—*white, female middle-level manager*

This is a hard question for me to answer because the child care is very close to home but far from work. But it is inconvenient in emergencies. It is very satisfying knowing the great care my daughter receives from her "home away from home."

—white, female middle-level manager

I am satisfied from the standpoint that it is the best available at this time, close to the elementary school, close to the doctor's office, and will take three children from the same family.

—white, female craftsworker

Hours for child care arrangements can have a tremendous impact on the ability of employees to work overtime, change schedules, make late and/or early meetings, and so on. The data show that men and women with young children, especially preschoolers, were least likely to be very satisfied with child care provider hours. About one out of three of the women and more than one out of two of the men with preschoolers were very satisfied with the hours, compared to more than one out of two women and about three out of five men with children over 12 who concurred.

A white, female middle-level manager wrote:

I have one major problem. The hours of my job do not correspond to the hours of my sitter.

A white, female lower–middle-level manager summed up her problems with transportation and child care provider hours in this way:

I have two children—both are in separate day care centers because of their age difference. I live five miles from my office. However, I drive sixteen miles before I arrive at work. This means that I must leave my home at 6:30 in order to provide plenty of time to get to work—which is usually around 7:45. I do have to leave very soon after 5:00 in order to pick both up by 6:00. (The fees after 6:00 are $2 every fifteen minutes.)

The last participant's comments, although they depict an extreme situation, do portray clearly what some employees must cope with in terms of transportation and child care provider hours.

Conclusions

The history of child care in the United States has been one of benign neglect until the 1980s, except for times of depression and war. In times of depression, child care issues became a national issue not because the society wanted women to work but because creating child care centers created jobs, especially for unemployed men. In the case of war, child care issues came to the fore because the nation needed women to work in order to produce the goods required for men to fight. The women's movement and civil rights laws on equal employment, which have steadily influenced increasing numbers of women to enter the work force on a permanent basis, have moved the United States from benign neglect to rhetoric on the subject of child care services; neither of these positions has dealt with the practical problems encountered by working parents, as the comments of many participants in this study demonstrate.

Most of the survey participants were generally satisfied with their child care arrangements in terms of cost, hours, location, and quality. However, a closer examination showed that such arrangements as care provided in someone else's home and center day care were a source of dissatisfaction to significant minorities of employees. With these facts in mind, it is not surprising that satisfaction with child care was significantly influenced by the age of the child.

We have seen very clearly in this chapter that women regardless of marital status, and single men who participated in the survey used similar types of child care arrangements and had similar concerns. We have also seen that married men, for the most part, were in a group by themselves. Having spouses whose only or major role is homemaking freed these men from child care concerns, and they were thus much more satisfied and less likely to experience problems with child care than their peers. Having established the ways in which survey participants coped with their child care responsibilities, and having reviewed their concerns and the extent of their satisfaction with their present arrangements, we will examine in the next chapter how child care and family/work problems affect corporate productivity.

3
Child Care Problems: Impact on Employee Productivity

Assisting employees with family/work conflicts and, in particular, with child care problems has never been a priority for corporate America. In this chapter we will look at some of the reasons why corporations have turned their backs on these issues—and, more important, what the cost of that rejection has been in terms of lowered work productivity. Data from the survey population, coupled with observations of others who have studied the subject, suggest that the provision of support for problems posed by dual-career and single-parent family structures and by the increasingly heterogeneous work force of the 1980s makes good business sense, since both employers and employees will benefit from that support.

Considering the historical attitude of government toward these issues, and the general perception that women are not—and should not be—permanent, "serious" members of the work force, it is not surprising that as recently as 1971, company-sponsored child care was virtually unknown in the United States. Only eleven companies in the nation provided some form of child care assistance for the children of their employees. By 1978 the number had increased tenfold, to 105. Today, about 2,000 companies provide some type of child care assistance to employees—a striking increase over past years but still a small percentage of the 6,000,000 firms in corporate America. The increases between 1971 and 1978 occurred primarily in hospitals, where there was a high demand for women to fill so-called women's jobs on a twenty-four-hour daily basis. Nurses were in short supply, and the lack of adequate child care, particularly for graveyard shifts, made the situation even more critical. As a result, hospitals have pioneered on-site child care facilities. In 1978, 71 percent of the providers of child care assistance were hospitals, and only 9 percent were industrial firms. In 1982, according to the National Employer-Supported Child Care Project, industry accounted for nearly half of the providers,[1] and today, corporations represent a significant majority of employers who recognize child care assistance as a pressing need—a promising trend, considering that businesses far outnumber hospitals in this country.

With the number of women holding permanent jobs in the work force on the rise, why has it taken corporations so long to address family/work conflicts, especially child care issues? And why, even today, are relatively few employers actually assisting their employees with these problems? A common justification propounded by many companies is that they doubt such assistance yields any real benefit to the corporation. They argue that providing on-site child care is extremely expensive and that no clear evidence exists to indicate that the benefits of such programs outweigh the costs. Although on-site child care is not the only solution to child care and family/work problems, for many executives, assisting employees in these areas means utilizing those options involving on-site centers exclusively.

Executives cite an article in *Personnel Psychology* in which T.I. Miller of the Division of Research and Evaluation in Boulder, Colorado, discussed the need for such services:

> In most discussions about employer-sponsored child care, little solid evidence is offered to support the widely expressed conventional wisdom that care for employees' children improves employees' work behaviors and attitudes.[2]

Miller's position is supported by a Bureau of National Affairs report, which said:

> Little sound analysis of the costs and benefits of child care assistance has been conducted, despite the great interest in the issue. Experts say many employers cannot correctly calculate the cost of providing the benefit because they do not know the value of space, employee time, and in-kind services that may be involved. The gains, such as improved morale and greater job satisfaction, generally have been documented subjectively.[3]

While no wide body of reliable scientific data supports the notion that corporate involvement in child care pays off, there is growing concrete evidence to suggest that this is the case. S.A. Youngblood and K. Chambers-Cook noted that absences decreased by 19 percent after the company under study instituted a day care center. In addition, the turnover rate in the same company decreased dramatically, from 8 percent before day care to 3 percent in the year following the adoption of the day care facility—representing a 63 percent drop in the annual turnover rate.[4]

One of the most massive studies of corporate initiatives in the area of child care was conducted by the National Employer-Supported Child Care Project in 1982. The organizations surveyed included 197 industrial corporations, 195 health care organizations, 17 public agencies, and 6 labor unions. The type of assistance offered varied from on-site child care centers and family day care networks to referral services, support for community-based programs, and educational programs for parents. Although not all of the queried organizations responded to all questions, 42 of the industrial firms reported on-site centers, 10 provided reimbursement programs, 19 offered child care information and referral services, 23 had parent education programs, and 103 supported community child care programs. Half or more of the respondents found that company support of child care services increased productivity and reduced absenteeism and employee turnover. Almost as many—39 percent of the total sample and 45 percent of the industrial respondents—also found that providing child care assistance reduced tardiness.[5]

In response to the question of whether the cost of their child care initiatives equaled or outweighed the benefits to the organization or vice versa, R.Y. Magid noted that 75 percent of the companies in her study believed that the benefits of the child care initiatives far outweighed the cost. They believed that such efforts led to a lower rate of absenteeism, greater stability and loyalty, improved employee morale, enhancement of the company's image, improved recruitment and retention of quality employees, less employee stress and distraction, and the earlier return of employees from maternity leave back to the work force.[6]

As these three reports demonstrate, corporate involvement in child care can produce significant financial dividends. With this information in mind, we will review some of the other reasons besides cost that are used by corporations to explain why they have not progressed beyond the talking stage—if they have progressed that far—toward implementing supportive programs.

Some corporations say that the cause of their lack of involvement in the child care concerns of their employees is their fear that providing child care assistance would discriminate against employees who have no children. If we help employees with young children, they ask, are we not also obligated to help those who must take care of older parents?

In reality, there is little basis for this fear. Of the thirty-five companies in the National Employer-Supported Child Care Project whose executives felt that equity would be a problem, only four companies (11 percent) found equity to be an issue with their employees.[7] Like most corporations who provide child care benefits, the majority found that childless workers also benefit when absenteeism and tardiness are reduced and their peers are relieved of stress. Furthermore, companies and their employees recognize that all benefits are not used equally by all employees, even when they are offered to all. Lastly, corporate America is not an egalitarian organization; the higher one's position, the more perks one gets. No one has argued that this unequal treatment should be abolished because not all employees can be recipients of those perks!

There are other reasons besides money and the equity issue that employers advance for their resistance to becoming involved with the personal family issues of child care problems and family/work conflicts. Some employers simply deny that these problems are within their company's purview, regardless of the possible cost in lost time and lowered productivity. Their reticence is rooted in an antiquated view of woman's role in society. Vivid expression of this attitude appears in the comments of three white male managers who participated in the survey:

> Just as the company promotes promiscuity among females and not males by providing maternity benefits to the unmarried women, child care assistance

would reduce the responsibilities of parenting to a point that kids become a by-product of 8-to-5. Kids require parents; their care is a responsibility of the parent, not the company! [Wife does not work and has one child in grade school and one in junior high.]

The two-income household is destroying the traditional family unit. Do men a favor—read some of Dr. James Dobson's books!!! [Wife works part-time and has two preschoolers.]

Women's place is in the home to care for the family. Men's place is at work to bring home the money. [Wife does not work and children are teenagers.]

Fortunately not all corporate managers share this view. Attitudes change slowly, but there is growing evidence of dialogue on the subject, as the following comments demonstrate.

I don't have any children, but I can see that a day care center within the company would help my coworkers. Women are here to stay in the work force, and companies should help.

—black, female middle-level manager

Corporate involvement in child care helps the employees by giving them peace of mind that their children are being taken care of properly. This will help their productivity.

—white, male middle-level manager

The main reason corporate America has failed to deal with the family/work conflict, and with child care in particular, is that these are almost exclusively women's issues, and corporate America is still dominated by older men who come from traditional, sexist family role models and who still believe, consciously or unconsciously, that women should be at home taking care of their children. Women who defy tradition and insist on working, they believe, must simply accept as their own responsibility the problems of balancing dual family/work roles and resolving the issues of child care. These corporate managers have not yet realized that most women are in the work force to stay and that their numbers will continue to increase. As the *Wall Street Journal* observed, "Many male executives persist in believing that working mothers, now a majority of women in the work force, are only working temporarily and that women in management positions who decide to have children aren't really committed to their careers."[8] (Chapter 7, in the second part of this book, elaborates on this view.)

Considering the obvious facts of women's presence in the work force, child care and family/work problems cannot be dismissed by means of philosophy or ideology, nor are these problems going to go away. If corporate America wants a productive work force that will enable their companies to compete effectively in an ever more competitive world, it must come to grips with these issues. The question is not one of equity or woman's proper role; it is, purely and simply, a matter of corporate bottom line profits.

Survey Participants' Perceptions of Productivity

The vast majority of the 5,000 employees in the five companies surveyed showed a keen awareness of the potential benefits to corporations that become involved in the issues of child care and family/work problems. When asked whether increased corporate involvement in the area of child care would increase productivity, three-fourths of the women surveyed (76 percent) and more than half of the men (58 percent) asserted that it would.

To the more specific question whether child care problems are costing their companies a great deal of money in unproductive use of employees' minds and time, 67 percent of the employees—regardless of gender—responded in the affirmative. Although one might expect that single parents and parents with children 18 and under would be more conscious of the problem, this was not the case. Nor was the age of employees' children a significant factor in their responses to the question, and no significant differences emerged based on age, race, or marital status. The more stress-related child care and family/work problems the employees had, the more likely they were to believe that corporations are losing a great deal of money in lost productivity.

The following comments from respondents provide insight into productivity, role conflict, and child care issues:

> I don't have infants anymore, but child care assistance would have helped me a great deal years ago when I needed it badly. I don't think my attendance would have been so bad if I had had adequate child care.
>
> *—Hispanic, female lower-level manager*

> In cases where child care is a problem for an employee, I know it brings productivity down. I mean, how can you work to your fullest if you're worrying about who's going to watch your child?
>
> *—black, female lower-level manager*

> If parents feel their child is in a good environment, they concentrate more on the task at hand.
>
> *—black, male craftsworker*

> My job is high-powered and intensive. I have a young child. My husband helps, but the husband primary responsibility for child-rearing rests with me. Does it affect my job sometimes? Yes!
>
> *—white, female middle-level manager*

A single, male lower-level manager who had a six-year-old child noted:

> When I talk to my single woman friends about raising children, we have
> similar problems: getting the job done and being a good parent. I missed full
> days and parts of days because of my child.

Finally, a white, female middle-level manager who had no children
summed up recurring problems that affect productivity:

> Since I do not have children, I am not an expert on this issue. However, I
> strongly believe that reliable child care provided through the company would
> cut down on tardiness, missed days, accidents, lost work, and increase time at
> work and productivity at work through a happier and more at-ease employee.

Productivity Issues for All Employees

A.C. Emlen and P.E. Koren found in their survey of over 8,000 employees in
Portland, Oregon, that employees lost an average of nine days per year, representing 4 percent of the total number of days that could have been worked. In
addition, they found in most cases that both female and male employees with
children 18 and under missed more days of work than employees with no
children under 18, came to work late, left work early, and dealt with family
issues during working hours. For example, women with children under 18
missed work an average of 11.9 days, compared to 9.6 days missed for women
with no children under 18. Men with no children under 18 had missed an
average of 7.4 days of work in the preceding year, while men with children
under 18 had missed an average of about 8.6 days.[9]

The findings in this study revealed similar trends. Because most corporate
cultures take a negative view of any personal issue that affects job performance,
especially when it is considered a "woman's issue," the author recognized the
potential reluctance of some participants with children 18 and under to
acknowledge that any family/work conflicts or child care problems were affecting their productivity. In order to control for this potential difficulty and to
provide maximally accurate information, all employees, regardless of parental
status, were asked to respond to the following questions. (Correlations will be
presented shortly that give a very clear picture of the extent to which
employees' responses are directly related to their having children 18 and
under.) The participants were asked:

In the past year, approximately how many times have you:

1. *Missed work*

2. *Been late for work*

3. *Left early*

4. *Dealt with personal family-related issues during working hours?*

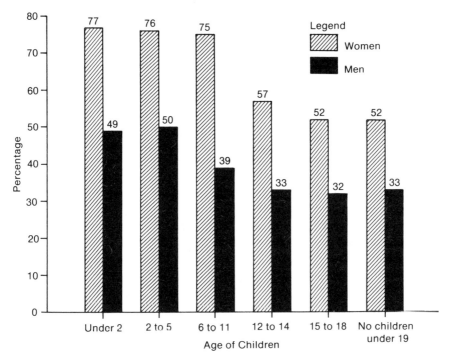

Figure 3–1. Percentage Who Missed At Least One Day of Work in the Previous Year

Employees were least likely to have been late and most likely to have dealt with personal family-related issues during working hours. Only 39 percent of the women and 33 percent of the men admitted to tardiness, while 63 percent of the women and 67 percent of the men had used work time for family matters. Sixty percent of the women and 58 percent of the men had left work early. The only significant divergence in responses of men and women appeared with regard to the question of absenteeism. Fifty-seven percent of the women, compared to only 38 percent of the men, said they had been absent during the previous year.

When the responses of the participants were analyzed in greater detail, some obvious trends began to emerge.

Missed Work

A review of employees' responses regarding absenteeism showed that when ages of employees' children were correlated with missed work, women and men with younger children were more likely to have missed work than were those with older children. Figure 3–1 demonstrates this finding. Notice that while the rate of absenteeism was consistently higher for women than for men, the rate decreased sharply for women with children 12 years old or older. For men, a significant decrease occurred after the children became 5 or older. In addition, the differences in absenteeism between those with children 12 to 18 and those with *no* children 18 or under were very small.

Except in the case of male managers, there was very little difference between single and married employees in specific groups. Crafts employees were more likely than their management counterparts, regardless of marital status, to have missed work. Also, male managers who were married were by far least likely to have missed work in the previous year.

Explanations for the difference between male managers and the other groups can be partially attributed to the fact that most women perform dual family/work roles; more craftsmen were younger and had wives who worked, whereas many managers were older and had wives who were full-time home-makers. Of the managers' wives who did work, a very high percentage worked only part-time. A plausible explanation for greater absenteeism among crafts employees than among managers, regardless of gender, is that the former have less discretion in decision-making power than the latter and, consequently, less flexibility to deal with various family situations during the workday. In other words, rather than deal with a boss who will not tolerate one's coming to work late, leaving early, or dealing with family situations on the phone, a crafts-worker is more likely to miss an entire day of work when a problem arises, as the following excerpts indicate:

> I make my arrangements before coming to work and if I can't, then I don't go to work, since I am the *only* parent. My boss doesn't understand.
> —*white, female craftsworker*

> Management has no child and child care problems. When was the last time a middle manager got his ass chewed because he stayed home with his kid?
> —*white, male craftsworker*

Because a higher percentage of black women are single heads of household, it is predictable that they will miss work more frequently than women who are white or of other color. For example, only 30 percent of the black women, as compared to 38 percent of the other women of color and 45 percent of the white women, had never missed work in the past year. Among men, however, race seemed to be a negligible factor: the range for missed work for all races was 58 to 62 percent. (These figures, as well as those cited in the next two paragraphs, pertain only to employees who had children 18 and under.)

As figure 3–1 showed, age of the children had a significant impact on missed work. One of the chief circumstances the participants cited for absences was the need to care for a sick child, as a Hispanic lower-level supervisor noted:

> If you view the absence records, you'll find a lot of occurrences because of children's sickness and their child care programs.

The survey data support this conclusion. Nearly half (44 percent) of the crafts-workers who had children 18 and under and who missed at least one day of work, and 29 percent of those who missed no work at all, acknowledged that providing for a sick child was at least somewhat of a problem. Figures for managers were 31 and 17 percent, respectively.

Caring for a sick child was the reason given for missed work by 56 percent of the women who were absent one to three times during the previous year, 78 percent of those with between four and six absences, and 82 percent of those who missed more than six days of work. The comparable figures for men were dramatically lower, but the trend was the same: 33, 54, and 58 percent, respectively.

Another problem that correlated highly with absenteeism was that of dual family/work roles. Almost half of the women who had missed at least one day of work and nearly one third of those with perfect attendance cited "handling dual roles" as a problem to some extent. Men's responses followed a similar pattern: one out of six and one out of ten, respectively.

Arriving at Work Late

A child wakes up with a fever, or the babysitter cancels out at the last minute, or the children miss the school bus. These and dozens of other early-morning emergencies can cause an employee to be late for work. Nevertheless, nearly two-thirds of the workers surveyed said they had not been late even once in the previous year.

The percentage differences between the responses of those employees with children 18 and under and those without were small. That some tardiness experienced by employees with children 18 and under was related to child care and family/work problems is reflected in the following comments by a supervisor and will become more evident later. A black, female middle-level manager made these observations about difficulties being experienced by her immediate subordinate:

> Having to get another babysitter at the last minute can cause an employee to come in late—as can children becoming sick and babysitters not knowing what to do. Husbands are sometimes unwilling to babysit when the employee is needed to work overtime, or the babysitter may be unable to keep the child after hours when overtime is needed.

As with absenteeism, age and race were factors in employees' responses to questions on tardiness and on the next category, leaving early.

Leaving Work Early

As previously described data indicate, craftsworkers were more likely than their counterparts in management to deal with family problems by arriving late for work or missing whole days, but the tables were turned for the record on leaving early. More than half of the craftsworkers surveyed (52 percent of the women and 63 percent of the men) reported that they had never left work early, as compared to only 26 percent of female managers and 34 percent of male managers.

A chief reason for this reversal is that crafts employees, for the most part, must request permission in order to leave work early, and since they are more likely to believe that supervisors will not grant them permission to leave early in order to deal with family concerns, they are more likely to come in late or to not come in at all. As stated previously, managers have more flexibility than craftsworkers and are therefore more likely to leave work early. A black, female lower-level manager made this comment:

> I hear the company should come first. *I* think, one, God, two, family, and three, work. If my child is at a sitter's and is seriously ill, I will leave to see that child to the hospital myself.

There was no difference between men with children 18 and under (42 percent) and without (43 percent) with regard to leaving early, but a substantial difference emerged between women who had children 18 and under (34 percent) and those who did not (47 percent) in this respect. In addition, the age of children 18 and under had an impact on women with regard to leaving early, but not on men. A higher percentage of women with children over 12 were likely to leave work early than of those with children under 5. For men there was no difference related to age of children. In discussions with women employees about this reversal of trend in comparison to the figures for missed work, the vast majority indicated that older children in many cases cared for themselves, which means that when problems or emergencies arise, parents must often leave work early to deal with them. In addition, school activities, which mothers are expected to attend, accelerate in the junior and senior high school years, and thirty-nine percent of the women said that attending school conferences and activities posed at least some degree of difficulty. This is the third most frequently cited problem among women and the one identified by the highest percentage of men in the area of child care and family/work concerns.

Another supervisor's comments demonstrated the relationship between child care and family/work problems and some employees' need to leave early. In this instance, the supervisor was a white, male middle-manager who supervised a predominantly female department:

> I try to be sympathetic about the requests I receive from my people to leave work early because of family problems, but sometimes it gets to be too much, especially in the winter, when colds are going around, and in the summer, when kids are out of school.

Dealing with Family-Related Issues during Working Hours

About two out of three employees indicated that they had dealt with family issues during working hours in the previous year. Management employees, younger workers, and women were much more likely than craftsworkers, older employees, and men to have found themselves in this position. As noted earlier, the differences between management and crafts occur because managers are granted a flexibility that craftworkers are not—with regard, for example, to dealing with issues over the telephone while at work.

This issue is one of the few in the survey to which married and single women responded differently from each other. About equal percentages of single parents and married parents, regardless of gender, had dealt with family issues during working hours. Further, it is indisputably clear that parental status had a strong influence on employees' responses. Forty-seven percent of the women and 56 percent of the men who had dealt with family issues during working hours had *no* children 18 and under, but the figures for women and men *with* children 18 and under were 77 and 73 percent, respectively. Just as employees with younger children tend to miss work and come to work late more frequently than employees with older children, so also do employees with younger children deal more with family issues during working hours.

Among the women, blacks were least likely to deal with family problems on the job. Nearly half of the black female craftsworkers (47 percent) and more than one-third of the black female managers (36 percent) denied that they had ever handled family problems while they were at work. This reversal of the trends apparent in the other three questions in this section is due in part to the fact that black women tend to be in jobs that make it difficult to deal with family issues on the job. Another explanation may be that black women employ other means, such as staying at home, to handle such matters. The percentages on this issue for craftsworkers and managers were as follows: white women, 46 and 27 percent; other women of color, 39 and 22 percent; black men, 55 and 18 percent; white men, 47 and 28 percent; and other men of color, 47 and 25 percent, respectively.

A white, female lower–middle-level manager explained why she used time at work for family issues:

> The company should have child care facilities at major work locations. Since they don't, they need to realize that a sick child, babysitter problems, etc., will take up a parent's time.

And a white, female/peer of hers remarked:

> Before placing my son in organized day care, I had a continuous bevy of personal calls from my babysitter. In addition to that problem, my work schedule was reliant on not only my child's health but on that of all the other children the sitter took care of.

Dealing with family issues on the job encompasses a wide spectrum of issues, but two primary factors emerged as major problems for those employees with children 18 and under: caring for sick children and handling dual family/work roles. Chapters 4 and 5 will deal with these factors in greater detail.

Productivity Issues for Employees with Children 18 and Under

Child Care Problems and Dual-Role Conflicts

The previous section focused on questions that were posed to all employees, regardless of whether they had children, and responses indicated that employees with children 18 and under were particularly likely to miss work, come to work late, leave early, and deal with family issues during working hours because of family/work conflicts and child care problems.

In this section we will analyze the responses only of employees with children 18 and under to a series of questions on family/work conflicts in general and on child care problems in particular. As the evidence accumulates, it becomes increasingly clear that these issues are costing corporations a great deal of money in terms of unproductive work time.

In examining the data, it is important to bear in mind several basic facts:

Only 12 percent of American households are comprised of a father who is the sole breadwinner and a mother who is a full-time housewife. The U.S. Census Bureau noted that 60 percent of U.S. families have both partners working full-time.

Sixty-six percent of single women who are parents are working full-time.

Overall, 33 million children have mothers who work full-time.

At any given time, 25 to 30 percent of all children live in single-parent households.[10]

What these statistics tell us is that corporate America has a significant number of employees who are faced with child care responsibilities and family/work conflicts that can dramatically affect corporate productivity and, thus, the corporate bottom line of profit. The extent to which the survey participants experienced family/work conflicts and child care problems is shown in table 3–1.

Women were most likely to believe that providing care for a sick child (45 percent) and handling the child's daytime dentist and doctor appointments (42 percent) posed at least somewhat of a problem. Women also found handling

Table 3–1
Child Care and Family/Work Problems
(percentages)

	Big Problem		Somewhat of a Problem		Small Problem		No Problem	
	Women	*Men*	*Women*	*Men*	*Women*	*Men*	*Women*	*Men*
Providing care for sick child	22	5	23	12	26	23	29	60
Child's dentist or doctor appointments	12	4	30	13	30	24	28	59
Going to school conferences or programs	14	6	25	18	24	28	37	48
Handling dual parent/ employee roles	8	2	31	11	37	30	25	57
Sudden loss of child care provider	19	6	15	8	16	12	50	75
Talking to child about his/her problems during work hours	11	4	20	13	28	22	41	61
Overnight travel	14	4	14	7	18	16	54	73
Child care during school vacations or holidays	9	3	17	7	22	13	53	77
Finding child care for evenings	15	4	10	6	12	8	64	82
Selecting best child care	8	2	17	6	21	13	55	68
Finding quality child care	10	3	15	7	18	11	57	80
Picking up child from care provider during work hours	10	3	11	5	14	9	66	83
Financing child care	7	2	14	5	16	11	64	83
Transporting child between care provider and home	3	1	10	4	15	9	72	86
Continuing present arrangements	2	0	8	4	13	8	77	88

dual family/work roles (39 percent) and going to school conferences and programs during working hours (also 39 percent) to be somewhat of a problem. The smallest percentage of women found transporting the children between the provider and home (13 percent) and continuing their present arrangements (10 percent) to be problems.

The highest percentage of men—but only 24 percent of them—found it somewhat of a problem to go to school conferences or programs during the workday. Three other areas that presented at least some problem to 17 percent of the men were providing care for a sick child, handling medical and dental appointments during the day, and communicating with the child about his or her problems during the day. Only 4 percent of the men saw any difficulty in continuing with their present arrangements, 5 percent in transporting the child between provider and home, and 7 percent in handling the costs involved in child care.

What we can infer from the employees' responses is that much higher percentages of women than men perceived that they had child care problems, and that the women's perception of the nature of those problems differed considerably from that of the men. The differences demonstrate clearly that many of the women had to be not only full-time workers but also full-time parents, whereas many of the men were free to concentrate on their jobs and were not required to become involved in much more than, perhaps, the financing of child care.

Other studies support these findings. One of them, done in 1982 by a high-tech company with which the author is familiar, noted that among 750 employees with children under 13, more than half (60 percent) of parents indicated they experienced difficulties when their children were ill. One-third (35 percent) indicated they had problems with the lack of available child care, and 38 percent listed the cost of care as a problem. Transportation to child care facilities (cited by 28 percent) and the quality of care (noted by 24 percent) also presented significant problems for parents in the sample.[11]

The *Wall Street Journal* in October 1984 asked executive women working full-time how they and their spouses handled home responsibilities. Fifty-four percent of the female executives surveyed responded that they handled household bill-paying on their own; 25 percent shared the task with their husbands; and 21 percent left the task to their husbands to handle. Fifty-two percent of the women surveyed saw to it by themselves, or with only a little help from their husbands, that the laundry was done, whereas only 7 percent of the men took care of the laundry by themselves. (Twenty-eight percent of the women said they shared the responsibility, and 13 percent "couldn't say" who was responsible.) As for grocery shopping, 47 percent of the women reported that they went to the store primarily or exclusively alone; 41 percent shared the task with their husbands; 8 percent let their husbands do the shopping, and 4 percent "couldn't say." When it comes to sharing responsibility, as we shall see further in chapter 4, women did most of the "sharing."

Seventy percent of the female executives surveyed by the *Wall Street Journal* were the sole or primary parent involved in shopping for children's clothes, although 17 percent of them occasionally received help from their husbands with this responsibility; 3 percent left this task to their husbands, and 10 percent "couldn't say" who handled it.

Husbands became involved more in taking care of a sick child. Only 30 percent of female executives surveyed shouldered this burden alone or primarily by themselves, and 49 percent said their husbands shared in the responsibility. Five percent said their husbands were solely responsible for the care of a sick child, and 16 percent "couldn't say."

Discipline was the most male dominated of parental responsibilities in the survey. Only 13 percent of the women said they handled discipline alone or virtually alone, and 73 percent said they shared the responsibility with their husbands. Four percent left the disciplining to Dad, and 10 percent "couldn't say" how the responsibility was divided.

"Despite their demanding work schedules," the *Wall Street Journal* concluded, "many of the women carry more of the burden of family and domestic responsibilities than their husbands do.... In households with children, most of the executives' husbands help out with raising the children. But very few of the husbands—only 5 percent or less—assume chief responsibility for any duty involving the children."[12]

To summarize, studies clearly demonstrate that although drastic changes have occurred in the numbers of women working, corresponding changes have not taken place in the division of labor in the home. In terms of shouldering domestic responsibilities, the woman is the primary parent. Several of the survey participants' comments about the dual-role conflict, or lack thereof, were insightful:

> Most men don't realize that the children are theirs, too, when the child is sick or needs day care; that, to them, is just another facet of "women's work." Most women take the responsibility for their children and handle it extremely well, a fact which, in my opinion, proves they are capable, strong employees whom the company should be glad to have on its payroll!
>
> *—white, female upper-middle-level manager*

> I do not want to downplay or criticize persons who wish to stay at home and care for children. Child care and homemaking is very hard work. However, I do resent society's feeling that this should be strictly the woman's role. My husband does a lot of child care and housework. And I continually get comments about him like, "Isn't he depressed?" "Isn't his ego deflated?" He doesn't need people's pity; he needs their support.
>
> *—female lower-middle-level manager*

> I feel fortunate that I can afford to have my mate stay home with the kids. I was brought up this way and expected no less.
>
> *—white, male lower-middle-level manager*

The fact that a percentage of men in this study—albeit much smaller than the percentage of women—did, indeed, have problems in these areas, demonstrates that slowly increasing numbers of men are taking on more responsibilities at home. When the responses to questions about child care problems were indexed and controls were established for marital status, the findings revealed that single men (16 percent) were least likely to say they had no problem in this area, followed by single women (23 percent) and married women (28 percent). Married men (60 percent) were by far the most likely not to have family/work conflicts and child care problems.

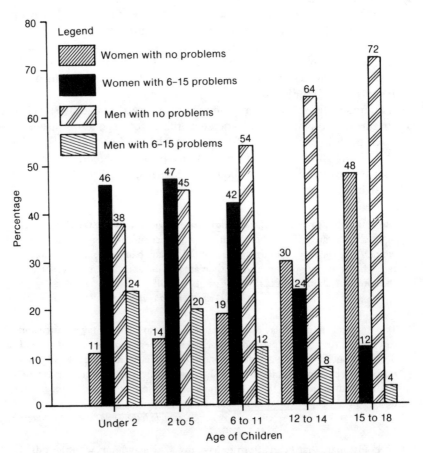

Figure 3–2. Percentage Who Have Family/Work and Child Care Problems

Table 3–2
Relationship between Family/Work Problems and Lost Work Time
(percentages[a])

	No Problems		Few Problems (1–5)		Some Problems (6–10)		Many Problems (11–15)	
	Women	*Men*	*Women*	*Men*	*Women*	*Men*	*Women*	*Men*
Missed work	49	35	64	40	66	48	71	68
Late for work	33	30	43	42	51	47	58	57
Left work early	55	56	67	61	71	61	82	59
Dealt with child care issues during work hours	60	68	80	80	84	81	94	77

[a]Percentages of parents who missed work, were late for work, or left work early because of child care, or dealt with child care issues during work hours, in the previous year.

No significant differences occurred by occupational level with child care problems for women (29 percent had none), but 43 percent of male crafts-workers, compared to between 64 and 66 percent of male managers, had no problems with child care.

Figure 3–2 shows the relationship between children's ages and family/work and child care problems. It is clear that the younger the children, the higher the percentage of employees was who said they experienced difficulties. For example, 46 percent of the women and 24 percent of the men with children under 2, compared to 12 percent of the women and 4 percent of the men with children 15 to 18, said they experienced at least six out of fifteen problems referred to.

Among women there were no significant differences by race, but race was a factor among men. Black men (43 percent) were least likely to say they had no problems with child care and family/work issues, compared to 53 percent of other men of color and 60 percent of white men.

The explanation for the different responses of the men from the various racial groups is partly that black men represented a much higher proportion of single heads of household and were, therefore, more susceptible to these problems than were men of color or white men. In addition, a higher percentage of the wives of black men were working part- or full-time than were the wives of other men.

Unproductive Time at Work Due to Child Care Problems

The relationship between employees who reported that they had child care problems and family/work conflicts and who also had lost productive time at work is clearly demonstrated in table 3–2. For example, almost twice the percentage (68 percent) of men who had a great many problems in these areas as those who had none (35 percent) had not missed work in the previous year. Also, more than one and a half times the percentage of women (94 percent) with a great many problems than those with no family/work or child care problems (60 percent) had dealt with family issues during working hours in the previous year.

Table 3–3 demonstrates the significant impact the age of children had on employees' productive time. For example, a large majority of the women with preschoolers and about one out of three men with preschoolers had spent unproductive time at work because of child care concerns. As one might expect, marital status did not affect the responses of women. Forty-eight percent said they had spent unproductive time at work because of child-related concerns. Forty-two percent of single men responded quite similarly to these women. On the other hand, only 24 percent of the married men said that child-related concerns had affected their productivity.

The large discrepancy in percentages for married men and women provides more evidence that women are still by far the major child care providers in dual-career families and that many men have wives who either do not work or work only part-time and who handle the primary provision of child care. The following comments by men with wives who stayed at home substantiate this conclusion:

My wife stays home to take care of our children.

—black lower-level manager

If a child has to see a doctor, I call home to see what's wrong. My wife doesn't work, so she handles all child care while I'm at work.

—Hispanic lower-middle-level manager

Child care for me is only two hours per week, so this isn't a problem.

—Hispanic, male craftsworker

Table 3–3
Parents Who Have Spent Unproductive Time at Work Due to Child Care Concerns
(percentages)

Age of Child	Women (N = 1,225)	Men (N = 1,597)
Under 2	58	33
2 to 5	57	34
6 to 11	52	27
12 to 14	44	22
15 to 18	39	17

My wife doesn't work. She is a fine child care provider.
—white, lower-middle-level manager

For those who are not in the same position as the men just quoted, other comments from the survey participants may shed additional light on the issue of unproductive time:

You feel obligated to your children and to work. There are too many times when you feel that you should be home with your children and not working. Therefore, you end up making mistakes in your work because of these concerns.
—white, female craftsworker

Typically, the spouse is at home so that day-to-day needs can be met. My concern about my child's health still affects me regardless of by whom or how child care is provided.
—black, male upper-middle-level manager

Always worrying about a sick child.... Managers tell you to leave personal problems at home, but you can never separate child from mind.
— white, female craftsworker

M.F. Fox and S. Hesse-Biber sum up the present situation with regard to the primacy of work for many women by stating that the family role is allowed to interfere with the work role; for men, the opposite is true—the work role is allowed to interfere with the family role.[13]

Although women carry the major burden in the area of child care, about one in four men responded affirmatively to the question on unproductive time at work due to child care problems, which supports the claim that in a minority of homes, men do play a supportive role in child care. That some men are becoming more accepting of their wives' employment, even to the extent of sharing household duties, is suggested by a recent study which found that men today are at home an average of twelve to fourteen more hours per week than they were in 1965. "The main conclusion is that men are spending more time caring for their children and doing housework than ever before."[14]

The percentage of employees who answered in the affirmative about spending unproductive time on the job might have been higher, especially for women, were it not for the number of jobs that make it virtually impossible for employees to leave their work stations—even to make a telephone call. As one black craftswoman observed, "How much *unproductive* time can be spent in information services, when everybody is worrying about the time it takes you to handle a customer?"

The responses to this question were also skewed by the number of employees who refused to admit to spending unproductive time because they felt that they had made up the time. For example, two white, lower–middle-level managers, one female and the other male, said:

I may spend unproductive hours, but I make up lost time over lunch hours, weekends, and evenings to meet deadlines.

You fail to ask how many times I have been called on the phone at home in the middle of the night to answer work questions, how many times I have had to go in to work at night or on weekends. These occurrences all affect employee productivity.

A black craftswoman said that she kept unproductive time to a bare minimum by using her breaks and lunch hours to make telephone calls and tend to personal matters. And a white, male middle-level manager remarked:

It has been my experience that school visits, medical problems when a parent has to leave the job, etc., are more than paid back by the employee's willingness to work extra time.

A few employees said openly that the reason they did not spend unproductive time on the job is because unsympathetic supervisors did not allow them to. A native American craftswoman commented, "If my child does call, I simply tell her to get off the phone, and I'll talk to her when I get home. That bothers me, but my supervisor gives me a hard time about my daughter calling." As we will see in chapter 6, employees whose supervisors cooperate in allowing them to address their child care needs often are the most productive workers because (a) they work doubly hard to make up the lost time, and (b) they are freer of stress and family/work conflicts.

Another factor minimizing unproductive time was assistance received from the extended family—especially, but not exclusively, among blacks—as demonstrated by the following comments from two black craftswomen and one white female lower-level manager:

Child-related concerns are shared by other family members, including grandparents, in order to avoid disruption of work.

I can't afford to have quality care for my children, so I have my brother take care of [them]. He is experienced but doesn't teach them well.

Very little unproductive time. My mother will watch them if necessary.

Some employers, especially white men, believed they could totally separate the issues of work and family, and therefore felt they put in no unproductive time. The comments of a white middle-level manager whose wife stayed at home exemplified this conviction: "My job at the company is to work; my job at home is to care for my family. I don't mix the two."

As one might expect, the more often employees did deal with family problems at the workplace, the less likely they were to claim that they spent no unproductive time at work. Similar trends occurred when responses to the question about unproductive time were cross-tabulated with those related to leaving work early, arriving late, and missing work.

There was another predictable relationship: employees who admitted that they put in unproductive time at work were much more likely than those who did not to agree that child care problems cost their company dearly in lost productive time.

Conclusions

The data clearly suggest that significant majorities of employees, regardless of age, race, marital status, occupational level, or parenthood status, believed that corporations could greatly benefit from assisting parents with child care. Significant majorities also believed that their companies were losing a great deal of money in unproductive time because of family/work conflicts and child care problems. The data unquestionably showed that many of the same empoyees cost their companies money in terms of their attendance and attention to work because of problems with child care and dual family/work roles. A study done in 1983 at a major technological firm supports the findings presented in this chapter. The report said:

> Child care-related problems...have caused almost half (48 percent) of the respondents with children to be late for work. The median number of late days in the sample due to child care–related problems was 3.6 days. We also asked respondents if problems with child care had ever caused them to miss work entirely. Again almost half of the respondents (47 percent) said yes. The median number of days missed was 2.1 per year due to problems with child care.[15]

The previously cited data demonstrate that gender, parenthood status, and children's ages had the greatest impact on absenteeism and much less of an effect on the frequency with which employees left work early or came late to work. While the age of children 18 and under had some effect on employees' proclivity to deal with family issues during work hours, the key determinant in this area was the presence in the family of children 18 and under, rather than the specific ages of children within that category.

Data in this chapter show further that while women have entered the work force in large numbers on a permanent, full-time basis, they are in most cases holding down a full-time job at home as well, with little if any help from their husbands or mates. Thus, it is not surprising that married women responded similarly to single women about child care and family/work problems and about loss of productivity at work. Many married women are, in fact, "single" when it comes to balancing work and family/child care responsibilities.

The 1983 study of a major technological firm stated further:

> Gender differences also emerged.... Child care problems caused slightly more women than men to be late for work. However, 70 percent of women with children had to miss work at least one time, while only 36 percent of the male parents had missed work due to child care problems. Finally, problems with child care have caused significantly more women than men to quit a job, refuse an offer of employment, or work fewer hours. Thirty-nine percent of women with children had experienced these problems, compared to 9 percent of the men with children.[16]

It is worth repeating the finding that single male parents are experiencing difficulties in their attempts to be both parent and worker that are similar to the problems experienced by women in this endeavor. The data on single men in this study were supported by G.L. Greif who, in his survey of 1,136 single male parents, said that "the changes most often experienced were having to arrive late or leave early (35 percent), and having to miss work (34 percent).[17]

For all groups, the stress inherent in the conflicts between family and work issues is taking its toll on corporate productivity. The next chapter will focus on the impact of stress on productive work time owing to child care and family/work problems.

4
Family/Work Conflicts and Stress: Impact on Employee Productivity

Previous chapters showed how problems with child care cost employers hours—and, in many cases, entire days—of unproductive time or time actually lost on the job. Absenteeism, lateness, early departures, even the use of the telephone to resolve problems during the workday are all relatively easy to document and measure. What many corporations fail to realize is that the delicate balancing of home and work responsibilities creates stress, which also greatly affects corporate productivity. The data and responses of survey participants in this chapter will firmly establish this as fact.

Social scientists have long recognized that work plays an essential role in the lives of human beings. Work is at the center of most adults' lives, providing them with a sense of identity, self-esteem, and order, or, in other words, fulfilling both egoistic and social needs. With regard to the latter, psychologists and sociologists have stressed the importance of good working relationships—characterized by a high degree of trust and by supportiveness, friendship, and interest among subordinates, peers, and superiors—in maintaining productive, efficient corporations. The most important egoistic need is the sense of fulfillment in terms of accomplishment—that is, the individual's sense of the importance of his or her own work, rate of progress, completion of work, and productivity.

While work is extremely important to Americans, family is even more important in most cases, especially for women. Partners want to provide the best for their mates and children, not only materially, but psychologically as well. When the two powerful forces of work and family come into conflict with one another, the resultant stress can be overwhelming, especially for upwardly mobile women and men; and since the responsibility for the handling of dual family/work roles falls primarily to the woman, it is clear who experiences the greatest degree of stress.

A feeling of guilt underlies the stress experienced by many working women. The feeling stems primarily from leaving young children in order to go to work. It is sometimes self-inflicted but is often imposed on women by family members, friends, neighbors who stay at home with their children, coworkers (mostly male), and researchers who insist that working mothers are damaging their children and destroying the family unit. Any employed woman is a target for blame should anything go amiss with her children, even the ordinary, everyday problems inherent in growing up. The feeling of guilt surfaced repeatedly in the comments of the survey participants. A young, white, female manager summed it up this way: "When he [the child] is ill, he wants me at home. It's always a hassle with my parents and in-laws. Anything that goes wrong they blame on my working, especially when he gets sick." Should marital problems occur, they too are construed as the fault of the working mother: had she been home where she belonged, the critics imply, all would be well.

Women are not the sole victims of stress caused by conflicting roles. Men too are pressured by relatives, neighbors, and friends who tell them, directly or indirectly, that "real men" don't let their wives work and, if their wives are working, real men certainly don't allow themselves to be dragged into doing women's work around the house. Too often they are ridiculed or even ostracized for taking care of their children, going shopping, or helping with household chores.

Many men apparently are heeding the advice of their peers and are refusing to share the work at home, and women, understandably, are attempting to cope with their dual workload by reducing the amount of time they spend on household tasks. A number of studies on time budgeting clearly show that women who are employed do less housework than women who are not employed and that the number of household tasks performed by women decreases in proportion to the increase in the number of hours they work outside the home. Even so, working women spend a significant number of hours on household family tasks.[1] For example, in 1974 J.J. Vanek noted that unemployed women spent fifty-five hours per week on household tasks, compared to about twenty-six hours for women employed full-time.[2] Computation of the total amount of work time shows that a fully employed woman works sixty or more hours a week. There is little evidence to show that men increase their contributions to household chores when their wives go to work.

Findings and conclusions in another study were similar. S.F. Berk wrote in 1985 that women employed full-time outside the home spent approximately thirty hours per week on household tasks and that women who were not employed outside the home spent about sixty hours a week on such tasks. She also noted that 70 percent of the total time spent on household chores was contributed by women, 15 percent by men, and the remainder by other members of the household.[3]

Berk wrote further that husbands with working wives did about 10 percent more work in the form of monthly household tasks than did husbands whose wives stayed home. This translated into an average of only about five minutes more a day on household tasks than for men with nonworking wives. Thus, men with nonworking wives spent about three hours and fifteen minutes, while those with working wives spent about three hours and twenty minutes.[4]

Besides bearing the primary responsibility for household tasks whether they are employed or full-time homemakers, many women whose husbands hold management positions also do much to advance their husbands' careers. J. London and J.T. Mortimer cited two case studies showing that the pressures and opportunities of managerial and professional work place additional burdens on wives, who often undertake clerical or bookkeeping tasks, perform extensive entertaining designed to enhance their husbands' images, or serve as community volunteers, both for the purpose of image-building and to make contacts to bolster their husbands' business and professional practices. Not the least of wives' contributions is their role as sounding board or informal consultant, soothing their husbands after a long hard day at work; but the support is not often reciprocal, and many wives complain that their husbands are psychologically unavailable to family members and, because of extensive absorption in their careers, have little energy left with which to become actively involved with wives and children.[5]

Leaving aside the support or lack thereof of husbands whose wives enter the work force—particularly on a full-time, career-path basis—working women's new economic independence and evolving career aspirations often create new stresses and conflicts in the home. Society is slowly accepting the idea that women have a right to work outside the home, but the widely held conviction that women should be the primary or exclusive child care providers and homemakers in a family has not changed in any perceptible degree. The incongruence of these two views is a major source of family/work conflict. In short, there has been little departure from traditional roles in the home in dual-career families: a woman must be Supermom, wife, worker, and confidante. As Ellen Goodman pointed out:

> Supermom...always had "something lovin'" in the oven. She was always nurturing. For years we have carried her around in our heads, just for the guilt of it. Now we have replaced her with Superwoman or Supermom II, whose typical day is something like the following: She wakes up to her 2.6 children. They go downstairs and she gives them a Grade A nutritional breakfast, which they eat, and they all go off to school.... She goes upstairs to get dressed in her $300 Anne Klein suit and goes off to her $25,000 job which is both creative and socially useful. After work she comes home and spends a wonderful hour relating with the children....She then prepares a gourmet dinner for her husband. They spend time working on their meaningful relationship, after which they go upstairs where she has multiple orgasms until midnight.[6]

The picture of home life among some of the respondents to our survey reflected the notion of Supermom. A Hispanic craftswoman reported that her husband "feels that his job away from home should release him from any sharing of the work responsibility of chores at home." A single, black woman who was a lower-level manager confessed that "when I'm at work, I worry about the chores that await me when I get home and the little time I have to do them because I work the split shift." A white, married woman who was a lower-level manager concurred:

> I find it very difficult to switch roles from worker to mother when I get home. From five o'clock until eight o'clock, I'm still working—cooking, watching the baby, playing with her. When she goes to bed at eight, I can finally have some time to myself. I find this to be more a mental than a physical strain; it creates a great deal of tension.

As we saw earlier, some men are breaking away from traditional roles and are taking on increasing responsibilities in the home. In a 1977 representative national sample of dual-career families, J.H. Pleck found that "employed husbands with employed wives reported spending 1.8 hours per week more in housework ... and 2.7 hours per week more in child care than did employed husbands with non-employed wives. When converted to minutes per day, these increments are obviously not large. Nonetheless, they appear to be one of the first findings of non-trivial increments in husbands' family work associated with wives' employment."[7]

Comments of some women in our study supported this conclusion. A black, female lower-level manager said that because of her husband's help, she had no problem balancing home and work responsibilities. "I have worked out a pretty good schedule so far as this is concerned," she stated. "My husband is very good about sharing responsibilities." A white, male lower-level manager noted that he and his wife "both work and both share home duties with few conflicts." A white, female middle-level manager explained: "My spouse and I agree we have *chosen* dual roles and spend some of our income to make both tasks easier (car pool, microwave, new sewing machine because I like making children's clothes, educational toys, family vacations, and the cleaning person are great)."

In fact, a small segment of society has been developing Superdad to help Supermom. Superdad does his fair share of cooking, cleaning, and child care. He has to be a witty and intelligent host when his wife entertains, a devoted father, a loving husband capable of giving his wife multiple orgasms every night and, on top of everything else, he must be promoted every year and become a vice president by the age of thirty-eight.

The emerging trend toward greater involvement on the part of men in household chores notwithstanding, Pleck and others have failed to note the selective aspect of the involvement. Most men restrict their homemaking duties to the easier, "clean" tasks like cooking, watching the children, and occasional light dusting or folding the laundry. The "dirty work"—washing and waxing floors, cleaning the toilet, and ironing the clothes—remain the woman's work in most households. What is more, many men are becoming involved in household chores not so much out of a spirit of voluntarism or generosity as out of sheer necessity. More and more working women are flatly refusing to be the "spic 'n' span" superwife of past generations. Their attitude is, quite simply, that if the husband doesn't help, the house won't be cleaned.

Dual careers and dual family/work roles create stress and conflict both at home and on the job. A certain level of on-the-job stress, caused by employment uncertainty, office politics, budget crunches, tight time frames, lack of corporate resources, and, sometimes, long hours, is inherent for most employees. For upwardly mobile employees, factors such as employment insecurity, office politics, and long hours are added to extraordinary workloads, a great deal of pressure, and more than average responsibility. For all employees, on-the-job stress along with family stress can create an overload: too much to do, with too little time in which to do it. Ultimately, owing to both physical and mental problems that are its by-products, overload leads to lowered corporate productivity.

J. Grimaldi and B.P. Schnapper made this observation on the eventual negative impact of stress on employees:

> The relationship between stress and illness is well documented. In fact, high blood pressure, ulcers, stomach disorders, and heart disease are familiar examples of stress-related health problems. Low back pain and even colds and flu can result from stress. In fact, some medical experts have estimated that as many as 60 to 80 percent of their patients have stress-related complaints.[8]

R. Rapoport and R.N. Rapoport suggested that the degree of overload is in some part self-imposed and is dependent on a number of factors, including the parental status of employees, their desire to be occupationally and economically mobile, the extent to which household tasks are shared, and the degree to which social-psychological issues and physical issues interact with and compound one another.[9]

A closer look at the survey participants' perceptions of family/work stress and its impact on corporate productivity follows.

Overall Effects of Stress on Productivity

In order to understand the tremendous impact of dual careers on family/work stress and corporate productivity, an index of questions related to these areas, and then three individual questions related to stress, will be analyzed.

The questions that comprised the index were:

1. To what extent has balancing family and work responsibilities created stress on the job?
2. To what extent has balancing family and work responsibilities created stress at home?
3. With regard to your child care needs, how much of a problem is handling dual roles as parent and employee?
4. How frequently have you spent unproductive time at work because of child-care related concerns?

Table 4–1 shows that, overall, 57 percent of the women, single or married, and 60 percent of the single men, experienced problems in at least one of the above areas at least to some extent. In addition, about 22 percent of these groups had problems in three or four of the areas. On the other hand, only about 29 percent of the married men had problems in at least one area, and only 5 percent of the married men experienced difficulties in three or more areas. "Degree of stress" was based on the number of questions to which participants responded positively at least to some extent.

The table demonstrates dramatically the unique and comfortable position in which many of the married men in management found themselves; but that comfort may be short-lived. As career opportunities for women increase and as the pressures of these careers intensify, wives will become increasingly intolerant of the extreme imbalance in responsibilities at home, and more and more married men will begin to feel the stress and conflict of dual-career lives. As this happens, married men may find themselves no longer immune to dealing with family problems in the workplace.

When responses were analyzed by race, little variation emerged among men of different races, but the data indicated that black women felt less stress

Table 4–1
Overall Stress Related to Family/Work Conflicts
(*percentages*)

Degree of Stress[a]	Single Women (N = 269)	Married Women (N = 958)	Single Men (N = 45)	Married Men (N = 1,558)
0	44	42	40	71
1	14	19	24	14
2	20	15	16	9
3	16	19	20	5
4	6	4	0	0

[a]Range is from no stress (0) to a great deal of stress (4).

than did other women of color or white women. Percentages of those with no stress problems were:

	Women	Men
Black	54%	73%
Other color	43%	67%
White	41%	70%

While a very small percentage of all men surveyed found that three or four of these areas posed problems, white men scored the lowest: only 6 percent responded positively to at least three of the questions. White women, on the other hand, were most likely of the race/gender groups to respond positively. Percentages of those with three or four stress problem areas were:

	Women	Men
Black	11%	10%
Other color	22%	9%
White	25%	6%

The relatively low stress level recorded for black women came as no surprise to a group of black female participants with whom the survey results were discussed in early 1985. Black women, they said, have traditionally performed a balancing act and are, therefore, better able to cope with family/work stress. The women also acknowledged that the presence of an extended family also helps to relieve stress for black women. As one woman put it, "My job is not very demanding, and I usually have all my family responsibilities worked out, with some help from my own family." Finally, they suggested that many more black men than other men of color or white men are "liberated" and help around the house.

Scarr, supporting the notion of the extended family, wrote that many black families include siblings of the parents, grandparents, brothers, sisters, aunts, uncles, and other immediate and not-so-immediate relatives. While the biological mothers have responsibilities for the care of the children, other relatives are available to take over that responsibility when the need arises.[10]

That white males are least likely to have problems overall can be attributed to their high status in the corporation and the likelihood that their wives are full-time homemakers.

The stress felt by respondents had a great impact on corporate productivity in terms of lost work time. In order to illustrate this important fact beyond a shadow of a doubt, the three specifically stress-related questions were formed into an index, which was correlated with questions asked employees about missing work, coming to work late, leaving work early, and dealing with family issues during working hours. As table 4-2 shows, there was an extremely high correlation between the index and these questions. Note that the percentage for women who experienced no stress, compared to those women who experienced the most stress, was more than double in terms of missed work (45 versus 22 percent). For men, the difference was not as dramatic, but it was still significant: 66 versus 50 percent.

These data clearly demonstrate the impact of the balancing act on employees' attendance and productivity. Now we will take a look at the three questions that comprised the index in order to better understand why the participants responded as they did.

Stress from Handling Dual Roles

Not surprisingly, women found dual roles far more of a problem than men did, and women in management were more sensitive to the issue than were craftswomen. Overall, 39 percent of the women, compared to 13 percent of the men, believed that handling dual family/work roles was at least somewhat of a problem. Thirty-five percent of the craftswomen, compared to only 16 percent of the craftsmen, perceived the necessity to handle dual roles as at least somewhat problematic. Forty-three percent of the female managers and 12 percent of male managers concurred.

There are several possible reasons that female managers would be more likely than their counterparts in crafts to experience balancing dual roles as a problem. One explanation is that female managers' jobs are usually much more demanding in terms of time and commitment. By and large, positions in management are more intense, complex, and difficult, requiring a great deal of thought both on and off the job. Finally, women in management are in a more competitive environment than are craftswomen. Female managers are career-oriented and are holding down jobs that are more demanding, difficult, intense,

Table 4-2
Relationship between Specific Stress Index and Lost Work Time
(*percentages*[a])

Degree of Stress[b]	Never Missed Work		Never Late for Work		Never Left Work Early		Never Dealt with Child Care Issues during Work Hours	
	Women	Men	Women	Men	Women	Men	Women	Men
0	45	66	65	66	41	44	35	30
1	36	55	55	60	32	39	20	22
2	34	47	47	53	22	32	8	14
3	22	50	42	47	24	33	2	1

[a]Percentages of parents who never missed work, came to work late, or left work early because of child care, or dealt with child care issues during work hours, in the previous year.
[b]Range is from no stress (0) to a great deal of stress (3).

and time-consuming. They tend to have fewer hours and less energy to devote to home tasks and are, therefore, more vulnerable to the stress of balancing dual roles.

A white, female middle-level manager summed up her situation and that of many other women in this way:

> My job is not an eight-hour-a-day job. It requires planning and very often some work in the evenings at home. It is difficult to be all things to everyone—spouse, children, employer, and others (school, other family members, neighbors, and friends). My husband also works for the company and is in a high-stress, time-demanding job requiring frequent travel.

As one might expect, handling dual roles is greatly influenced by the age of children both for men and women, as figure 4–1 indicates.

The percentage of women who had problems at least to some extent with handling dual roles was twice or more the percentage of men. According to a survey of 20,000 employees from thirty-three companies, with 8,000 responding to the questionnaire, 38 percent of the women with children under 12,

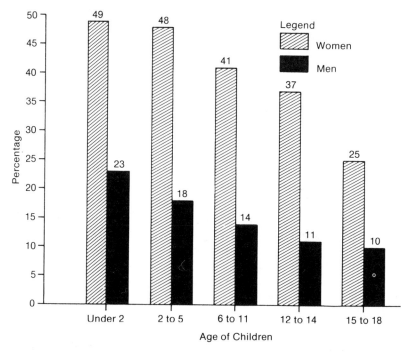

Figure 4–1. Percentage Who Are Having Difficulty Balancing Family and Work Responsibilities

21 percent with children 12 to 18, and 9 percent with no children under 18 found it difficult to combine home and job responsibilities. For men in the same study, the figures were 23, 14, and 8 percent, respectively.[11] These findings support the observations of some social scientists, including D.A. Skinner, who noted that "an overwhelming proportion of the literature reports that the impact of dual-career stress is felt most by women....A man can combine a professional career and parenting more easily than a woman can because less is expected of the man with regard to familial responsibilities."[12] J.G. Hunt and L.L. Hunt concurred. "The lives of dual-career men are essentially similar to those of other career men," they wrote, "while the lives of dual-career wives were juggling acts that provided a measure of career involvement as long as it did not inconvenience the family."[13]

A review of some employees' comments will help to clarify the problems they are experiencing with dual family/work roles.

A major area of concern for parents, and especially for women, was worrying about their children while they themselves were working. A clear source of this worry is the double bind in which women are placed by society's conflicting messages about their child care and working roles. A white, male lower-level manager echoed the women's sentiments with his observation that "having children in day care is hard on working parents, especially working mothers." His wife, he said, "always feels that she's cheating our children out of a normal childhood."

A Hispanic craftswoman reported that she worries a great deal about her children. "There's nothing else that comes first," she said, "and when I talk to customers, I'm often thinking about the kids and I stumble over the words." A white craftswoman put it this way: "I'm always wondering if [my child] is being taken care of properly, because with every sitter, all he does is cry all day. I've changed sitters five times and he's only one year old, and that's not good for him."

Sick children create a lot of stress and worry which, as two white craftswomen observed, can be major sources of unproductive time on the job. "When a child is sick, you feel guilty if you work and you feel guilty if you stay at home," said one of them. "Some bosses are not very understanding." The other confessed that she sometimes sends a sick child to day care anyway. "It's very difficult not feeling guilty," she said. "My children are important to me and so is my job. There are many times that I feel I can't stay with them because of my job responsibility."

Their children's safety is another source of worry for many parents. A white, male lower-level manager and a black, female lower–middle-level manager added:

Concerns about child safety are always present...on the job. The children come first under all circumstances.

If I have to leave my child at home alone for a little while to [get to] work on time, I worry about whether he'll be all right until the older kids arrive to care for him.

A white craftswoman had her son call her at work daily to "check in." She worried about him, but she "can't afford day care."

A white, female middle-level manager, on the other hand, found that a day care center solved her problems. "The day care I am currently using is wonderful," she says. "When I used a private sitter, my mind was often cluttered with problems. We pay dearly for the care, but the weight of the world is off my shoulders."

Even a good day care center is not enough to relieve many working women of the guilt society has foisted upon them. A black, female lower–middle-level manager whose one-year-old child is in such a center still worries a lot. "I feel very guilty about leaving my child—he is so young," she wrote. "The day care center is really good, but I feel that I don't spend enough time with him."

Those employees who worry about their children for whatever reason are bound to be limited in their ability to function effectively as working parents. Worrying about children is just one of the many reasons employees gave for having difficulties balancing work and family responsibilities. The following quotations demonstrate some of the other reasons:

Family problems always stay in my mind until they are solved.

—*white, male craftsworker*

When your job is also very stressful, it just is very hard to deal with by itself. When you add the family stress, you sometimes feel like you're going to break apart.

—*white, female lower–middle-level manager*

I bring home work frequently and am called back to work outside "normal" hours.

—*white, male lower-level manager*

Balancing work and family responsibilities leaves no time for anything else— no fun, relaxing times.

—*white, female craftsworker*

Add to the so-called normal strains of parenting the not-uncommon additional problems of substance abuse, and the stress becomes even more overwhelming, as one white, female lower–middle-level manager pointed out. "When you live in a chemically dependent family, there is always stress," she wrote. "We now have two chemically dependent people out of three. (One has been recovering for two and one half years, and the other is now in treatment.)

You try to learn to deal with it, but it does create stress. How you handle the stress is your only key to survival." Two black craftswomen acknowledged that their productivity was affected by the additional stress of being single parents. One stated her greatest problem to be "a lack of energy." As a single parent, she found that all the responsibility fell to her, "creating at times a problem with outside recreation and possible overtime." The other craftswoman commented simply: "It is hard to do a good job when there are problems at home. I'm sure that is true with anyone." A black, male lower-level manager found it hard to "balance responsibilities—home cleaning, repairs, parenting, and work."

Employees who believed that child care problems were costing their companies a great deal of money in unproductive time were much more likely than those who did not to say that handling dual family/work roles presented at least somewhat of a problem for them. For example, 41 percent of employees who strongly agreed that child care problems were costing their companies money also found handling dual roles at least somewhat a problem, compared to 14 percent who strongly disagreed that child care problems were costing their companies money and who said that handling dual roles was at least somewhat of a problem. These statistics reveal that many employees who are experiencing difficulty in handling dual roles are aware of the cost being incurred to their companies as a result of their problem.

Male respondents who said they had no difficulty in balancing dual roles attributed this to the fact that their wives either did not work outside the home at all or did not work full-time. Women who responded the same way pointed to the availability of competent, reliable child care services. A white, male upper-level manager commented: "My wife does only volunteer work; therefore, she is able to take care of most of the family and household chores." A black, female lower-level manager wrote: "If it were not for the excellent day care center my children attend and its long hours, I don't know how I could handle my job."

Besides the fact that many men have wives at home, a number of them are adamant about their ability to separate work and family. The following comments state the case very clearly:

> My family does not, and should never, create any stress on my job. I don't bring my problems from home to work and, on the other hand, I don't take any of my problems home from work.
>
> —*white, male lower-level manager*

> When I am at work, I devote my full attention to work. When I am at home, I devote my attention to my family.
>
> —*white, male lower-level manager*

> I separate totally my work and my family.
>
> —*black, male lower-level manager*

Contrary to the comments of these men, most social scientists believe it is impossible to separate totally work and family. They contend that numerous aspects of work can create such stress and dissatisfaction in employees that they cannot be left at the corporate doorstep. How many of us, they ask, can return home after work in a good frame of mind when we fail to get the promotion, pay raise, or job we felt we should have gotten, or if our jobs require us to deal constantly with corporate politics, conflicting directions, and dissension within our work group or are so taxing and draining that they leave us little energy to give to our families? The answer surely is that very few of us can effectively segment our lives in this fashion.

The view that family conflicts and problems spill over into the work environment is not easily challenged. How many of us can go in to work with a clear, dedicated mind if our children are sick or if we feel we are neglecting them? How many of us can produce to our fullest extent at work if we are experiencing mental stress due to family/work role conflicts and work overload, or if we must constantly put in sixteen-hour days because of family/work responsibilities? Again, the answer is very few. A white, female lower-middle manager summed up the problem: "Balancing responsibilities is stressful in the home as well as on the job. That stress is bound to affect quality in both areas."

The next two sections present considerable data indicating that job stress creates problems at home, and home stress creates problems at work, for significant numbers of employees with children 18 and under. (Although these questions were not posed to employees who did not have children under 18, one can speculate that stress also occurs in dual-career families with no children 18 and under. The stress is probably greatest for families in which roles are still strictly divided according to gender and/or in which husbands and wives have high-level, complex, competitive, time-consuming management positions.)

Stress on the Job

Earlier in this chapter it was noted that many jobs are inherently stressful, especially for the upwardly mobile. When this stress is added to family responsibilities and conflicting messages given to employees, particularly female employees, about their proper roles, the total stress level on the job for some employees is extremely high, as we will see.

Social scientists have pointed out that women's work is still considered secondary to and less important than men's. Fox, Biber, and Pleck, elaborating on this concept, argued that for women, family responsibilities often take priority over work responsibilities, and that for men, work responsibilities almost always take precedence over family. Placing women in this role leads to a catch-22 and a major source of conflict and stress. On the one hand, women are brought up to believe that family responsibilities must come first; but on the other hand, when women employees do give top priority to their families, corporate executives—who would most certainly expect their own wives to do the same—use this as an excuse to relegate them to lower positions of responsibility and to view them as undependable, non–career-oriented employees.[14]

Women's role in society is not the only source of family stress and conflict. Demands that are made evident through socialization as well as external pressures are placed on men constantly to relegate their families to a secondary position, while they work at jobs that require them to put in long hours, bring work home, and travel extensively. By shifting all responsibility for the home to the wife, this male role model leads to family estrangement and, for growing numbers of men, a sense of increasing guilt. A Hispanic, male lower-level manager, for example, expressed the feeling that he is short-changing his family: "I work a lot, so I worry that I should really be with my family. I've put my job before my family hoping to get ahead."

Considering that many married women are in effect single when it comes to handling family and work issues, it is not surprising that there is no significant difference between the responses of married and single women with respect to the extent to which balancing work and family responsibilities is a cause of on-the-job stress. Seventy-six percent said handling dual family/work roles did create stress for them at work. The figure was the same for single men; but only fifty-two percent of married men asserted that family problems interfered with job performance.

Table 4–3 shows that the age of children had more of an impact on the responses of men than women as to whether the balancing act created at least some stress on the job. For example, only a five percentage point difference (42 to 37 percent) occurred in the responses of women with children under 15; the range for men (26 to 13 percent) was much greater. It is important to note, nevertheless, that while the age of the children appeared to have less influence for women on this question, women were almost twice as likely as men to report that they *did* experience at least some stress on the job as the result of family problems.

Table 4–3
Parents Who Have At Least Some Stress on the Job because of Balancing Family and Work Responsibilities
(*percentages*)

Age of Child	Women (N = 1,255)	Men (N = 1,597)
Under 2	42	26
2 to 5	42	22
6 to 11	41	17
12 to 14	37	13
15 to 18	27	12

Some typical comments from the women were revealing:

> You feel obligated to your children and to work. There are too many times you feel that you should be home with your children and not working. Therefore you end up making mistakes in your work because of concerns.
> —*white, female lower-level manager*

> There has to be some stress on your job when there are children involved and you're a one-parent family, regardless of what kind of job you have.
> —*black, female lower-level manager*

> Family problems are sometimes brought to work. Sometimes you're late because of children problems. Emergencies come up and you have to leave. No pay for a lot of things necessary to the family.
> —*black, female craftsworker*

> Mornings are *so* hectic. I am seldom ever late. However, many times I come in very keyed up from trying to get kids and husband and self off to work, school, day care, etc. Especially hard when husband is not there to help, but I am lucky that way.
> —*Hispanic, female lower-level manager*

> While it's ideal to separate home and work problems, it's not reality. It's difficult to work when you know your child is throwing up at home or misbehaving at the babysitter's. I have to force myself to work sometimes.
> —*white, female upper-level manager*

Many women faithfully attempted to make up for the work time lost to family problems and responsibilities, but most of them felt that this was not adequate, particularly in the eyes of their employers. "Sometimes I must cram to meet work deadlines if I've been away from work because of a sick child," a white, female lower–middle-level manager said. "All I do is take as much work as possible home with me when this happens." Another white female manager, who, incidentally, denied that the balancing act affected job stress or productivity, remarked that "people see only the negative things, like when I leave at three p.m. to take my daughter to the dentist. No one saw me work on Christmas Eve or when I bring my daughter back to work with me in the evening. Am I invisible then?"

Stress at Home

Just as work has some inherent stresses regardless of marital or parental status of the employees, home life also can be stressful regardless of the demands of work. The normal stress of family life is greatly increased in American society because of the conflicting messages given in this society both to men and women. The impossible standard set for women in terms of their dual disproportionate amount of responsibility in the home has already been discussed. Many women are made to feel guilty for working and leaving their children, and others are accused of actually destroying their husband's masculinity, especially if they are more successful than their husbands.

Some men, as we have seen, believe that they are less than real men if their wives work and fear they will be considered effeminate if they help around the house. A small but increasing number of men are striving to be Superdad: the perfect, upwardly mobile husband making $100,000 at age thirty-five, the perfect father who spends a lot of quality time with his children, and the perfect marriage partner who shares equally in all of the household tasks and plays the role of the great host to assist his wife's advancement.

A major study in 1982 of 32,500 people found that 59 percent of those surveyed believed that work pressures on themselves or on their spouses occasionally created a serious strain on their marriage. Eleven percent cited work pressures as a frequent problem, and only 30 percent said they never experienced such pressures.[15]

In the survey on which this book is based, balancing work and family responsibilities appeared to create more stress at home than at work: 43 percent of the women and 22 percent of the men said that at least to some extent they believed that balancing family roles and work roles created stress at home, while 37 percent of the women and 16 percent of the men asserted that the balancing act created stress at work. When the data were analyzed by gender and occupation, it became evident that more female managers (49 percent) than female craftsworkers (39 percent) experienced stress at home because of the balancing act.

Figure 4–2 illustrates the impact of children's ages on the degree of stress experienced by their parents at home because of the balancing act. Note that more than double the percentage of men with children under age 2, as compared to those whose children were between 15 and 18, experienced at least some stress at home.

Why did employees affirm that the balancing act created stress at home? What they wrote was revealing and was consistent with other comments quoted in this chapter. Their remarks varied greatly, ranging among topics from feeling guilty about leaving children, feeling drained from dealing with sick children and household tasks after long hours at work, to simply trying to balance the demands of home and office.

Why don't you try being Mommy and Daddy to two boys? Their father is a computer programmer on call at all times. If I don't work overtime when and if it is offered (which is seven days a week at this point in time), I will never get ahead. The time their father spends with them is obviously very sporadic. Therefore, the time I spend with my sons is precious to both of them and to me. You're damned if you do and damned if you don't.

—*white, female craftsworker*

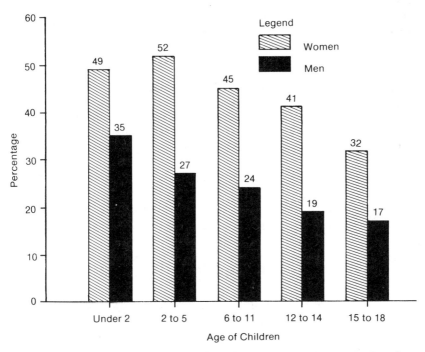

Figure 4–2. Percentage Who Are Having Stress at Home Balancing Family and Work Responsibilities

Child feels neglected when I work overtime. If I have a bad day at work, child feels the stress through conversation. A working parent can't go to daily school functions as often as she would like to.

—*white, female lower-level manager*

If I lose sleep with sick children, I'm crabby. And sometimes children don't understand that you can't always get off work to attend school events.

—*white, female lower-level manager*

In 1983 my workload was outrageous. Very often (once a week) I would pick up my child by 5:00, take him home, and after he was asleep (at 9:00) call in a sitter and go back to work for a few hours. Finding a sitter on a Saturday is also difficult.

—*white, female middle-level manager*

Children never give me a break. They feel like I'm always on the go, working splits, but if I worked straight shifts, the hours would be so bad that I would see less of them than I do now, and day care is a problem when I work late hours.

—*black, female lower-level manager*

The hours I work make it difficult to spend time with my children. When I come home, it's time for them to go to bed. In the morning when I'm home, they're in school. Sometimes when I am needed at home, I can't be there, so I get to work and worry about them.

—black, female craftsworker

I never see my son except coming and going on Monday through Friday. I get up in the a.m. to see him off to school, and I see him again when waking him up to bring him home from the sitter. Any problems or concerns or business we need to conduct gets done with a phone call from or to work.

—white, female lower-level manager

Every mother's deepest concern is expressed by the lower-level female manager who said, "Children want attention. I worry about whether my working has affected my children to an extent that they will be poor citizens and unproductive human beings." A white craftswoman wrote: "I find myself taking out my work-related 'bad' days on my kids."

Not only are children possibly affected when their parents attempt this balancing act of family and work roles, but the relationship between the parents themselves may also be affected. As one white, female middle-level manager noted candidly, "When both spouses work and have difficulties at work, it is hard for both to have an 'open ear' when one needs to talk."

"I am often too irritable because there never seems to be enough time," said a white craftswoman. A white, female lower-level manager who never got help from her husband noted: "It's hard to keep a clean house, take care of kids, work all day, fix meals. . . . things keep demanding, including my husband."

Males recognize the problem, too. Two Hispanic men, both lower-level managers, commented: "My wife and I argue more now that we are working the same hours," and "I bring my work to home, meaning I worry about this problem or that at home." Others wrote:

Even though my mate is not employed outside the home, she likes to thrust family responsibility on me as soon as I set foot through the door. Her rationale is that *she* had an exhausting day with the kids.

—black, male craftsworker

Our "workday" begins at 5 a.m. and ends after 6 p.m. because of the drive time to a qualified sitter: thirteen hours to put in an eight-hour day? What's left? You come home to a kitchen full of dirty dishes and meals to prepare.

—white, male lower-level manager

And, according to the women, men are also part of the problem:

My husband wants relief from the baby at an expected time. When I work extra hours, he gets crabby.

—white, female craftsworker

Towards the end of every month we get a lot of work and I feel under a lot of stress when everyone wants about five different things at once. It is not physically possible to go to work under those conditions and then go home to housework and taking care of a two-year-old. It is very difficult, and I go home with a lot of stress piled on me.

—Hispanic, female lower-level manager

My husband resents the company having evening meetings and/or parties that do not include spouses.

—white, female middle-level manager

Skinner identified an interesting paradox in parents' concern about the impact of their working on their children. He said that in the attempt to protect children from the strains of a dual-career family, parents sometimes unwittingly create more strain for themselves and, thus, indirectly, more for the children.[16]

Those families that did not report stress problems at home said that the lack of stress was owing in large part to supportive, helpful partners. "My husband and I share all responsibilities—cooking, housekeeping, kids, yard, laundry, etc.," wrote a white craftswoman. "Without him, I'm sure the stress would be great." Another said: "My husband can more easily stay home from his job, so it is a responsibility that always falls to him. The same for school visits and the like."

Most men who gave explanations for why they did not experience stress took what could be considered a conservative, nonreflective stance. For example, one white craftsman said, "If I felt that my job was creating a problem for my family, I would look for a job that I could handle without stress." A white, male middle-level manager described it all very straightforwardly: "My priorities are simple: my God, myself, my family, my country and my work. My work is important in fulfilling my responsibilities toward my other priorities, but my life must be integrated with all of them."

Ultimately, stress can result in unproductive work time if it is so overwhelming that the employee becomes ill. Several respondents in the survey reported stomach ulcers and other health problems which they attributed directly to family/work stress. A white female manager stated simply: "Stress reaches peak levels, resulting in illness and fatigue." Similarly, a black craftswoman commented: "Being a single parent and working with outside interests both for yourself and your children can cause you stress and health problems."

G. Ritzer supported these views while writing about upwardly mobile managers: "I believe it can apply to dual career families, especially women and single parents regardless of occupational status. The fact is that stress is associated with a number of personal problems. . . . Upwardly mobile managers, who typically have extraordinary workloads and great pressure and responsibility, have far greater incidence of heart disease, ulcers, arthritis, stroke, and various forms of mental illness. Then, too, job-related stress may manifest itself in a series of behaviors such as alcoholism, drug abuse, and even suicide."[17]

In this chapter we have observed the problems that are created for employees when they attempt to balance work roles and family roles. That these problems create stress, which in turn affects corporate productivity, is very clear. When family/work conflicts create stress that lead to health problems, emotional or physical, companies forfeit a tremendous amount of money not only in lost productivity but also in increased medical and health insurance costs.

Particular Problems of Single Parents

The data in this chapter and chapter 3 have shown that single male parents, overall, were least likely (16 percent) to say they had *no* problems with child care, and most likely to have experienced stress (more than 60 percent said they had experienced at least one out of the four problems that made up the overall stress index in this chapter). The data also showed that women who were single parents (23 percent) were second only to single men in having had no problems with child care and in reporting at least one stress-related problem. (The percentage of both single and married women reporting at least some stress was 57.)

The problems of the "true" single parents (as opposed to married women who are in effect single with respect to domestic responsibilities) and of married women are going to increase in the years to come, resulting in an even greater impact on corporate productivity. Working women will continue to move up the corporate ladder into jobs that will be more demanding. This will cause some of them to try to make their marriages less sexist in terms of family, household, and child-rearing tasks, and the difficulty that couples will have in adjusting to the new nonsexist roles will create more stress and conflicts in marriages. Single parents' problems will multiply as their numbers increase. Between 1970 and 1983, there was a 180 percent increase in the number of divorced and separated single fathers who were rearing children under 18 years of age. In 1983, 600,000 fathers were rearing almost 1,000,000 children. During the same time frame, there were 4,256,000 divorced and separated single mothers, representing a 165 percent increase.[18] Because of the increasing divorce rate as well as the growing number of illegitimate births, single-parent families had increased to the extent that in 1980 almost one out of five children of school age lived with a single parent. Ten years ago, the figure was one in eight. Among black children, 46 percent live with one parent and an additional 9 percent with neither parent. Of children born in the 1980s, it has been estimated that nearly half will live for a period of time with a single parent before they reach adulthood.

For the single parent, the problem of "role overload"—the combination of full-time employment and family work—is especially severe. Although husbands in dual-earner families may not do much housework, they do make some contribution, chiefly in performing traditionally male tasks and, to some extent, in helping with the children. The single parent, in contrast, has no one to provide this assistance. Following are comments from several single parents in the survey:

> Since I'm a single parent, I worry about whether I'm spending enough time with my children. I want them to feel they are more important in my life than this job.
>
> —*black, female lower-level manager*

> My child is old enough to understand that I am solely responsible for our support and thus my work usually has to come first. He is, for the most part, supportive.
>
> —*white, female lower-level manager*

> I feel that I've used most of my vacation time to take care of business, and I feel cheated.
>
> —*black, female craftsworker*

> As a single parent, I am constantly concerned about sufficient money for child care. I try to do the best for my kids, but sometimes I feel I am a miserable failure.
>
> —*black, female lower-level manager*

Conclusions

In this chapter, we discussed in some detail the extremely conflicting societal messages given to working men and women about their roles as workers, parents, and partners. In brief, U.S. laws state that women have an equal right to participate in the work force, but the society as a whole is still very ambivalent about the impact working women have on their families and even about whether women should be working at all, especially on a permanent, full-time basis. Some individuals in this society blame all familial problems, including the high divorce rate and juvenile delinquency, on working women.

Men also feel the effects of society's ambivalence toward female/male roles, and many of them ask themselves: Should my wife work? How should I feel about her working? What role should I play in child-rearing? What role should I play in household chores? How should I feel about a wife who is more successful than I am? What kind of a man do I want to be? What kind of a man does society say I should be?

Conflicting role messages have led to significant conflicts not only in the home but also at work, largely because the sexist socialization of women and men maintains traditional role patterns in a time when they are outmoded.

Data were presented in support of evidence indicating that working women, married and single, are still carrying the greatest responsibility for the family. It is also clear that single male parents are experiencing slightly more difficulty than women are in balancing dual family/work roles.

Many married men have considerable advantages over women and single men because their wives stay at home or work only part-time, thus relieving them of many home and family tasks. Other married men whose wives work full-time are most likely to leave them with almost total responsibility for child care and family tasks. The result of this sexist role segregation is that women experience a higher incidence of missed days, tardiness, leaving work early, and dealing with family issues during working hours than do married men. Ultimately, women experience more stress, which negatively affects corporate productivity. Many women try to make up for their lowered productivity by taking work home and coming in to work on weekends; but this effort, while laudable, further increases stress and family/work conflicts by consuming valuable limited time. Solutions to these problems will be put forth in the second part of this book, but in the next two chapters, before we address the solutions, we will look more closely at the issues of corporate productivity.

5
Child Care and Scheduling Problems: Impact on Employee Productivity

Family/work conflicts are intensified by the competing needs of parents, by the inequitable distribution of household tasks, and by the sheer lack of time to accomplish everything that needs to be done in the home and in an increasingly competitive and demanding workplace. Still another source of family stress is the task of scheduling—delivering and picking up children from the day care center, arranging for their care when the usual caretaker or the children are ill, making special arrangements for overnight care when one or both parents must travel on business, meeting doctor and dentist appointments, and attending school programs and conferences.

In their survey on the quality of employment, R.P. Quinn and G.L. Staines found that the most frequent types of interference in family and work life were an excessive amount of work preventing the worker from spending enough time with the family (39 percent) and the work schedule interfering with family life (25 percent).[1]

In the 1981 *General Mills American Family Report,* the most frequent strains working parents experienced were "lack of time with family/children and less time to see each other." The second largest response (16 percent) noted long hours on the job and too much overtime.[2]

E. Galinsky writes in a chapter from a forthcoming book on stress and support for families, *Family Life and Corporate Policies:*

> Ask any group of working parents to describe their biggest concern and most likely it will be time. Research confirms this: time studies show that when a mother enters the labor force, 40 to 50 hours of extra work are added to the family system per week. In a census conducted in one plant of a high technology corporation as part of Bank Street's Work and Family Life Studies, employees were asked to indicate the work condition that most negatively affected their home life. The work condition receiving the highest response (or 25 percent of all respondents) was work hours. Several studies have found that the total hours spent at work each week was the most significant predictor of family strain; yet other studies have determined that the number of work hours in interaction with other factors such as one's mood at work or lack of job control is significant.[3]

Whatever view one espouses concerning the strains experienced by working parents, the fact remains that time and scheduling problems are of major concern, especially to working mothers. A study of 32,000 individuals clearly supports the conclusions of these social scientists. The respondents were asked to declare who was primarily responsible for such issues as child care, attending school conferences and meetings, and getting the children to doctor and dentist appointments. In each category, the percentage of women carrying the primary responsibility was at least three to five times higher than the percentage of men doing the same. For example, 61 percent of the women and 11 percent of the men said they bore the primary responsibility for child care.[4]

The 1981 *General Mills American Family Report* showed that nearly twice as many employed wives (39 percent) as employed husbands (22 percent) reported experiencing family/work scheduling conflicts. Those in families with children age 12 and under said they used some form of day care, and of these, about 23 percent of the mothers said the child care arrangement caused them to be late for work, to miss work, or to experience other work scheduling problems. However, only 2 percent of the fathers in two-earner families agreed. Women, obviously, are the ones who must adapt their schedules when conflicts arise.[5]

In analyzing the survey results, Mortimer et al. reached the same conclusions. "Issues surrounding work time and scheduling, coupled with the difficulties surrounding child care, seem the most problematic stressors in the dual provider family," they noted. Like other social scientists, they observed that the primary burden falls to the wife who, they said, must get the children off to school, make arrangements for after-school care, and stay home with them when they are ill. Women, they noted, are expected to disrupt their work to attend to their families, while it is acceptable for men to do just the opposite: disrupt their family lives in pursuit of occupational advancement. This, they pointed out, has "important implications for the socioeconomic attainment of men and women."[6]

Fox and Hesse-Biber noted that housekeeping standards and career goals can be lowered in order to deal with the problems of balancing dual roles and the overload that results; however, the notion that parental care itself can be lessened is not tenable. Since maternal care is the primary source of care for children, the additional pressures for working women to deal with children and their scheduling needs can be overwhelming.[7]

Overview of Scheduling Problems

As noted in chapter 3, the survey participants were given a series of questions relating to child care scheduling issues. The frequency distributions for those who responded that a selected area was at least somewhat of a problem are illustrated in table 5–1.

In all but two cases, more than double the percentage of women than men said that they had at least somewhat of a problem. This extreme difference clearly demonstrates and supports the notions put forth by the previously quoted researchers and in earlier chapters of this book.

When the data were analyzed according to gender and marital status, significant differences emerged in the perception of problems on the part of married and single men in all areas, but in only two of the areas did significant differences occur between single and married women. Further, the spread in each of these areas—attending school conferences and traveling overnight—was only 11 percentage points. Forty-seven percent of the single women, compared to 36 percent of the married women, said that attending school conferences was a problem; 37 percent of the single women, compared to 26 percent of the married women, said overnight travel was a problem.

On the other hand, there was a difference of at least 26 points in the responses of married and single men to these two questions. The largest percentage difference—43 points—emerged on the question of traveling overnight: 53 percent of single men, compared to 10 percent of married men, said that this presented a problem; but in all areas, single men responded positively at a rate that was at least three times higher than that of married men. For example, 51 percent of the single men, compared to 16 percent of the married men, acknowledged that they had problems with scheduling children's doctor appointments. In most cases, the responses of single men were very similar to those of women. In fact, a slightly higher percentage of single men perceived these areas as problematical than did women.

In the next several sections, some of the scheduling problems will be analyzed in further detail.

Table 5-1
Parents for Whom Scheduling Is At Least Somewhat of a Problem
(percentages)

	Women	*Men*
Providing care for sick child	45	17
Child's dentist or doctor appointments	42	17
Going to school conferences or programs during the day	39	24
Sudden loss of child care provider	34	14
Talking to child about his/her problems during work hours	31	17
Overnight travel	28	11
Child care during school vacations or holidays	26	10
Picking up child from child care provider during work hours	21	8
Transporting child between child care provider and home	13	5

Caring for Sick Children

One area that merits closer examination is children's health care. It is the principal cause of scheduling problems and also, of all child care concerns, potentially has the biggest influence on productivity.

Forty-five percent of the women, regardless of marital status, said that providing care for a sick child was at least somewhat of a problem; and 47 percent of the single men, compared to 16 percent of the married men, concurred. Race had no significant impact on employees' responses.

Table 5–2 shows employees' responses on the question of caring for sick children by gender and by age of children. As one might expect, the age of the child had a tremendous impact on employees' responses. More than three times the percentage of women with preschool children (5 and under), compared to women with children 15 to 18, said that caring for a sick child was at least somewhat of a problem (62 versus 20 percent). The percentage of men with preschool children who agreed that caring for a sick child was at least somewhat of a problem was more than three times that of men with children 15 to 18 (27 versus 8 percent). Table 5–2 also demonstrates the extreme gap in percentages for women and men for all children' age groups.

The comments made by employees reveal the considerable problems that caring for sick children creates for working parents:

> It is very difficult, especially for single parents, to handle sick child care. The company does not seem to be very understanding, especially if the child gets sick a lot. And they *really* don't understand if the parent gets sick, too.
>
> —*white, female craftsworker*

> When your child has a 102° temperature, but you've taken her to the sitter because you *must* be at work, who can give their all to the job?
>
> —*white, female middle-level manager*

Table 5–2
Parents Who Say Caring for Sick Children Is At Least Somewhat of a Problem
(*percentages*)

Age of Child	Women (N = 1,225)	Men (N = 1,597)
Under 2	61	32
2 to 5	63	25
6 to 11	53	18
12 to 14	37	13
15 to 18	20	8

More and more often, I send the sick child to day care and wait for them to call me to get him. I am sick of wasting all my vacation days to care for a sick child, and that has happened every year. The day care center does not like what I do, and I don't like it myself either.

> —*white, female lower-level manager*

I would like my husband to share staying home from work with sick kids, but he works in a two-man office as a dispatcher, so he feels that he cannot miss work as easily as I can.

> —*white, female lower-level manager*

My job was in jeopardy a year ago because my daughter had a series of bouts with the flu.

> —*single, black, male craftsworker*

My wife and I share taking vacation days off because our sitter does not take sick children. At times it really becomes a hassle because we are both in high-pressure, visible jobs.

> —*white, male lower–middle-level manager*

These remarks suggest strongly or state outright that sick children create productivity problems for employees, who miss work and suffer stress because of difficulties in making appropriate arrangements for the children or worrying about their well-being. Data drawn from the analysis of the survey support individuals' perceptions that sick children affect productivity: 48 percent of the women, compared to 15 percent of the men, missed work in the previous year because of a sick child. Again, while no sigificant differences emerged in the responses of married and single women, a noticeable difference appeared between single and married men: 29 percent of single men, compared to 15 percent of married men, said they had missed work because of a sick child.

Young children cannot take care of themselves when they are sick, and many child care providers will not take in sick children; one could speculate, therefore, that the younger the child who is ill, the more likely the parent is to miss work. Figure 5–1 bears out this hypothesis. Note the dramatic drop in percentages of positive responses for both both women and men when children are over 11. The figure also demonstrates that when one parent must stay at home with a sick child, the odds are at least two to one in favor of that parent's being the mother.

These findings were supported by Quinn and Staines in their *1977 Quality of Employment Survey*. They found that when both partners were working and one parent had to be at home with a sick child, only 13 percent of the men, compared to 79 percent of the women, stayed at home.[8]

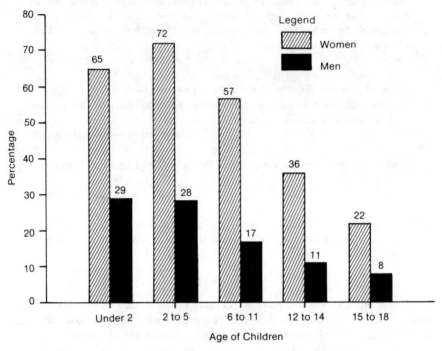

Figure 5-1. Percentage Who Have Missed Work to Care for a Sick Child

There is a high correlation not only between missed work and caring for a sick child, but also between caring for a sick child and leaving work early, coming in late, dealing with family issues during working hours, and on- and off-the-job stress. These comments about serious child care problems reinforce the conclusion that such problems potentially have an extensive impact on parents' frame of mind and, consequently, on their productivity as employees:

> I recently sent a child with pneumonia to day care. This is only February, and I cannot face another year with no vacation days. The center called me every day for five days. I worried but did not leave work.
> —*white, female craftsworker*

> Worrying about a sick child. . . . Managers say leave your personal problems at home, but I can never separate my child from my mind. I have to use vacation time to stay at home. This is not a fair policy.
> —*white, male craftsworker*

When your child is sick, you worry most of the day and can't wait to call home to be sure everything is OK. Many times in our office, sitters can't get through, or if they do, I receive no message until the next day.

—white, male lower-level manager

When they are sick, it's hard to concentrate. When your sitter gives you notice, it's hard to concentrate.

—black, female lower-level manager

At times there's a need to be at home with sick children, but there is also the necessity for a paycheck. I go to work, even though I am not as productive, when my child is sick.

—single, white, female lower-level manager

Back when he was at a day care center, I did have a lot of problems with his being sick and also worrying if he was getting the right kind of care. I would see the kids screaming and crying because they did not want to stay at that day care center, and that really bothered both my husband and me.

—Hispanic, female craftsworker

A parent cannot work to a full extent when you know your child is ill and you can't take him to a doctor until Saturday.

—Hispanic, female lower-level manager

When the types of child care arrangements used for sick children are analyzed, it becomes clear that the parent's gender and marital status play important roles in determining who provides the care. Table 5–3 shows that, overall, the percentage of single women who stayed at home when a child was

Table 5-3
Child Care Arrangements When Children Are Sick
(percentages)

	Single Women (N = 269)	Married Women (N = 938)	Single Men (N = 45)	Married Men (N = 1,518)
You stay home	39	15	20	1
Mate stays home	1	4	5	20
You or mate stays home	4	38	10	17
No problem	2	4	7	43
Current care adequate	26	19	26	12
Other	29	21	31	7

sick was much higher than for other employees. (Only 1 percent of married men stayed at home with sick children.) The high percentage of married men (compared to the percentages of women and single men) who said that caring for a sick child was not a problem because a mate was at home with the child indicates again the number of full-time, or nearly full-time, homemakers among married male employees' wives. The table also shows that single men and women were more likely to stay at home with a sick child than were their married counterparts. For example, 39 percent of the single women, compared to 15 percent of the married women, stayed at home with a sick child.

The most common types of care employees indicated under "other" were that the children were old enough to take care of themselves and that relatives helped in caring for sick children. The younger the child, the more likely it was that a parent would stay at home with him or her. For example, female respondents said that 70 percent of the time, when a preschool child was sick, he or she was cared for by the parents, and, in the vast majority of cases, it was the mother who stayed at home. For children 12 and over, the percentage for parental care dropped to 37, and the most frequently selected response (38 percent) was "other"—meaning, in most cases, that the children took care of themselves. For married men, regardless of children's ages, unemployed wives were by far the primary caretakers of sick children.

In terms of race, blacks (17 percent) were most likely to stay at home with a sick child, as compared to other people of color (13 percent) and whites (9 percent). This helps to explain why black women were most likely of all the race/gender groups to miss work, as we saw in chapter 3.

When the number of times employees missed work was correlated with the type of child care arrangement for sick children, the survey showed that 80 percent of the parents who shared staying at home had missed work, compared to 21 percent and fewer of those who used other forms of care. (This excludes respondents who named themselves as the only source of child care.) Seventy-three percent of men who said they shared care of sick children with their wives, compared to 5 percent and fewer who used other forms of care, missed work, showing that some men are taking responsibility for child care arrangements when children are sick.

Following are some of the respondents' descriptions of their arrangements for the care of sick children:

In the office where I work, the management people hassle the employees about having to stay home with sick children. For a child's doctor appointments, we miss work to solve the problem, and we get scolded. Therefore, we worry about jeopardizing our jobs to take care of a sick child.

—white, female craftsworker

I take a vacation day so that the absence doesn't go against my attendance record.

—Hispanic, female craftsworker

My sister lives next door and checks on my child if I can't stay at home.

—white, female craftsworker

I take various courses of action: (1) my ex-husband comes to stay with her; (2) if someone else from my immediate family is home, she stays with them; (3) I have a babysitter who is not geographically near who will keep the child when she is sick.

—single, white, female middle-level manager

I take a vacation day, a longer lunch, or go home for part of the day.

—white, female lower-level manager

If there is ever any serious problem at home, my employer has been great about giving me time to take care of things. My husband works nights, so if there is a problem, we can handle it.

—black, female lower-level manager

My children are at the age where they can usually stay by themselves.

—black, female lower-level manager

Since my wife is self-employed, it adds a great deal of flexibility to our status.

—black, male middle-level manager

Grandparents (out of town) may assist for a several-day bout of illness. My mate and I often "split days," each working a half day.

—white, female lower-level manager

Children's Doctor and Dentist Appointments

Even those parents whose children rarely become ill are faced with a scheduling problem when young children need to go for routine checkups with doctors and dentists, few of whom have office hours on weekends or evenings. This problem ranked second among female respondents' list of situations that presented at least somewhat of a problem.

For men, handling children's doctor and dentist appointments was roughly comparable to the problem of caring for a sick child, but for women, the relative age of the child had more bearing on the issue of care for a sick child than it did on this issue. Table 5–4 shows responses according to gender of the participants and ages of their children.

It is not surprising that more than double the percentage of men, compared to women, viewed the handling of children's dentist and doctor appointments as *no* problem at all (59 versus 28 percent). Again, there was no significant difference in the responses of women, married or single, but there was a marked difference in the responses of single and married men.

As one might expect, craftswomen (47 percent) were more likely than women in management (23 to 31 percent) to say that they had at least somewhat of a problem in handling these appointments. Thirty percent of craftsmen, compared to 7 to 14 percent of men in management, had a problem in this area (lower-level managers were more likely than higher-level managers to have difficulties).

Race was a significant factor. White women and women of color other than black responded the same (41 percent), compared to black women, 55 percent of whom said this was at least somewhat of a problem. Thirty-two percent of black men, 39 percent of other men of color, and 15 percent of white men said they experienced somewhat of a problem in handling children's dentist and doctor appointments.

Table 5–5 illustrates that problems handling these appointments lead to missed work. Seventy-four percent of the women and 57 percent of the men who said that handling these appointments was a big problem had missed work at least one day in the previous year.

A Hispanic, female lower-level manager who missed work occasionally because of her children's illnesses or appointments had a husband who showed his supportiveness by doing the ironing, making breakfast, and delivering the children to day care services and to school, but, she said, "he feels *I* should be involved *every time* an illness or a doctor appointment occurs." A white peer

Table 5–4
Parents Who Say Children's Dentist and Doctor Appointments Are At Least Somewhat of a Problem
(percentages)

Age of Child	Women (N = 1,234)	Men (N = 1,597)
Under 2	44	29
2 to 5	50	26
6 to 11	48	19
12 to 14	43	15
15 to 18	33	8

Table 5–5
Relationship between Children's Dentist and
Doctor Appointments and Absenteeism
(percentages who have missed work)

	Women (N = 1,234)	Men (N = 1,594)
Appoints are a big problem	74	57
Appointments are somewhat of a problem	67	53
Appointments are a little problem	55	40
Appointments are no problem	56	34

reported that such appointments were the source of hassles with her supervisor. "I get some real uncomfortable threats," she said.

Jobs Requiring Travel and Overtime

Traveling overnight because of work can present some serious scheduling problems for parents, especially for single parents and for women whose husbands contribute little, if anything, to the care of the children (as we have seen, this represented a significant majority of the women surveyed). Overall, 33 percent of the women and 66 percent of the men had jobs that required overnight travel.

A major explanation for the differences between men and women whose jobs required them to travel overnight is that a higher percentage of women in the sample held crafts rather than management jobs; the opposite was true for men. In addition, even those women who were in management held positions traditionally given to women, which meant that they were seldom required to travel; very few women hold jobs in the higher levels of management that require extensive travel.

R. Kanter observed that frequent overnight travel poses a multitude of problems for families: husbands and fathers have little time left for their families during the normal working week; when they travel, they have no time for wives and children. She also noted that in a survey of 128 managers and their wives, all but two felt "burdened and stressed" by extensive travel requirements; those two exceptions were a female manager who was single and a man who used travel to escape from his family. Others have cited such problems as "disconnected social relations, increasing responsibility for the wives, guilt on the part of husbands for deserting their families, fatigue from the travel itself, wives' fear of being alone, and the potential for infidelity."[9]

Although Kanter's comments focus primarily on the problems of men who must travel, they pertain at least equally to women in the same situation, who, in fact, probably suffer more stress and dislocation than do their male counterparts. They are, after all, already made to feel guilty for being away from home for eight hours a day; an overnight or prolonged business trip can spark even stronger feelings of guilt for their failure to fulfill their traditional role as wife and mother. The inconvenience of a wife's absence, coupled with her own guilt feelings, can place a heavy strain on a marriage, particularly in instances where the husband has few or no homemaking, child care, or cooking skills. Attempting to find appropriate care outside the home for young children under such circumstances can be extremely difficult, and, as we have seen, most of the time this responsibility falls squarely on the woman's shoulders.

The survey data support Kanter's findings: 28 percent of the women who had children 18 and under, compared to only 11 percent of the men who had children in this age group, said that overnight travel was at least somewhat of a problem. In this area, a significantly lower percentage of both married men and married women experienced problems than did single men and single women: 56 percent of the single women, compared to 43 percent of the married women, viewed overnight travel as at least a small problem; for men, the discrepancy between singles and marrieds was even more dramatic: 79 compared to 26 percent, respectively.

Employees' comments on the overnight travel issue delineate the problem:

Most stress is caused when my job conflicts with family responsibilities. Evening meetings and overnight travel are the hardest to handle without stress. I don't voice my stress on the job, but I feel it.

—white, female lower-middle-level manager

Going out of town for more than one day is stressful for the people at home. However, I usually enjoy a short trip now and then.

—white, female lower-middle-level manager

My job requires travel, which sometimes leads to my missing special days—birthdays, school functions, etc.—but I accept that as part of my job! The stress I feel is inside.

—white, female lower-level manager

Too little time to relax on weekdays and weekends. Overnight trips and overtime are *very* unwelcome.

—white, male lower-level manager

Before my present assignment, I was handed a full-time traveling assignment, one that could have been given to a single person or a volunteer. This lasted three years. I am 34 years old and have four children. Makes for a great family life!

—white male lower-middle-level manager

Closely related to the overnight travel problem are the issues of overtime and late meetings, which require parents to make child care arrangments in the evening. One out of four women and one out of ten men said this posed at least somewhat of a problem. Sixteen percent of those employees who were satisfied with child care service hours said that finding a child care provider for the evening was at least somewhat of a problem, but 57 percent of employees who said that they were *not* satisfied with child care service hours found that securing a child care provider for the evening was somewhat of a problem.

The operating hours of a day care center can also create problems. "I can't stay late at the office because day care closes at six p.m. and it takes forty minutes to get there," one white craftswoman said. A white female manager, expressing a variation on the same theme, explained that she has a need for dependable help in the evening since both she and her husband work well beyond 5:00 or 6:00 p.m. every night.

As increasing numbers of women move up the corporate ladder, an even higher percentage of them will find themselves facing child care scheduling problems if more men do not begin to play a larger role in the family. Employees' shifts affect the problem further. Here are four comments:

> I try to handle all problems away from work or at lunch time. My husband travels; however, he is very supportive and has a much more flexible schedule.
>
> —*native American, female craftsworker*

> My husband and I have worked out specific responsibilities for us and each of our children. I work nights, and my husband works days in order to minimize lost work time due to child care.
>
> —*Hispanic, female lower-level manager*

> Since I work at 5:00 p.m., I have plenty of time for all my family needs, even my cats. When I work days, I'll take an E day [day off without pay] to take care of home needs.
>
> —*black, female craftsworker*

> I just was promoted four months ago and my job requires a lot more hours and some travel. My husband and I have had several discussions on the new strains in our relationship.
>
> —*white, female middle-level manager*

Children's School Conferences and Programs

The area that the largest percentage—nearly one-fourth—of the men in the sample saw as at least somewhat of a problem was attending school conferences and programs. Thirty-nine percent of the women concurred.

Marital status had a significant effect on the responses of both men and women. Twenty-eight percent of the single women, compared to 40 percent of the married women, said that the handling of children's school conferences was *no* problem; for men, the corresponding figures were 23 and 49 percent, respectively. Note how close the percentages were for men and women, depending on marital status, in this case.

Table 5–6 shows the impact of the age of the child on the degree to which parents experienced difficulties with attending school conferences and programs. The age of the child was far less of a factor here than it was with other issues, presumably because all children (excluding toddlers) want their parents to attend school affairs.

The survey's findings seem to indicate that men deal with and experience difficulties with the more peripheral areas of child care and parenting. It is a father's duty, apparently, to show interest in the children's education and in their social activities, but not to provide care to a sick child or to perform other such "womanly" tasks.

Conclusions

The information presented in this chapter reinforces the hypothesis that a high percentage of women have difficulty in handling dual roles and experience stress both at work and at home because they carry the primary responsibility for dealing with child care scheduling problems. Much higher percentages of women, regardless of marital status, than married men, but not single men, experienced scheduling tasks such as child care for sick children, dentist and doctor appointments, and school conferences and programs as more than just a minor problem. Children's ages had a great impact on most of these issues.

These additional tasks, when not shared by the spouse, are a major cause of lowered productivity at work for women—proportionately more so than for

Table 5–6
Parents Who Say School Conferences and Programs Are At Least Somewhat of a Problem
(percentages)

Age of Child	Women (N = 1,234)	Men (N = 1,594)
Under 2	32	27
2 to 5	46	31
6 to 11	47	29
12 to 14	42	24
15 to 18	31	16

men. Data on men who are single parents shows that their scheduling problems are similar to those of women, regardless of women's marital status, repeating a correlation seen before between these groups. Thus, single men's problems with lowered productivity and increased stress, owing to child care scheduling problems, are also similar to those of both married and single women.

All child care scheduling problems lead to a cost to the corporation in terms of lost productivity due to missed work, tardiness, leaving work early, dealing with family issues during working hours, and employee stress.

6
Other Evidence That Child Care and Family/Work Problems Affect Productivity

For the past thirty years, social scientists have recognized the importance of good working relationships in order for people to function at their most productive level. The most satisfying and productive work environment is one in which employees feel that there is a high degree of openness, honesty, trust, supportiveness, and sensitivity, and a feeling of fairness. In order to provide such an environment, a company must be sensitive to the changing make-up and needs of its work force. Probably the major change in the make-up of the work force is the increasing number of working mothers. If companies utilize outmoded employment policies and practices to deal with the new realities of women's employment, work group stress and tension will most assuredly increase. If companies do have updated policies but no firm commitment to the philosophy supporting them, many supervisors will ignore them because their sexist attitudes and stereotypes about working women will be at odds with the policies. In either case, as the following material will show, legitimate child care needs and the family/work problems of employees will not be dealt with in a fair and effective manner, to the ultimate detriment both of employees and corporations.

Limited as it is, most of the research that has been conducted on the relationship between child care and family/work problems, on the one hand, and productivity on the other has focused on the productivity levels of individual employees. In this chapter data will be presented to demonstrate that child care and family/work issues affect not only employees' productivity but also that of the supervisors and, in some cases, the entire work group. In addition, we will see how supervisors' methods of handling these problems can significantly affect the productivity of those employees who are experiencing them. Finally, we will examine the extent to which these problems influence employees' decisions about whether to accept promotions, if and when to return to work after childbirth, and whether to leave the company.

Impact of Child Care Problems on Supervisors

It is reasonable to assume that if a supervisor is spending a considerable amount of time dealing with a subordinate's child care and family/work issues, his or her own productivity as well as that of the subordinate could be negatively affected. In this study, only 25 percent of the female managers and 39 percent of the male managers said they had *never* dealt with child care problems of subordinates. More than double the percentage of female than male managers said they have had at least frequently to deal with their subordinates' child care problems (35 and 16 percent, respectively). While the percentage of men who dealt with employees' child care and family problems remained constant at about 16 up through middle management, it dropped precipitously at that point to almost 0 percent. The figures for women were much higher, but women, too, were more likely to deal with these problems if they were at the lower levels of management. The percentage for women ranged from 38 percent at the lower level to 30 percent at the lower-middle level and less than 16 percent at the middle level and above.

The drastic decrease in the number of higher-level supervisors dealing with child care problems of subordinates could be attributed to the conviction held by many upper-level managers that a person who experiences problems with child care is likely to have poor management skills. If an individual cannot manage his or her family problems, they reason, how can he or she successfully manage a job? A white, male middle-level manager put it bluntly: "It is generally understood that if you want to get ahead in this company, you'd better keep any family concerns to yourself." There is another explanation for the lack of involvement in child care problems among higher-level supervisors: Most women in corporations are located at the lower levels of the corporate hierarchy, and they also shoulder the major burden of child care. Therefore, it is not surprising that lower-level female supervisors deal more with subordinates' problems than do upper-level male supervisors.

An analysis of the supervisors' comments about the child care and family/ work problems they face complements and supplements many of the comments reported in previous chapters. For example, a white, male lower–middle-level manager said: "Sitters—private ones at least—are not dependable. They get sick, they have doctor appointments, etc., and you are left up in the air with no sitter for that day or however long. They also call you at the last minute to tell you they won't be able to babysit that day."

A black, female lower–middle-level manager who had both male and female single parents as subordinates noted that, understandably, these employees' "minds were often not on the job. Anytime you are a single parent and a concerned parent," she explained, "you are going to worry about your child."

A white, female lower-level manager agreed. "Having seven of eleven clerks with children under 18," she wrote, "I have scarcely a week go by that one of them doesn't have a sick child, conferences at school, or babysitting problems."

A white, female lower-level manager noted that sick children can affect employees' sleep and, thus, their productivity levels on the job. "Employee had little or no sleep during previous night because of sick child. Employee was absent because the babysitter cancelled out."

Other comments painted a similar picture: "Overtime is out—has to find a babysitter." "Sick child—has to stay home." "School is out for a day or so— has to take time off." "Problems in school." "Babysitter is sick or out of town or can't keep the child after regular working hours."

Finally, a black, female lower-level manager wrote: "In cases where child care is a problem for an employee, I know it brings productivity down. I mean, how can you work to your fullest if you are worrying about who's going to watch your child?"

These sorts of comments were made repeatedly, especially by female supervisors. Some of their male counterparts, on the other hand, who did not believe that child care problems were costing their companies money in terms of lowered productivity, insisted that *their* subordinates "have made whatever arrangements that are necessary on their own, and no problems have arisen." Employees whose spouses do not work, of course, will present no problems. One supervisor believes that he avoids problems simply by "allowing no time off with pay."

One can assume that most of these "trouble-free" subordinates are males. Ironically, the self-satisfied supervisor who refuses to grant time off with pay may be causing an even greater loss in productivity by damaging employee morale and by forcing those employees who must and do miss work on account of child care and family/work problems to lie about the reason for their absence in order to be paid for the time.

Supervisors' Support for Child Care Needs

Single and married women responded similarly when asked "To what extent does your supervisor support you and your child care needs?" About 66 percent in both groups felt that their supervisors were at least somewhat support- ive. A higher percentage of single men (74 percent) than married men (59 percent) described their supervisors as supportive. Overall, men (23 percent) were more likely than women (15 percent) to say that their supervisors were *not at all* supportive.

Greif offered a possible explanation for the fact that single men are more likely than married men to take their child care problems to their bosses. He suggested that a single father is looked upon as an extraordinary man who must be extremely dedicated. People wonder, he said, "how he can do all the things he has to do: work, run the house, cook, take care of the children."[1] Need it be pointed out that large numbers of women have always done all this and that very few of them have been praised for their "extraordinary" effort? Furthermore, Greif noted, America has a dichotomous attitude toward single male parents: they are seen simultaneously as pillars of strength and as poor souls in need of help. "How can he know how to cook, clean and shop for clothes for two children? How can he know how to discuss sexuality with an adolescent daughter? People feel sorry for him and run to his aid. . . . They say to him in the same breath, 'You're great,' and 'Let me help you.'"[2]

Women were more likely than married men were to sense the support of a supervisor, which could be attributed to two factors. First, women are more often supervised by other women than men are—a result of the job segregation that these companies have not totally overcome. Second, women are expected to be the major child care provider, which leads their bosses to be more sensitive to and more tolerant of the demands this role places on them.

Table 6-1 clearly demonstrates that supervisors can affect the stress levels of their employees. It correlates the extent to which bosses were supportive with the number of employees who experienced at least some stress at home and at work because of balancing family/work responsibilities. Thirty percent of the women whose boss was supportive to a great extent, compared to 46 percent whose boss was not very supportive, indicated that they had at least some stress on the job. Nineteen percent of the men whose boss was supportive to a great extent, compared to about 29 percent whose bosses were not very supportive, experienced some degree of stress at home.

The following comments reveal why some employees believed their supervisors were not supportive, as well as the impact employees experienced from their supervisors' negative attitudes:

> The stress comes from my supervisor's failure to accept this. He does not understand a sick child's need of his mother and the problem we have, with no relatives nearby, in finding someone to care for him.
>
> —*white, female craftsworker*

Table 6-1
Relationship between Supportive Supervisors and Employee Stress Due to Family/Work Conflicts
(*percentages*)

Boss Is Supportive:	Women (N = 1,226)		Men (N = 1,596)	
	Stress on the Job	*Stress at Home*	*Stress on the Job*	*Stress at Home*
To a great extent	30	35	13	19
To some extent	36	42	17	24
To a small extent	46	53	23	27
Not at all	46	48	24	29

My supervisor is always on my back about time missed, and I worry about whether my child is being mistreated.

—black, male lower-level manager

With one supervisor I would have preferred calling in sick for myself rather than take a day of nonpay or a day of my vacation. He was very discriminatory when it came to child care.

—white, female craftsworker

Present boss is so-so. He's married, with children, a wife who doesn't work and a mother living with them so he's never had child care problems. Sometimes has a hard time dealing with mine. I'm also the first person he's supervised in his twenty years as manager that has had children. Other bosses I've had, both with and without children, have been understanding.

—white, female lower-middle-level manager

I don't think my supervisor has any real knowledge of rearing teens. His only teen child is with the mother. Ongoing crises are unknown to him.

—white, female middle-level manager

My supervisors have expressed interest individually, but I always felt that interest was just to make sure that I didn't interrupt the status quo at work. People with chemical dependency problems get great family counseling assistance, I think. However, it's too bad that we wait until there's a full-blown problem before we do anything for families.

—white, female craftsworker

My supervisor and the company could care less if my kids are sick, dying, or having problems. All they care about is that I show up to do their work.

—white, female craftsworker

Although it is true that many male supervisors are unsupportive of employees with child care problems, women also can be less than sympathetic, as these two comments by white craftswomen indicate:

My supervisor has never been married and has no children. She has difficulty discussing any kind of personal problems.

She [the supervisor] has no children and her attitude is one of "Your job comes first—no matter what." This creates a lot of stress.

What all these comments indicate is that an unsupportive supervisor will force caring parents to lie about child care problems, which in turn can affect their ability to perform at their best on the job. Another possible consequence is that employees with child care problems may miss an entire day's work rather than try to make alternative plans. Consider the following remarks:

My immediate supervisor now is very understanding and fair. I've worked for her for about two years. Before that I was *never* comfortable about my needs for child care with other supervisors. I would take days off rather than tell them about the problems I was having.

—white, female craftsworker

I believe my supervisor would be fair, but not very patient with the time I would need to make arrangements in case of a very dramatic need (short-term illness extending to a week or two, or injuries requiring longer-term care). Because I *am* a concerned parent, I save vacation days for such unplanned events; even so, emergency child care is viewed skeptically. When my vacation ran out last year, I called in sick when I needed time to care for a sick child.

—white, female lower-level manager

I've had no problem with this supervisor. I did with my last one when my wife was working. There is even a note in my personnel file that she wrote because of a couple of family problems I had to attend to.

—white, male lower-level manager

Three comments follow from employees who found their supervisors supportive:

Personally, my supervisor is exceptionally good about child sick days and child care problems. I am not made to feel guilty about missing work for sick children. I can also use vacation days if I can't afford a nonpay day. I don't know if this is company policy but I feel it should be up to the employee and would really benefit all.

—white, female craftsworker

My supervisor is great. He has a real understanding of my role as a single male parent.

—white, male lower-level manager

If you need time off you either make it up or take it without pay. It has never been a sticky situation.

—white, female craftsworker

When supervisors are supportive, their companies can reap some very positive benefits. A white, female lower-level manager said she tries to "return 125 percent on the 'concern investment'" of her supervisor who, she feels, "tries to be flexible and tolerant of my situation." Her previous supervisor, by contrast, showed "disdain for handling personal needs and created a very stressful situation."

Employees' Ability to Discuss Child Care Problems with Their Supervisors

Directly tied to the issue of support from supervisors is the concept of feeling free to discuss child care issues with them. Some employees may not know what the attitude of their supervisor is because they have never asked for help or understanding, as this statement from a Hispanic, female lower-level manager demonstrates:

> I do not want my supervisor feeling he has an added burden with an employee who has 'home/family/children' problems—especially since I am the only female out of the eight he supervises.

Almost three out of ten women and more than one out of five men responded that they did *not* feel very free, when asked "How free do you feel to discuss your child care needs with your immediate supervisors?" Table 6–2 shows the employees' responses.

When employees do not feel free to discuss child care needs with their supervisors, the consequences can duplicate those resulting from unsupportive bosses. Statistical analysis indicated a significant relationship between how free employees felt to talk to their supervisors about child care problems and the amount of stress employees experienced on the job. For example, with regard to the latter, 50 percent of the women who did not feel free to talk to their immediate superiors about these issues, compared to 34 percent who did, said they had at least some stress on the job because of trying to balance family/work responsibilities. The figures for men were 25 and 14 percent, respectively.

In addition, 55 percent of the women who did not feel very free to talk to their supervisors about their child care needs, compared to 38 percent who did, had difficulty handling doctor and dentist appointments. The same pattern held for men (36 percent, compared to 14 percent).

That only about one-third of the employees felt very free to discuss these problems indicates that many supervisors were not even made aware of situations in which they might have been of some assistance. The reasons employees did not feel free to discuss these matters ranged from the simple observation of "My boss could care less" to this experience related by a female, white lower-level manager:

> I just left a job where, on my final appraisal, I was marked down for nonregular attendance because I left early occasionally for children's doctor appointments.

Table 6–2
Freedom to Discuss Child Care Issues with Supervisors
(percentages)

	Women *(N = 1,225)*	*Men* *(N = 1,576)*
Very free	32	31
Free	39	47
Not very free	18	11
Not at all free	11	11

The truth was that I had made up all of this time through overtime, either before or after the scheduled appointment, but I was told that I should have taken vacation time instead of leaving early. Nobody had told me about this policy.

Other survey participants responded as follows:

My supervisor believes in leaving your problems at home. Don't bring them to work, he tells us.

—black, female craftsworker

I do not feel at all free to discuss my problems. My supervisor has no children and doesn't understand. He is a workaholic.

—Hispanic, female craftsworker

He is a new supervisor and I don't think he knows what it is to be a single working mother, with demands from both job and children.

—Hispanic, female lower-level manager

The primary reason employees gave for feeling free to discuss these problems was that their supervisors had children themselves and understood the situation. "I'm lucky to have a supervisor with two small ones of his own," commented a white, male lower-level manager, who added, however, that the supervisor's wife stayed at home to watch his children. A black, male lower-level manager felt free to talk about his problems "because my supervisor has kids, too, and I'm sure he understands the position a parent is in."

Nevertheless, supervisors do not have to have children of their own to be supportive. "My boss has no children but she understands people's needs," commented one black craftsman.

Sometimes the problem rests not with the immediate supervisor but with "higher-ups" in the company. A white, male middle-level manager believed that most supervisors felt concern for employees' problems but "our policies sometimes prevent them from being flexible enough to handle individual cases." A white, female lower-level manager observed, "My immediate supervisor has been responsive to my needs, but higher management hasn't." And a white craftsman remarked, "I don't feel very free because I feel the company does not give the supervisor much option to be personal or flexible."

Other employees might have felt free to speak to supervisors had they not been fearful about the consequences for their careers. "I feel free to talk to my immediate supervisor," wrote a white, female middle-level manager, "but I would probably not make a big issue over any child care concerns or needs I have, as I feel it might possibly jeopardize my present job or future advancement."

What all this information implies is that a positive approach on the part of supervisors can lead to productivity benefits for companies as the result of reduced employee stress and absenteeism.

Impact of Child Care Problems on the Work Group

If supervisors do not effectively handle their work group's child care and family/work problems, these issues can affect not only the employee with the problem and the supervisor but also the entire work group. When work groups are under stress or in conflict over any problem, their ability to perform to their maximum potential is severely inhibited.

A white, female lower-level manager remarked, "Sick children have caused problems and hard feelings because of the mother's staying home or not staying at work the full work tour." A white, female lower-middle level manager noted that when any employee is absent due to child care problems, "it creates a work problem affecting productivity because of scheduling changes and workload shifts." One of her peers added: "The number one problem of our department is fair and equal treatment of all company employees in relation to time off and days paid for sick children and doctors' appointments. Every department handles this differently, and mothers are getting bitter. We need a uniform policy."

Enlightened management could go a long way toward resolving the issues cited by these three survey participants. Managers who accept these issues as part of the natural work environment and realize that they are not simply going to go away will be able to develop contingency plans for the entire work group when sudden child care or family problems disrupt the schedules of individual employees. Involving members of the work group itself in the development of such plans will, in fact, help them to develop more cooperative attitudes toward their peers and will aid in bringing about quick resolutions to problems that call for a redistribution of the workload.

Impact of Child Care Problems on Promotions

Family responsibilities can affect the capacity of both men and women to compete in the climb up the career ladder, as K.A. Moore and I.V. Sawhill pointed out: "A woman's job commitment has traditionally been viewed as secondary to her domestic responsibilities." They went on to say, "As the wife's employment begins to require more and more contribution at home from the husband, he may find it increasingly difficult to leave on business trips and work overtime.... The man with a working wife may find himself at a competitive disadvantage compared to a man who can work sixty or seventy hours a week because his wife takes complete charge of the home front."[3] Even though the sharing of domestic tasks may dull the husband's competitive edge, it is absolutely essential for the success of a dual-career marriage, as the comment of a white, male middle-level manager demonstrated: "My wife and I found it very difficult to have our careers, raise the kids, and take care of the home. Our compromise was for me to turn down a promotion because of the time demands of the job."

It is not surprising, in view of all we have seen thus far, that more than double the percentage of women than men (53 versus 25 percent) said that child care needs could affect their decisions to accept a promotion at least to a small extent. It is interesting to note that women who were single parents were less likely than their married counterparts to believe this to be the case. (Forty-five percent of the single women, compared to 55 percent of the married women, said that child care needs could affect their willingness to move up the corporate ladder.) A plausible explanation for this difference is that the financial needs of many single women are greater than those of many married women; thus, a promotion would be of greater importance to them. More money could mean better child care services and less stress. For men, the opposite was true: 46 percent of the single men, compared to 25 percent of the married men, believed that child care could affect their taking a promotion. The difference in statistics for men can be explained in part by the fact that single men are already in better-paying jobs than women, so the financial rewards of a promotion may not outweigh the additional stress, time, and competitiveness of a higher-level position. Race had no significant impact on the employees' responses.

Table 6–3 shows responses by gender and by age of child with respect to the influence child care problems would have on employees' decisions whether to accept a promotion at least to some extent. Note the very significant impact the ages of children had on the responses of female employees. For example, double the percentage of women (49 percent) with preschoolers, compared to 23 percent of those with children 15 to 18, believed that their child care needs would affect this decision at least to some extent.

A white, female lower–middle-level manager said she would turn down a promotion if it were offered. "At my present level I am finding it very difficult to balance work and family problems, and I already make more money than my husband does. A promotion would just create more time and family problems— although a day care center close to work might make me change my mind."

Table 6–3
Parents Who Say Child Care Needs Would
Affect Their Decision to Accept a
Promotion At Least to Some Extent
(percentages)

Age of Child	Women (N = 1,225)	Men (N = 1,597)
Under 2	46	23
2 to 5	51	20
6 to 11	40	15
12 to 14	34	15
15 to 18	23	16

A male counterpart agreed. "I put in enough hours already. This job takes away from my family life. A promotion is not what I want."

A Hispanic, female lower-level manager felt she was already "working full-time at home and work," and she saw the additional responsibilities that a promotion would entail as "just too much to handle."

A white, female lower-level manager anticipated that a promotion could mean more traveling. She would not accept a promotion, she said, unless the company "helped out with overnight child care costs." (The five companies that participated in this survey, as a direct result of the survey findings, now pay for overnight child care when employees travel on business.)

When employees turn down promotions for any reason, corporate productivity suffers because management has lost the opportunity to place "the right person" in the job. As women become increasingly permanent members of the work force and as more men take on additional family responsibilities, employees' reluctance to accept promotions will be costly to companies that provide no assistance or inadequate assistance with family/work problems. There is still more at stake in this issue than the reluctance of employees to undertake greater responsibility within their companies; some employees actually leave their companies entirely to take jobs with organizations that offer better child care assistance.

Impact of Child Care Problems on Resignations

Ultimately, one of the most costly consequences of unresolved child care issues is for well-trained employees to quit the company. When the question about quitting their jobs was posed to the survey participants, married women (38 percent) were significantly more likely than single women (17 percent) to consider quitting, and the reverse was true for men: 11 percent of the single men, compared to 4 percent of the married men, had considered quitting.

Figure 6-1 shows the significant effect of gender and children's ages on employees' consideration of whether to leave the company; children's ages particularly affect mothers' consideration of quitting. Despite low percentages, the children's ages also had some effect on men's responses.

An analysis of the responses by race showed that white and craftswomen of color other than black were most likely to have given some consideration to quitting (36 percent). On the low end were female managers of color other than black (6 percent), followed by 14 percent of the black female managers and 25 percent of the black craftswomen and white female managers. Not surprisingly, white male managers (6 percent) were least likely to have considered leaving; the percentages for other men in this response category ranged from 11 to 20 percent.

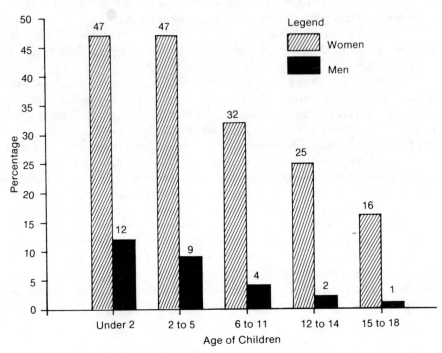

Figure 6–1. Percentage Who Have Considered Quitting Because of Child Care Problems

What were some of the reasons employees gave for quitting or thinking about quitting? One of the major themes was the impact of work on family life. Here are a few employees' comments:

Not so much because of child care problems as just problems in general. During the strike, my family's lives were calm. Not always rush, rush, rush. We had *time* for each other.

—*white, female craftsworker*

If I could afford to quit, I would. This is the greatest balancing act I've ever managed. I thoroughly enjoy my work and try to work 100 percent at work and be 100 percent at home. My home "suffers" more than work!

—*White, female lower–middle-level manager*

I considered quitting during the first two years of both my children's lives. This was due to my confusion about personal priorities. I resolved the issue successfully both times.

—*white, female lower-level manager*

I feel that I do not adequately perform my job because of child care hassles. I often choose the welfare of my job over the welfare of my children and then feel inadequate as a mother. I am tired of making these choices.

—white, female middle-level manager

My daughter went through a very bad time four years ago, and I almost quit because I felt she needed me at home. Fortunately my managers allowed me to work part-time for about ten months. Unfortunately they have not been quite so understanding of other related problems.

—white, female craftsworker

When counseling was discontinued by my previous manager, the problems increased greatly at home. Shortly thereafter, I walked off the job.

—white, female craftsworker

Having to deal not only with work problems but with child care issues is at times almost unbearable. I don't feel that anyone wins in these situations. Frustration runs rampant and staying home looks increasingly appealing.

—white, female craftsworker

Sometimes the financing of child care was the most crucial problem, as the following respondents reported:

It's hard to find a good sitter, and the ones you do find herd them in like cattle, spend no time with the child, and besides, my baby hates sitters. He has cried all day since I've come back to work, and he is only two months old. We have finally found a sitter with no other children, and he likes it a little better—but the money they want is outrageous.

—white, female craftworker

At first, because of unsuccessful child care situations, the thought had entered my mind. But now the situation of discovering a fine child care facility has been resolved, and the only problem is affording it.

—black, female craftsworker

My child care cost takes most of my pay. I would be better off on welfare.

—single, white, female craftsworker

The age of the child and the availability of family members to babysit were factors contributing to whether some employees had seriously considered quitting. A black craftswoman thought about giving up her job when her "daughter was younger and both grandparents worked." A black craftsman whose wife worked thought of quitting when they could not find a day care center that would take a very young child. One Hispanic craftswoman proclaimed, "I know that I could *never* find a better arrangement than I have by having my parents. If it came to leaving my child with a stranger or private day care, I would seriously consider quitting my job." Another Hispanic woman was discouraged because she felt her day care center was not genuinely concerned about the children's safety. "They never check to make sure that all the kids returned home from school." She also found it hard to locate sitters who "treat all the children the same, without favoritism for certain youngsters."

Guilt is a burden for many employees who blame inadequate child care for problems their children develop. A Hispanic woman explained:

> I worked hard and early to get proper care for my 4-year-old. I went back to work when he was 4 months old, and he has had discipline and developmental problems ever since. We've seen a child psychologist. Now I am six months pregnant and plan to return to work six weeks after the baby is born. The guilt and responsibility weigh heavily on me. Exceptional day care would ease the burden.

For a white, male lower-level manager, the company's attitude made all the difference.

> If my company was impersonal about my family concerns, I would consider drastic action, up to and including resigning, but I have not found the company to be uncaring. When my youngest child was born two months prematurely and we had many problems, my supervisor was super. He went beyond company guidelines to accommodate me.

What were some of the reasons employees would not quit? Financial needs, of course, were a major consideration, but many women wanted to work because to them work had an intrinsic value:

> As a single parent, I *can't* quit working.
> —*white, female lower-level manager*

> I seriously considered it, but financially it is out of the question. If only I could get more flexible hours or a six-hour workday.
> —*white, female lower-level manager*

> I cannot afford to even consider quitting because I am the provider for my family. I just feel sooner or later I will be able to work early straight hours on a regular basis.
> —*black, female lower-level manager*

> I like my job, I need my job. I have, however, tried to talk my husband into leaving his job to care for our son.
> —*white, female middle-level manager*

Even if I weren't monetarily motivated to work, I would do so because I love my job and I like working. I would just keep working at a solution to my child care problems until they were resolved, but quitting my job would *not* be a viable alternative for me.

—white, female middle-level manager

I can't quit: I'm a single parent. But there are days when I'd like that option. Despite all the difficulties, however, I like to have a career. I'm proud of that.

—single, white, female lower-level manager

Having to work is a reality, not a choice. My children have been taught to accept reality. In order for their lives to be easier, money is the only choice to achieve one's goals.

—Hispanic, female craftsworker

Most of the responses from men are predictable. "That question must be directed to women," one wrote. "I am a father. I have no choice but to work." Another acknowledged that he had no child care problems to tempt him to quit because his wife took care of the children. A third, whose wife also stayed at home, not only felt no urge to quit but was impatient with those who did. "Employees who seriously consider quitting should be encouraged to do so. They probably aren't worth keeping."

Worth keeping or not, employees represent a solid dollar value to corporations. On the average, it costs a corporation $25,000 to properly train an employee for most jobs and $50,000 to train a highly skilled professional. To lose an experienced worker and invest another $25,000 to $50,000 in his or her replacement seems a foolish extravagance when it is apparent that corporations can address many of the problems that cause employees to consider quitting— and for far less than what it costs to train a replacement.

Effect of Child Care Arrangements on Women Returning to Work after Childbirth

A Catalyst study of 1,300 top corporations found that women return to work shortly after giving birth. The median time for maternity leave was three months, and almost seven out of ten women returned to work within four months. Women said they kept maternity leaves short mainly to avoid jeopardizing promotions, merit raises, and overall career goals.[4] This study went one step further by eliciting from female respondents two factors that influenced whether they would return to work at even an earlier date: their concerns about the availability of quality child care and about their work schedules. About half of the participants who had had children in the previous two years said that these two factors strongly influenced the timing of their return after maternity leave. If corporations could assist women to return to work sooner after the birth of a baby, they would pay out less money in benefits and would increase employee productivity.

Do Employees' Child Care Problems Jeopardize Their Jobs?

Considering all of the problems and concerns parents have, it is a testament to their abilities to cope that almost 90 percent of the employees (84 percent of the women and 94 percent of the men) believed that child care problems had *not* jeopardized their jobs to a significant degree.

No significant difference emerged on this issue in the percentages for married and single women, but a seven times greater percentage of single men than married men said that child care had jeopardized their jobs (36 versus 5 percent), more than double the percentage of women. What this says is that many single men are not well prepared to cope with child care issues. Again, children's ages had a significant influence on the responses of both men and women. Twenty-one percent of the women with children under 2 and 11 percent of the women with children 15 and older said that child care problems had jeopardized their jobs. The figures for men with children in the same age categories were 10 and 3 percent, respectively.

Conclusions

This chapter vividly illustrates the reality that child care and family/work problems affect employees who are parents and their supervisors as well. The vast majority of the supervisors had dealt with child care issues of their subordinates and of their work groups, and it was clear that in cases where supportive supervisors created an open, honest environment in which their subordinates felt free to discuss their child care concerns, employees turned in less unproductive time.

We also saw that child care problems and family/work conflicts influenced employees' decisions whether to accept promotions that might place additional demands on their already burdensome schedules.

Data also showed that many women decided when they would return to work after childbirth on the basis of the availability of quality child care and the potential for flexible work schedules.

The ultimate impact of these problems is that good employees may quit the company because of them. And most of these employees will not leave the work force. As we will see in chapter 11, having already been trained at great expense, they will go to companies that offer more reasonable and progressive child care policies and benefits.

The responses of men who were single parents continued to confirm the hypothesis that their problems are similar to those of women regardless of women's marital status. Greif wrote that the 1,136 men in his study of single parents found the balancing of dual roles to be their most difficult problem. His findings concerning single men reinforced what many women regardless of marital status have known for generations.

> The father, who was raised in a time when status was measured by his success in the work world, could put everything into his job. When the father ended up with sole custody, all that changed. He could no longer work overtime if it interfered with his child-care schedule....Perhaps most significantly, he had to change his priorities. Instead of fulfilling the childhood goal of working his way up the career ladder and measuring himself by his success in the work world, he had to become a full-time parent and choose which of the two roles he was going to be most successful at: parent or work.[5]

Greif concluded that many fathers in his study could not perform both roles well and that one of the two had to suffer.

As increasing numbers of families become dual career, as increasing numbers of men become single parents and child care becomes less exclusively a woman's issue, corporate America may move forward more rapidly in this area. In the first six chapters, we have looked at the issues involved in child care problems and family/work conflicts. The next five chapters will offer concrete solutions to these problems.

Part II
Solutions to Child Care and Family/Work Problems

7
What Should Corporations Do About Child Care and Family/Work Problems?

T he reasons that survey participants believed their companies should or should not provide their employees with various types of assistance for child care and family/work conflicts were directly related to their perceptions of women who work and of the ways in which various child care arrangements affect children developmentally, emotionally, and socially. In this chapter we will analyze these perceptions and then evaluate how interested employees believed their companies were in assisting them with child care, and how actively they believed companies should be involved in child care and family/work problems.

In a 1938 Gallup survey, only one out of five Americans (21 percent) looked favorably on a married woman's working, provided her husband could support the family, according to an article by J. Immerwahr. Within forty years, the tables had been turned, he reported. By 1978, 72 percent of Americans believed that it was appropriate for married women to work.[1]

However, Quinn and Staines, in their study on the quality of employment, found that 56 percent of single men, 66 percent of married men with wives who worked, and 83 percent of men whose wives did not work believed that "it is much better for everyone involved if the man earns the money and the woman takes care of the home and children."[2]

Immerwahr cited the Public Agenda Survey in 1983, which showed that most Americans still qualify their approval of women's working. Ninety-three percent of the respondents believed that a woman's first responsibility is to her children, and 50 percent asserted that a woman who wants to work instead of staying at home and raising children should not have children in the first place.[3]

Another survey conducted in 1983 on 846 working Americans found that 48 percent of those participants who considered themselves liberal and 62 percent of those who saw themselves as conservative believed that it is bad for children to have a mother who works outside the home.[4]

One might hypothesize that employees who believe that nonparental child care has a negative impact on children and those who believe that women should not be working outside the home would not want their company or any company to be involved in assisting employees with their child care needs or with family/work conflicts. Obviously, the reverse would be true for employees who believe that nonparental child care is beneficial, or at least not harmful, to children.

A review of the literature on this subject shows that views on these issues vary extensively, and conflicting opinions about the impact of working mothers on their children are encouraged by a wide variety of so-called childhood specialists. In a sexist society like ours, the dominant view, until recently, has been that only biological mothers could properly rear their children in an atmosphere of bonding and attachment. As Scarr wrote, "The concepts of bonding and attachment fit conveniently into the notion that mothers have special responsibility for children's emotional development. They give 'reasons' for the notion, because mothers are special caregivers, both because they themselves are *supposed* to have special feelings for their babies (called bonding) and because infants are *supposed* to have special feelings for their mothers (called attachment). These concepts came to human lore from ethology, the study of animal behavior, but they have served other masters."[5]

This argument ignores the millions of legally adopted children who have grown up as good, healthy people and who have been raised by relatives, as well as the millions of children who are abused every day by their biological mothers. Finally, it ignores the fact that many fathers are as loving and caring toward their children as their mothers are.

As more and more children grow up in two-career and single-parent households, it becomes increasingly evident that researchers espousing the notion that *any* child care outside the home is bad are primarily men who are, purely and simply, sexist. Nonsexist-oriented male and female researchers are publishing more and more data showing that children can develop perfectly well-adjusted personalities in a variety of child care settings and that they are able to form healthy attachments to others besides their biological mothers without suffering a loss of attachment to the latter.

For years it was assumed that children whose mothers worked would have psychological problems that children whose mothers stayed at home would not have, and that they would do poorly in school because their mothers were not available to nourish their intellects. A great deal of research contradicts these assumptions. L.W. Hoffman, for example, reviewed more than fifty years of research related to the impact of employed mothers on their children. She concluded that most researchers set out predisposed to find "how bad off" these children were. In reviewing all the research reports, she found that most daughters of working mothers were better off in terms of self-confidence, academic performance, and career motivation than were the daughters of full-time homemakers, and that most of the researchers had chosen to ignore the positive responses.[6] M. Rutter, after an extensive review of the literature, concluded that early pronouncements that child care other than mother care had a negative impact on a child's mental health were premature and wrong.[7]

Expanding on these concepts, Hoffman has argued that mothering, in fact, does not have an infinitely positive effect on a child's mental health. She cited a longitudinal study by Moore (1975) begun in the 1950s which indicated that full-time mothering "had its vulnerabilities even then." Boys who spent their preschool years with their mothers were more intellectually able but also more conforming, fearful, and inhibited as adolescents. She also pointed to Birnbaum's 1975 study that covered the same period and suggested that the educated nonworking mother may "overinvest in her children" by worrying too much and failing to encourage independence. "It seems even more likely," she observed, "that the current non-working mother might provide more mothering than a child can profitably handle."[8] She also noted, along with F.I. Nye, that their data, on the whole, suggested that the working mother who obtains personal satisfaction from employment does not have excessive guilt, and, if she has adequate household arrangements, is likely to perform as well as the nonworking mother or better, and that the mother's emotional state is an important mediating variable.[9]

The real question is not whether women should be working, but rather what type of child care is provided—whether by mother, father, or caretaker. Parents who neglect their children, who are nonloving and not truly interested in their children's welfare and development, are not good parents, regardless of their job status. Furthermore, the potential damage to children in two-career homes stems not from the absence of the parents but from the guilt and stress that may accompany family/work conflicts. If tension becomes so severe that it affects family relationships, it may be wise for one parent to stay at home. For most single parents, however, this is obviously not an option.

On the other hand, a parent who is bored, unhappy, and resentful about staying at home (and that parent is most often the mother) can have an equally detrimental effect on children. And there is no guarantee that parents who are content to stay at home will actually spend any more time directly interacting with their children than will parents who work.

A Hispanic craftswoman in the survey sample observed that "children are the product of their relations with others. Parental domination ends when the children enter school. If parents expose their children to society before school age, the child can only benefit. We must deal in terms of quality and not quantity of time the parents spend with the children—and with reality."

This is not to suggest that all child care by persons other than parents is good care. The recent cases of child abuse, the fact some child care workers are ill-prepared and poorly trained, and the existence of child care settings that are not environmentally or physically appropriate for children are evidence that "third-party" child care can be as bad for children as parents who have not resolved their difficulties in balancing family and work roles.

Are children better off at home or in nonparental child care? A white, male middle-level manager believed that "it is all a matter of quality.... A good day care center will enrich children's development; a poor day care center will harm children's development. A good parent will enrich children's development; a poor parent will harm it." This view was echoed by a white, female middle-level manager: "Some parents are not the best in caring for their own children. Child care is a *skill* and requires a desire and commitment to excellence equal to any other professional role. Some children (and parents) do better, grow, and learn in more productive, human ways if [the children] are in the care of quality day care professionals."

It is important to recall that much of the controversy over child care arrangements and working women did not exist during World War II, when women had to work for the nation's defense. Nor was it found in those industries in which so-called women's jobs predominated. In other words, when it was in the interest of the male-dominated society for women to work, most Americans had little difficulty in setting aside their concerns about the supposed damage working mothers do to their children.

Impact of Working Women on Breakdown of the American Family

> I feel that many men are intimidated when their wives work. Men feel they are less of a man because they are not the sole breadwinner. Some men think a wife's place is at home, especially if they grew up in a home where their mother did *not* work outside the home.
>
> *—white, female craftsworker*

> I don't mean the breakdown of the "traditional" family. Many women are still unable to find good, well paying jobs, and I think this frustration creates a stress that might cause a breakdown in a normally harmonious family with two working adults.
>
> *—white, female lower-level manager*

> I think working women help their family grow and the time the family has together is used more productively than when the woman stays in the home.
>
> *—white, female lower-level manager*

> Society and the family have changed; that does not mean either has "broken down." In fact, a lot of positive things emerge as a result of change. Perhaps we need to think of working women as leading to the strengthening of the American family.
>
> *—white, female middle-level manager*

> Women today are still more responsible for the home and children. Since they are not there, I feel American families are suffering.
>
> *—black, female craftsworker*

I believe women should be at home and that men should be the breadwinners.
　　　　　　　　　　　　　　　　　—other color, male lower-level manager

Women working hasn't really broken down the American family. It has caused smaller families and a change in the way the American family functions, which has both good and bad points.
　　　　　　　　　　　　　　—white, male lower–middle-level manager

Many people have not resolved the conflict in priorities between a career and a marriage/family. This statement applies to *both* men and women and to families where only one parent works or where both work. Obviously, both parents working compounds the problem.
　　　　　　　　　　　　　　　　—white, male middle-level manager

The *General Mills American Family Report* noted:

> According to most family members, and to human resources executives, union leaders, and family traditionalists, the trend toward both parents working outside the home has had negative effects on families. Feminists disagree. The central issue is whether or not homes where both parents work are less able to provide children with proper supervision than are those where at least one parent is engaged in full-time child care. It is clear, however, that perceived changes in the quality of parenting are a greater source of worry than the issue of working parents alone.
>
> Almost twice as many family members feel that the effect of both parents working outside the home has been negative (52%) as feel it has been positive (28%) for families. Working women, by a much smaller plurality (44%), feel that the effect has been negative; 37% see a positive effect and 14% say that there has been no significant effect at all. Family traditionalists feel unanimously that the family has suffered; two-thirds of feminists, on the other hand, see benefits to the family.[10]

Survey participants were asked: "To what extent do you believe the increasing employment of women has led to the 'breakdown' of the American family?" Only 30 percent of the women and 15 percent of the men did not believe that the growing employment of women was responsible for the breakdown of the family in the United States. Thirty-seven percent of the women and 58 percent of the men believed that this cause-and-effect situation has occurred more than to just a small extent. Table 7–1 shows the responses of employees by gender.

When controls were established for occupational level, significant differences were apparent among women at the various levels. For example, 43 percent of the craftswomen, compared to 19 percent of the women above the lowest level of management, believed that women's employment was responsible at least to some extent for the breakdown of the family. Similar differences

Table 7-1
Beliefs That Working Women Lead to
Breakdown of the American Family
(*percentages*)

	Women (N = 2,353	Men (N = 2,547)
To a great extent	11	21
To some extent	26	37
To a small extent	34	27
Not at all	30	15

emerged among the men, but the differences among levels were less pronounced. Sixty-two percent of the craftsmen, 59 percent of the male lower-middle-level managers, and 50 percent of those men above middle management concurred. The fact that men at higher levels of management were somewhat less likely to blame working women for the breakdown of the family is a sign of hope that talk about child care may evolve into action.

There was no significant difference between the responses of single and married employees on this question, nor between the responses of employees who had children and those who did not.

The ages of children did not affect women's responses to this question, but men with younger children were less likely than men with older children to respond in the affirmative.

Considering the fact that over the decades women of color have had a higher participation rate than white women in the work force, it is not surprising that 42 percent of the black women, 35 percent of the other women of color, and 28 percent of the white women did not believe that women's working had led to the breakdown of the American family. The figures for men in the same categories were 33, 24, and 14 percent, respectively.

When the obviously sexist position represented by this question was correlated with what participants believed companies should be doing to assist parents, it was clear that employees who answered the question in the affirmative were much less likely than those who did not to indicate that companies should assist employees. Forty percent of the men who believed that women's working had a very negative impact on the family thought that companies should not provide any financial assistance to employees for their child care needs. Only half (20 percent) of the men who answered the question in the negative concurred with this opinion.

What these data disturbingly demonstrate is that significant percentages of the women and men surveyed were of the opinion that working women are responsible for the breakdown of the American family. Women who believe this, especially those who believe it strongly, must experience tremendous conflict and stress about working. Men who believe it must have a difficult time perceiving women as valuable contributors to the corporation, and they certainly will have great difficulty overcoming these feelings enough to become understanding of the child care needs and family/work conflicts faced by women.

Effects of Child Care Services on Children

To determine how the survey participants felt about the impact of child care services on children (and, by extension, why they did or did not want corporate involvement in this area), the following question was asked:

To what extent do you agree or disagree with the following statements?

1. *Children who spend a portion of their day in a day care arrangement develop and grow in ways that are similar to children who spend all of their time with a parent at home.*

2. *Child care does not disrupt the emotional bond between mother and child even when day care is initiated in the child's first year.*

3. *Child care often speeds up the development of a child's social skills.*

4. *Overall, the differences between children who are raised entirely at home and those attending a child care program appear to be slight.*

Despite the relatively strong feeling that working wives and mothers are responsible for family instability, the participants were less negative about the effects of child care *outside* the home. There was overwhelming agreement on the third 82 percent of the women and 72 percent of the men agreed with the statement. Disagreement was most prevalent in response to number one: only 48 percent of the women and 32 percent of the men agreed.

Responses by gender and marital status on the impact of child care arrangements on children were not significantly different among married and single women, but—as elsewhere—single men responded quite differently from married men. Fifty-one percent of the single men, compared to only 34 percent of the married men, agreed with the second statement, as did 66 percent of the women, regardless of their marital status.

When controls for gender and parental status were established, it became apparent that whether the participants had children 18 and under was not a significant factor in their perceptions about the effect of child care services on children. The most influential factor was gender. For example, of the women who had children 18 and under, 48 percent agreed with the first statement, as compared to 47 percent of the women with no children under 19. Of the men with children 18 and under, only 30 percent agreed with the first statement, as compared to 33 percent of those without children under 18.

When the four parts of this question were formed into an index in order to test the strength of employees' feelings, the responses revealed some definite trends. Table 7–2 illustrates that female managers (more than two out of five) were much less likely than craftswomen (one out of four) to view child care services as harmful to children. Similarly, table 7–3 shows that, overall, craftsmen were less likely than male managers to consider child care services harmful.

On the whole, blacks—followed by others of color and then whites—were least likely to believe that child care services were detrimental to children. The ages of employees had a minimal influence on their responses to this question, as compared to other questions. However, younger employees were less likely than older employees to believe that nonparental child care had a negative impact on children.

When employees' views on this issue were analyzed, it became apparent that many of the positive comments stemmed from the developmental changes parents saw taking place in their children in the areas of learning and social adjustability. Many employees whose comments were negative believed that children who are not brought up by their own parents have more emotional problems and more difficulties with adjustment than those who are. In addition, some stereotypical statements about women who work reflected the traditional sexist attitudes described earlier in this chapter.

Comments of participants who believed that child care services are desirable will be followed by comments of those who did not:

Child care has been beneficial for my children. They (ages 4 and 5½) have always been in a day care atmosphere. They have been taught things at the center they would not have learned from me: French, sign language, socializing with other children, preparation for kindergarten.

—*white, female middle-level manager*

From my own experience, I feel my children have benefited greatly from day care. They are more advanced intellectually and socially. They get along better with other children, are more independent, and have been exposed to more people of different backgrounds (national and religious) than I was at the age of 30.

—*white, female middle-level manager*

I have two children (one year and 3½ years old), both in day care. I feel, in my case, they are better all-around kids for it. They seem to get along better with other children and are advanced in other fields because of their day care adventures.

—*white, male lower–middle-level manager*

Table 7–2
Women's Beliefs about Effects of Child Care Services on Children
(percentages)

	0^a	1	2	3	4
Craftsworkers (N = 1,236)	6	20	25	23	25
First-level managers (N = 773)	2	14	22	23	39
Second-level managers (N = 271)	2	11	18	22	48
Third- and higher-level managers (N = 25)	0	0	32	24	44

[a]Range is from very negative effects (0) to no negative effects (4).

Table 7–3
Men's Beliefs about Effects of Child Care Services on Children
(percentages)

	0^a	1	2	3	4
Craftsworkers (N = 745)	16	24	25	21	14
First-level managers (N = 982)	18	26	22	16	18
Second-level managers (N = 550)	19	25	20	20	17
Third-level managers (N = 138)	11	25	12	21	30
Fourth-level managers (N = 48)	15	27	15	23	21
Fifth- and higher-level managers (N = 23)	17	22	30	9	22

[a]Range is from very negative effects (0) to no negative effects (4).

Children in child care become more independent and begin to understand responsibility. They can also interact with other children and begin to expand their worlds.

—black, female lower-level manager

My child has been in day care since she was six weeks old. Now, at three, she can do things that her pediatrician says are quite advanced for a child of her age. Also, she is quite receptive when placed in a new environment or around new people.

—black, female craftsworker

Children raised in a good day care center are very bright, well-adjusted children and better able to handle situations without parents. They are more outgoing and adapt better to school and society. Children raised at home are too dependent on their parents.

—Hispanic, female craftsworker

A white, lower–middle-level manager who had no children reemphasized the importance of quality, whether at home or in the day care center:

First, I am not a parent, so I have no personal experience and do not discuss the pros and cons as much as a parent would. Quality of day care versus quality of home life care is more important than merely day care versus home care. Negligent parents are no more help than negligent day care.

Many of the survey participants expressed reservations about the benefits of child care services, and some held views diametrically opposed to those just quoted. For example:

The competitiveness of the day care situation makes children too bold, and they tend to be disrespectful. . . . Children who don't have a "mother to come home to"—latch-key kids—suffer untold damage. Child care is OK, but it ends.

—white, female lower-level manager

Although a child's development in day care is similar to that of a child at home, it is definitely not the same! Studies have shown that latch-key children tend to exhibit an inordinate amount of stress and a perverse tendency to worry about "adult problems" (i.e., "a job when I grow up," "enough money," "somebody to love me when I get old"). This does not seem to differ greatly across economic lines.

—white, female lower-level manager

This is a social/cultural issue that has evolved not from social/cultural needs but from economic needs. It is, therefore, unnatural and possibly harmful to the family unit.

—white, male craftsworker

I have one child born when my wife was working. When the second was born, she quit working. The second child has more self-confidence and poses far fewer discipline problems than the first.

—white, male lower-middle-level manager

A child raised at home has a closer bond with his parents than one in a day care center because most parents feel that after the workday is over, their job is done.

—black, male lower-level manager

In my experience, a day care center was really bad. The language my children heard was terrible. They were exposed to some tales of raw home experiences. Punishment was dealt, and often the bruises showed. Long before our children were subjected to this, we removed them from child care.

—*native American, female lower-level manager*

Some of the employees, as the following comments show, had conflicting feelings about child care services. Some seemed to be struggling to maintain the stereotype of woman as the child care provider despite a growing recognition of the positive effects child care outside the home can have on children. Both the following comments were made by black male managers:

A child needs to have sufficient time with parents, particularly the mother. A *good* child care program could also help in developing social skills of the child. A child could spend from two to four hours a day in a child care program without adverse affects, but beyond that, the child needs to be with his parents.

A child raised in a program in its first years gets less tender loving care than would a child in its own home, but I believe it does help the child grow up faster, and it helps the child develop more for the outside world.

The hypothesis was advanced in the beginning of this chapter that sexist stereotypes are responsible for the belief that nonparental child care has a negative effect on children. This idea was substantiated by a cross-tabulation that was made regarding the effect of women's employment on the breakdown of the family. The conviction that families suffer as a direct result of the increasing participation of women in the work force goes hand in hand, according to the cross-tabulation, with the view that nonparental child care is harmful to children. Only 3 percent of the women who believed that, to a great extent, women's working had led to the breakdown of the family, also felt that nonparental child care had no negative impact on children, whereas fully 38 percent of women who did not believe women were responsible for the breakdown also believed that nonparent child care was not harmful to children. The figures for men—5 and 35 percent, respectively—were quite similar.

Some of the respondent's comments gave a clear picture of their stereotypical way of thinking. "The child care in the United States is a sad reflection of society's worship of money instead of God and family," wrote a white, male middle-level manager. A white, male lower-level manager said, "A child needs to know that at least one parent will be at home when he comes home. Also, the bond between parents and child is extremely important during the first seven years of life!" Another white male—a craftsworker—said, "Society asks for this, but I'm not sure it's the right thing to do. For me, it's not!"

White males are not alone in these views. A Hispanic, female lower-level manager commented, "Children are very impressionable in very young years, and they need to know their parents, especially the mother." A Hispanic male at the same level of management insisted that children reared by a sitter on a permanent basis "only lose by not being with their mother."

The General Mills study, however, noted the wide divergence of views in the conflicting responses of its participants. While 52 percent of those surveyed believed working women had a bad effect on the family, especially on the children, most participants believed that both mothers and fathers should play equal roles in child-rearing, and an extremely high percentage (86 percent) believed that "it's not the amount of time you spend with children that's important, but what you do with your children when you spend time with them".[11]

Survey Participants' Perception of Company Interest in Child Care

The corporate community and American society as a whole have become increasingly aware in the past ten to fifteen years that family/work conflicts and child care problems must be addressed in order to make this nation fully productive and to ensure that children will be properly cared for while their parents are at work. As we have already seen, this burgeoning interest has been accompanied by very little action either in corporate board rooms or in the chambers of the federal government. Of 6 million American employers, only 2,000 are providing any form of child care assistance to their employees. In a survey of 32,000 participants, only 35 percent believed their employers were sensitive to and supportive of employees' family life.[12]

Many of the survey participants believed that child care and family/work problems have a negative effect on productivity, and many were having a difficult time adjusting to dual roles. Employees with children 18 and under were asked to what extent they believed their companies were interested in their child care needs. The answer, particularly from women and single men, was "not very interested at all." Only about one-fourth of the women (23 percent) and less than one-fifth of the single men (19 percent) believed their company was interested even to some extent in their child care needs. The comparable figure for married men was 41 percent. On the other hand, 40 percent of the women and 29 percent of all the men said that their company had absolutely *no* interest in this issue. The remaining participants (37 percent of the women and 30 percent of the men) responded that the company was interested "to a small extent."

These responses reinforce earlier observations that women, regardless of whether they are married, and single men share common views and shoulder most of the responsibility for child-rearing. In this area in particular, the message to corporations is clear: as the ranks of men who are single parents increase, so does the likelihood of an alliance between them and women employees to press for greater assistance with child care needs.

The companies included in this study have begun to explore the possibility of providing assistance for child care and family/work problems, but at the time of the survey, they had not taken concrete steps in this direction. The responses of many participants, therefore, were based largely on the understanding and cooperation—or lack thereof—of their individual supervisors and on their perception that the company *was* concerned about productivity. Following are comments made by employees who believed that their companies were at least somewhat interested in their child care problems:

> My supervisor has been tremendous. She is very understanding about problems that working and raising a family can create.
>
> *—white, female lower-level manager*

> They are interested because if you have problems, it means that you miss work, are late, or do poorly at work. Attendance is very important.
>
> *—Hispanic, female craftsworker*

> I've been able to take all the nonpaid time I need. If a pregnant woman must quit working early, she gets paid for all the time she misses plus six weeks after the baby is born.
>
> *—white, female craftsworker*

> Our supervisors are great at understanding our child care problems and really try to help out.
>
> *—black, female craftsworker*

> It probably depends on the department you work in and the group of people!
>
> *—black, female lower-level manager*

> The company is interested because of the cost. If the problems cause a lot of nonproductive time, that's costly to the company.
>
> *—black, male lower-middle-level manager*

Here are some of the comments made by employees who believed that the company was *not* very supportive. Notice the crucial role played by the supervisor in these remarks:

> Here are the comments I have heard from my former supervisors: "If you want to have children, that's your business; running the company is our business." "The meeting starts at 5 p.m. sharp." "So how long will that maternity leave take? Should we load up the other people with your work?"
>
> *—white, female lower-level manager*

I've seen too many mothers of small children forced into jobs (including lateral transfers) requiring them to travel when they have specifically asked not to travel. Their desires always seem to be ignored.

—white, female middle-level manager

Management does not appear to care about the family—or God. Their God is the almighty dollar!

—white, male middle-level manager

The company has not shown any concern in the past. As a matter of fact, during the 1983 work stoppage, my spouse and I were routinely assigned work at separate, remote locations with no consideration for our child care needs. I would classify that attitude as one of callous disregard for our needs.

—white, male middle-level manager

If they were concerned, they would have done something years ago, instead of allowing supervisors to downgrade your work performance and transfers because of child care problems. I strongly believe that the company is interested only in having a body, preferably a warm one, here to do the job! I haven't seen any compassion about child care problems from management people, unless it was *their* child.

—black, female craftsworker

In short, a significant majority of the employees with children 18 and under did not believe that their companies were at all interested in assisting them with their child care problems, and most employees who felt differently were basing their perceptions on experiences they had had with sympathetic supervisors or on their understanding that because the company wanted to maintain a high level of productivity, it *had* to be concerned with issues of child care.

Should Companies Be Actively Involved in Child Care?

Unlike the previous question, the one about whether companies should be involved in the provision of child care assistance was posed to the entire survey population, since most employees in corporate America who are in a position to make policy decisions do not have young children. Several factors came into play here, including the ambivalence of many employees (even those with children) about whether mothers of young children should work outside the home, along with the large number of men whose wives were full-time homemakers and who did not believe that child care should be the responsibility of the company.

Table 7-4 shows employees' responses to the question "To what extent do you agree or disagree with the following statement: Your company should play an active, supportive role in assisting employees in their child care needs? Although more than half the total sample population believed their companies should be involved, it was women who felt most strongly about the issue. Seventy-seven percent of the women with children 18 and under and 60 percent of women without children under 19 agreed with the statement, compared to only 52 and 48 percent of the men, respectively. Interestingly, men in management—who could most effectively influence the company to take initiative in this area—were least likely to support the idea. Only 45 percent of male managers agreed with the statement, whereas 73 percent of the craftswomen, 62 percent of the craftsmen, and 64 percent of the management women gave positive responses.

It is a positive sign, nevertheless, that nearly half the men in management saw a need for their companies to provide assistance with child care, and it is more encouraging still that as the level of management rose, the responses generally became more positive. (Of the male managers who agreed that companies should be actively involved in child care, the breakdown by levels of management was as follows: 45 percent of lower, 41 percent of lower middle, 54 percent of middle, 53 percent of upper middle, and 62 percent of upper.)

Employees who believed that child care problems cost their company a great deal of money were more likely than those who did not to believe that their company should play an active role in helping employees with their child care needs. Among white male managers (the company's decision-makers), 53 percent of those who agreed that child care problems were very costly to companies also agreed that their companies should support child care services. On the other hand, only 23 percent of those who disagreed felt that their companies should become actively involved with the provision of child care. Thus, if corporations are to move beyond mere discussion, more corporate managers will have to become convinced that child care problems are very expensive for their companies.

Table 7–4
Should Companies Actively Support Employees' Child Care Needs?
(percentages)

	Women with Children 18 and under (N = 1,225)	Women without Children 18 and under (N = 1,103)	Men with Children 18 and under (N = 1,602)	Men without Children 18 and under (N = 926)
Strongly agree	29	15	11	7
Agree	48	45	41	41
Disagree	19	30	33	39
Strongly disagree	4	10	15	14

Why do employees believe their companies should become actively and supportively involved in child care issues? Following are comments from respondents who favored company involvement:

> The company should play an active role if they are committed to providing quality care. If they have the same amount of commitment as they do for affirmative action, I suggest that they not bother.
>
> *—white, female craftsworker*

> It's not a bad idea for the company to take a positive, supportive role in providing the best environment possible for children, when parents must work.
>
> *—white, male craftsworker*

> I strongly believe in company day care. Since both sexes are working these days, the company should start thinking more of the needs of *both* sexes. A day care program would relieve a lot of worry on my part if my child could be close at hand.
>
> *—Hispanic, female craftsworker*

> I really feel the employees who are faced with this problem would be more efficient in every way if the company provided some type of assistance in this area.
>
> *—black, female lower-level manager*

> I believe in this. I know it is hard to raise a child and work, but sometimes unproductive time is unavoidable. Employee and employer should each go halfway if necessary.
>
> *—black, male craftsworker*

The reasons employees gave for believing that companies should not be involved in child care varied, but a strong theme of sexist philosophy underlies many of the responses:

> Child care is an area where the company needs to stay away. The business world owes a person nothing but a paycheck when one works. Family problems should be kept away from the job. When you start doing this, you are entering a form of socialism.
>
> *—white, male upper-level manager*

> This I view as socialistic. Keep away from private family issues. Do not get involved with the family. We have a business to run; we are not here to become Big Brother.
>
> *—black, female lower-level manager*

I don't feel it's the company's business to be involved in child-rearing. Eventually the company and government will want to take the parents' role. It should stay with the parent.

—Hispanic, female lower-level manager

In order to accomplish our economic status and meet the needs of our family, it is necessary to establish some spending, saving, and earning priorities. This is not done without sacrifice [by] *all* family members, but the company did not create any of our financial commitments and should not be required to do more than pay the salary I earn.

—white, male lower-level manager

I don't think any employer should have to get involved in child care problems. The child is the parents' problem. If you need the extra income, you had better examine your own priorities: do you want money or children or both?

—white, male lower-level manager

Sure, parents are having hard times finding child care, but their job is not responsible for that. Their role as parents is to provide child care, to find it, and then, when they enter their work door, they shouldn't let it interfere.

—white, female lower–middle-level manager

Although a significant majority of the employees believed that affordable, quality child care is a serious problem in America, and although an equally impressive majority believed that their companies should be actively involved in providing child care assistance, it seems evident that many employees did not feel strongly enough about their company's involvement in child care to affect its policies.

Conclusions

There is an ongoing, raging controversy about the impact of working mothers on their children's emotional, social, and cognitive development. Like most social controversies, this one is fueled by the reports of so-called experts. Some experts argue that working mothers have no negative impact on their children, and others contend that working mothers are the cause of all their children's problems and many of society's as well.

The data presented in this chapter revealed divergent views about the impact of working women on the family and of child care services on children; but substantial numbers of the survey participants and increasing numbers of studies are pointing out that working women do not have a negative effect on the family structure and that quality child care outside the home can be very beneficial to the development of the child. Those who blamed the breakdown of the American family on the increasing numbers of working women displayed stereotypically sexist, hostile attitudes toward women. The real issue is not whether care by a biological parent or by a day care provider is best for the child, but whether the care itself—regardless who provides it—is of high quality. Despite the divergent views, a majority of the survey participants in these companies believed that their companies should be actively involved in assisting parents with child care needs. In addition, many employees were aware that the dual-career family has a growing impact on men.

Probably the single biggest reason these corporations and most other American corporations have not gotten beyond the stage of rhetoric is that they are controlled and run by white males whose wives, in most cases, have never held a full-time job outside the home. Most of these men have not had to concern themselves with child care or with balancing two jobs—one at work and one at home. Their wives always took full responsibility for child care and for the home, and they were expected only to "bring home the bacon." As child care problems and family conflicts come to be seen as family issues rather than as women's issues, corporations will be more likely to become involved in the solutions to these difficulties.

The next three chapters will examine a number of initiatives that companies can take to help employees resolve their child care and family/work problems while, in the process, increasing their own profits.

8
Flexible Work Options

Flex hours helped dramatically. Supervisors were somewhat supportive, but nevertheless I think my supervisors would not tolerate absence due to child care problems. (*Their* wives never worked!)
> —*white, female lower–middle-level manager*

If I could find a job I liked this much, making this kind of money, I would certainly consider the change, particularly for a job-sharing situation. At this time my company doesn't even offer part-time work with any security. As far as they are concerned, my family and children are *my* problems.
> —*Hispanic, female craftsworker*

A complete flexible program should be initiated to allow parents to use their vacation days one at a time as well as paid and unpaid leave days to take care of children's concerns. There should also be guidelines for making up time or for accumulation of compensatory time.
> —*white, female craftsworker*

My wife does a lot of work outside the home, but it's not income-producing. I feel there is a definite need for people to have the flexibility in scheduling their vacation, time off, and nonpaid leave to take care of family needs. I am generally opposed to company compensation for child care, but I'm in favor of company encouragement of supervisors to be flexible.
> —*white, male middle-level manager*

For doctors' and dentists' appointments for children, make-up time such as lunchtime, before or after scheduled hours, should be allowed.
> —*black, female lower-level manager*

In the previous discussions of productivity issues, we saw that the scheduling of family/work responsibilities was an area of tremendous concern for many employees. An extremely high correlation was apparent between the degree of difficulty employees had in balancing dual roles, providing care for sick children, handling doctor and dentist appointments during normal working hours, and attending school conferences and activities, and the extent to which they missed work, came to work late, left work early, and dealt with family issues during working hours.

One way an employer can help employees deal with these scheduling problems and the attendant stress is to provide flexible work options, such as permanent part-time work, job-sharing, flexible work hours, and half-day vacations. In this chapter, we will review the current status of flexible work options and what the survey participants believed that companies should do with regard to them, and then we will analyze the pros and cons of the various options.

A survey done in 1981 by Parents in the Workplace, a consulting firm serving businesses with employees who are parents, found that out of 473 firms in the Minneapolis and St. Paul area, 28 percent allowed job-sharing, 49 percent were considering doing so, and 23 percent rejected the idea completely. The survey also found that 54 percent of these companies offered flexible work schedules, 30 percent were considering this option, and 16 percent would not provide such a choice to employees; and that 81 percent of them offered part-time work, 14 percent were considering doing so, and 5 percent said they would not consider this option.[1]

The *General Mills American Family Report* noted that by 1985, 70 percent of the companies surveyed expected to offer job-sharing, and 66 percent expected to have reached the point at which their employees would be able to design their own work schedules as long as they put in thirty-five hours a week. Sixty percent of the companies expected that by 1985 they would offer flexible work hours (that is, employees would be able to select specific work schedules, such as 7:00 a.m. to 3:00 p.m., 8:30 a.m. to 4:30 p.m., or 9:00 a.m. to 5:00 p.m.). Lastly, 51 percent of the companies anticipated offering shorter work weeks with less pay—in other words, some form of part-time work.[2] These were lofty expectations in 1980–81, but the reality is that in 1985, the number of companies that have actually adopted such flexible work options is small.

A 1982 survey conducted by Employee Counseling Programs of New York regarding fast-track female corporate employees from various institutions found that only 18 percent of them were offered flexible work schedules, and another 18 percent were offered part-time work.[3]

Also in 1982, about 10 million full-time workers in the United States had flexible work schedules and compressed work weeks (that is, four ten-hour days rather than five eight-hour days). Many of these employees were government workers. In the same year, about 12 million workers held voluntary, permanent part-time jobs. The Bureau of National Affairs (BNA) 1984 report on employers and child care stated that in 1978, 13 percent of all nongovernmental organizations employing more than fifty workers permitted at least some employees to use flextime. In July 1984, the BNA found that 32 percent of employers surveyed offered flextime and that 16 percent of them allowed employees compressed work weeks.[4]

In a 1984 study, Catalyst noted the discrepancy between what work options employees had and what options they wanted to have but did not. For example, 37 percent of the 374 firms surveyed reported that they had flexible work hours, while 73 percent favored such an approach. With regard to flexible workplaces, 8 percent of the companies surveyed were offering such an option, while 35 percent said they favored doing so.[5]

N. Barko noted that in the United States in 1985 there were about 2 million part-time permanent professional employees, including doctors, economists, and lawyers. She further observed that in general, many corporate executives opposed permanent part-time employment for a host of reasons that will be discussed later in this chapter.[6]

Participants' Views

All survey participants, regardless of whether they had children, were asked the following question:

To what extent do you agree or disagree that companies should do the following things in order to assist in the child care/work/family needs of its employees?

Allow all employees the option:

1. *To choose to work part-time*

2. *To select various forms of job-sharing*

3. *To select flexible hours*

4. *To select half-day vacations*

Substantial percentages of the respondents, regardless of race, gender, and parenthood status, agreed that employers should offer these options.

In gross terms, more than 50 percent of the employees believed that each of the four options should be offered, but the percentages varied among all four options. The most popular option was the fourth; 93 percent of the women and 88 percent of the men agreed that half-day vacations should be allowed. Least popular were the first and second; 73 percent of the women and 59 percent of the men felt that part-time work should be an option; 79 percent of the women and 61 percent of the men supported the option of job-sharing.

Table 8–1 shows the responses of employees by gender and parenthood status on the question of flexible work options. Significant differences did not emerge within each gender group for employees with children and those without, but they did emerge between the genders. This is not surprising, considering the imbalance in family/work responsibilities. Still, these differences were overshadowed by the fact that such high percentages of both men and women, regardless of parenthood status, believed that all four options should be offered.

Table 8-1
Participants Who Believe Companies Should Offer Flexible
Work Options
(percentages)

Option	Women with Children 18 and under (N = 1,225)	Woman without Children 18 and under (N = 1,103)	Men with Children 18 and under (N = 1,600)	Men without Children 18 and under (N = 926)
Half-day vacations	96	89	89	87
Flexible hours	83	85	80	74
Job-sharing	83	73	63	56
Part-time work	77	69	61	55

This may be due in part to the growing desire of both sexes, and especially of younger employees, to exert more control and flexibility over their work and personal lives.

These four questions were formed into an index, with controls established for age and gender. Table 8-2 clearly illustrates the crucial role played by a child's age in determining employees' responses to the series of questions on flexible work options, and it reveals the gender gap as well. When controls were established for other factors such as age and occupational level, it became apparent that a higher percentage of younger employees and crafts employees than of older employees and management employees believed that all flexible work options should be offered.

A reasonable explanation for why crafts employees were much more likely to believe these options should be offered is that many of their jobs are extremely structured, with very little opportunity or time available to deal with various family/work responsibilities.

Even those craftsworkers whose jobs are less structured often do not have the freedom that management has to make decisions about how to deal with family/work conflicts. Adding to the difficulty of these problems is that many supervisors have not been encouraged or trained to understand the child care and family/work concerns of their employees. As a white craftswoman pointed out: "I would strongly agree with all of the options. Management has the flexibility craft doesn't. This is unfair. They have little understanding of our problem."

The ultimate effect of inflexibility and lack of understanding on the part of supervisors is that employees' productivity suffers. Many crafts employees and some managers will stay at home when they cannot resolve their child care problems and family/work conflicts. Even if they do go in to work, the stress they bring in with them because of these unresolved conflicts can affect not only their job performance but also, in severe cases, their health.

Table 8–2
Employees Who Believe Companies Should
Offer All Four Flexible Work Options
(percentages)

Age of Child	Women (N = 2,376)	Men (N = 2,561)
Less than 2	75	55
2 to 5	74	50
6 to 11	66	47
12 to 14	65	44
15 to 18	60	41
No children under 19	54	36

Not surprisingly higher-level employees were less likely than those at lower levels to believe that companies should offer all four flexible work options. For example, 52 percent of the craftsmen, compared to only 31 percent of the upper-level managers, concurred. Their reaction is predictable, since most of the upper-level managers had wives who assumed full responsibility for child care and homemaking. These men felt that since *they* successfully handled their family/work obligations and worked "normal" hours, others should be able to do the same thing. They also argued that most flexible work options would be too costly because of such factors as increased benefits, Workmen's Compensation, space and equipment. Finally, managers opposed to flexible work options, especially those involving part-time schedules, job-sharing, and working at home, said the options would create great disruption of work flow and would greatly harm employee morale. Many would concur with a peer who commented:

> Part-time work and job-sharing would just create havoc with getting the job done. There would be a lot of ill feelings about people not pulling their load. I suspect it would cost us dearly in terms of dollars.

These prophets of doom fail to recognize that as more and more women and single parents enter the work force and as more men accept a greater role with family tasks, the frequency of scheduling problems and their infringement on productivity will also continue to increase, if nothing is done to prevent it. The data showed that employees who experienced difficulty in handling child care problems and family/work conflicts were more likely than those who did not to believe that companies should offer all four options.

Family/Work Stress and Flexible Work Options

Figure 8–1 illustrates these points. Sixty percent of the women with children 18 and under who said that they felt *no* stress, compared to 89 percent who said

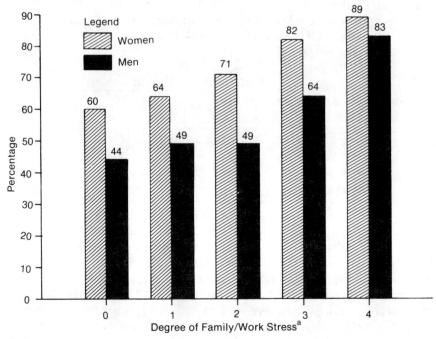

Figure 8-1 chart

aRange is from no stress (0) to a great deal of stress (4).

Figure 8-1. Percentage Who Believe Company Should Offer All Four Flexible Work Options

they felt a great deal of stress, wanted companies to offer all four work options. For men, the figures were even more dramatic: almost double the percentage of men who experienced a great deal of stress, compared to those who experienced none, wanted all four options (83 versus 44 percent).

A significantly strong relationship also existed between employees' beliefs about whether companies should provide flexible work options and tardiness, leaving work early, missing work, and dealing with family issues during working hours. Thus, those who had a lot of problems in these areas were more likely to want flexible work options than those who did not have many problems.

Following are some of the employees' comments about why they believed flexible work options should be provided:

> Since I am a switchboard operator and can change hours with other employees, I can adjust my work schedule to meet my family's needs. If I don't have a sitter, I can trade off days or hours.
>
> —*black, female craftsworker*

Let employees use sick, vacation, make-up time, and employee days when their children are sick.

—black male manager

If I had some of these options, I would never miss work.

—white, female craftsworker

Rather than using my vacation days, I'd like to be able to take time off during working hours for family-related activities/appointments and be able to make the time up later, perhaps on a Saturday.

—white, female craftsworker

As these remarks suggest, explicitly or implicitly, the major benefit employees would receive from flexible work options would be the ability to deal more effectively with their family/work demands, which, in turn, would decrease lost work time, lessen stress, and thus create a more productive employee; and the major gain for corporate America would be more productive employees. In short, the responses seem to indicate a potential win/win situation for employers *and* employees.

Although a large majority of the employees believed all four work options should be made available, some employees disagreed because, as two of them explained, "Corporations should not get involved in their employees' private lives," and "I got along without such benefits, so why should others get the benefits?" A white, male upper–middle-level manager who opposed any flexible work options argued, "Again, teach people to live with less. Why do both parents work? Not because they want to but because they feel they have to. They want to keep up with their neighbors." A black, male lower-level manager expressed similar sentiments: "My wife works and we handle our family needs with no help from the company. Why should others get it?" Managers who are in the business of making money for their firms cannot afford to take such irrelevant, nonthinking positions.

In the following sections, we will review in more detail the pros and cons of several flexible work options and the reasons that the survey participants did or did not support them.

Flextime

Flextime simply means that an employee has some choice about what time he or she begins and finishes work as long as the required number of hours are put in. Most companies establish specific time ranges for flextime. For example, an employee may begin anytime between 7:00 a.m. and 9:00 a.m. and may leave anytime between 4:00 p.m. and 6:00 p.m. (If the normal work week is forty hours—eight hours a day, with one hour off for lunch—an employee could begin at 7:00 a.m. and leave at 4:00 p.m., begin at 8:00 a.m. and leave at 5:00 p.m., and so forth.) With most flexible work plans, there are "core hours" in mid-morning and mid-afternoon when all employees must be present. Those who choose to use flextime must establish a regular routine and cannot arbitrarily alter the hours worked from day to day.[7]

The first major employer to institute flextime was the federal government, in 1974. In 1981 the government conducted a survey of 325,000 federal employees who participated in one of the 1,554 alternative work schedule programs in twenty different federal agencies. The study found that more than nine out of ten of the survey participants believed the program was at least somewhat important to their solving family/work problems. The specific benefits cited by the employees were the ability to take care of sick children's needs, lower baby-sitting fees, more time available to spend with children, and freedom to attend school conferences and programs and to spend time with their families.[8] One of the more recent innovative forms of flextime has been instituted on a trial basis by Connecticut Savings Bank in New Haven. The experimental plan allows thirty employees to leave work at 2:30 p.m. during the school year and to take summer vacations without pay. The employees cite advantages similar to those identified in the government study.[9]

The potential benefits of flextime for the employee are apparent, but there are also very likely advantages for the company. Less stress and a greater capacity to concentrate on the job, along with decreased absenteeism and tardiness, are good not only for employees' morale but also for corporate productivity. Other factors recommending the use of flextime are ease and minimal cost of administration: employees are continuing to work the same number of hours as they did on a previously inflexible schedule. Flextime that is based on a normal thirty-five- or forty-hour work week does not eliminate many of the child care problems, school conferences, and children's activities that go on during the core hours when employees must be at work, but it does give employees more flexibility to deal with these issues.

However, for women in dual-career families, flextime can be a double-edged sword. If both partners use it in order to increase their ability to share family/work responsibilities, the woman benefits greatly—more so, perhaps, than her partner, if he has previously shifted most of these responsibilities to her. If, however, a husband takes advantage of his wife's flextime schedule to dump his responsibilities on her, she may find herself solely responsible for all tasks that must be taken care of during the workday and, consequently, even more burdened than she was before.

H.H. Bohen and A. Viveros Long drew just that conclusion in their study on flextime. They noted that when there was no accompanying change in the traditional family roles, flextime did *not* lessen stress, allow parents to spend more time with their children, or better balance family/work roles, and that therefore corporations need to look beyond flextime to assist parents with family/work conflicts and child care needs.[10]

Another problem with flextime is that it is not a very workable concept in some types of work, such as assembly lines. Yet, despite its negatives, flextime has many positive aspects and can be most helpful to some employees. As Burud et al. put it so concisely:

> Flextime clearly does not offer the solution to the child care concerns of all working parents, but it can be useful in some situations. Flextime may be especially helpful to parents who share the responsibility of caring for children at home. It can work well, for instance, if one parent cares for the children in the morning before school and the other picks them up from school in the afternoon. It also may allow parents some latitude in matching the workday with the schedules of local child care providers (for instance, allowing parents to use a center that opens slightly later than the normal starting time).[11]

In brief, corporations that utilize flextime will be providing their employees with an option that is inexpensive to implement and easy to administer. Flextime can improve productivity by reducing absenteeism, tardiness, and early departures. The disadvantages are that it really does not deal with such pressing issues as the care of sick children or children on vacation. In addition, the inequitable distribution of family work between men and women is not affected unless the partners desire such a change.

Permanent Part-Time Work

For the purposes of this discussion, part-time work means a permanent job that is designed to require less than thirty-five or forty hours a week and that does not involve splitting or sharing the responsibilities with another person. The federal government has been the leader in offering employees both flexible work options and permanent part-time employment. In 1978, the U.S. Congress passed the Federal Employees Part-Time Career Employment Act, which encouraged government agencies to create part-time positions.

A report by the New York State Council on Children and Families showed considerable support for part-time work. It reported that only 2,190 of the full-time employees would not approve of a part-time work option. Over half of the women and more than one out of five men working full-time who had children under 18 indicated they would like to work less than full-time.[12]

Of the four flexible work options, the data showed this to be the least popular, although still viable. More than half the men (59 percent) and nearly three-fourth of the women (73 percent) agreed that part-time work should be an option offered to employees.

Part-time employment offers significant advantages to the employer as well as the employee. For the employee, the permanent part-time option provides advantages similar to those of flextime: more opportunity to balance family/work roles, which, in turn, translates into reductions in stress, absenteeism, and tardiness, and an increase in energy—all benefits to the employer. In addition, while few managers in the New York State survey on part-time employment felt that part-time workers' productivity was not as high as that of full-time workers, 27 percent of managers believed that part-time employees in the professional categories were more productive than full-time employees, and 40 percent reported that part-timers had much lower absenteeism than full-timers.[13]

For the corporation, part-time positions offer several other fringe benefits. They provide an opportunity to attract a pool of talented people (particularly women) who cannot or do not want to work full-time. Because of the attractiveness of such positions to women, companies will be better able to fulfill EEO goals by increasing the numbers of female employees. And, by providing a viable alternative for women returning to work soon after childbirth or for those with serious child care problems, part-time jobs offer the possibility of retaining valuable employees and avoiding the cost of training replacements for workers who would otherwise leave the company entirely.

The creation of a permanent part-time sector in a company's work force is not without initial cost to employer or employee, or both, and a careful reassessment of the organization's benefit program is essential before creating part-time positions. From the employer's standpoint, the simplest alternative—and one that is increasingly used as a cost-cutting tool—is to eliminate all benefits to part-time workers. What many employers fail to realize, however, is that such short-range savings usually result in greater costs in the long run in terms of rapid employee turnover, lowered morale and company loyalty, and ultimately, decreased productivity. Such negative approaches to the part-time option rarely serve to address family/work conflicts. In many cases, part-time work is not an option but the only alternative presented to minimally skilled workers.

Positive approaches to part-time work opportunities will, in many cases, involve a short-term cost to the employer, particularly when the positions are at the upper levels of management. The income ceiling for Social Security taxation (currently $39,600) allows employers a free ride for several months each year on employees whose salaries are above that figure; if the work of one full-time position worth over $39,600 is performed by two part-time employees, the full amount of both salaries would be subject to taxation. In addition, unemployment compensation costs, because they are based on numbers of employees, would increase—but Workmen's Compensation (which is based on a percentage of the payroll) would not in most instances.

Whether the cost of other benefits—health insurance, disability and life insurance, pension and savings plans, holidays, vacations, and sick leave—would increase would depend on how the employer handled the entitlements of part-time workers. To deny *all* benefits to part-time employees can serve as a disincentive to workers and may negate the potential benefit of the option. On the other hand, to provide *full* benefits can be costly to the corporation and create resentment among full-time employees. A full review of the company's personnel policies and benefits packages is essential, and such alternatives as increased employee participation in the payment of benefits or a "cafeteria" benefit plan in which part-time employees are entitled to a smaller tray than full-time workers are possibilities.

Increasing the number of employees by dividing full-time jobs among part-time workers may also initially increase recruitment and training costs. Further, extensive use of part-time employees may necessitate additional space and equipment, depending on the work schedules and the nature of the jobs, and most companies that have established part-time positions find it beneficial to hire a coordinator to oversee the program.

All of these potential costs must be evaluated in the context of the savings associated with lower turnover and training costs and with reduced absenteeism, tardiness, stress, and unproductive time of all sorts. Part-time work offers a significant advantage over flextime for some employees in that they are working fewer hours and thus have more time to deal with all of the child care and family/work problems discussed earlier. It compares less favorably to flextime in terms of the costs of implementation and administration. Still, part-time work options, when properly structured, offer a positive solution to many workers' child care and family problems.

Job-Sharing

Job-sharing is another part-time employment arrangement. The major difference between this option and permanent part-time work is that one "complete job" is done by one person in a part-time position, whereas in job-sharing, the work and responsibilities of one full-time job are divided between two or more employees, each with similar and overlapping duties and prorated salary and benefits. As we saw earlier, almost four out of five women and more than three out of five men in the sample believed that companies should offer some form of job-sharing.

Much of what was described for part-time employment in terms of benefits and cost can be applied to job-sharing, so we can go on to discuss the problems both work options can potentially create for work groups.

One criticism expressed by peers regarding part-time or job-sharing schedules is that the workers who take advantage of them are not carrying their share of the workload. Workers on these flexible plans, on the other hand, may feel that they are burdened with *more* work because of the new arrangements. Another primary concern of workers who choose these options is whether they will be treated fairly in terms of training, career planning, performance reviews, merit money awards, and promotions. Many part-timers believe that full-time employees will have distinct advantages in these areas.

Supervisors voice concerns about problems with scheduling training meetings and dealing with potential schedule conflicts of part-time and job-sharing employees. They also worry about reconciling these employees' schedules with those of customers in jobs that require customer contact, and about arranging overnight travel when necessary. Specifically with regard to job-sharing, the issue of compatibility between those who share a job is of paramount importance, and many supervisors have indicated that this is the most difficult area to deal with. Despite these problems, a study performed by one high-tech company noted that a majority of work group members were supportive of job-sharing and believed that, like permanent part-time arrangements, it offered a win/win situation to both employer and employee.[14]

Half-Day Vacations

The survey participants with children 18 and under consistently indicated that they would miss fewer days if their supervisors would permit them to take time off without pay, individual vacation days, or half-day vacations to deal with family problems. In the beginning of this chapter, we observed that more than nine out of ten women and almost as large a proportion of men believed that companies should allow employees to take vacation time in half-days. Unfortunately, many companies do not permit this, primarily because the corporation's time accounting system does not include a code for half days, or the union contract does not cover half days, or it simply is not company policy.

Of all the flexible work options, half-day vacations incur the least cost to the corporation, while offering the possibility of considerable savings. Employees who are permitted to take vacation time in half-days are much less likely to call in sick when there is a conflict between family and work schedules that would require only a few hours to deal with. In addition, the incidence of tardiness, leaving work early, and all the other related losses of productive time would be reduced.

Working at Home

Even though employees were not asked about working at home because executives of the participating companies did not want this included as a flexible work option, such an arrangement is becoming much more viable as new technology can hook up the "home worker" with the company network. Managers who refused to consider working at home as an option said that most workers need direct supervision as well as contact with other employees, and that there has been no demand for such an option. Today, about 15,000 workers at home have home work stations; however, by the 1990s as many as 10 million workers will have home work stations.[15]

The fact remains that working at home offers a number of advantages. For one thing, it would allow employees a great deal of discretion in scheduling their work hours and would therefore enable them to deal more effectively with the issue of balancing family and work responsibilities. In addition, child care costs and stress could be greatly reduced, even eliminated in some cases, and commuting time and expense would be disposed of.

As with other work options, working at home would have its disadvantages. Too much contact with the family can be as stressful as too little contact, and the isolation from other employees can indeed be problematic for some individuals. So can easy access to the refrigerator. Dr. David Nasatir, a sociologist and software developer, has said tht he has found that people who work at home tend to become lonely and overweight.

In terms of benefits to the corporation, some employees' working at home would mean lowered costs for space owing to the reduction in personnel in the office. It might also allow corporations to attract very talented individuals who, for a variety of reasons, are reluctant to engage in employment outside the home. Although working at home may require more self-discipline than traditional work site employment, Dr. Nasatir contends that people who work at home actually tend to put in more hours than office employees, regardless of the number of hours for which they are paid.[16] Working at home does pose difficulties in supervision and evaluation because of the lack of personal contact among superiors, peers, and subordinates. Obviously, new methods for monitoring and evaluation that are more task-oriented need to be developed.

Most of the disadvantages of working at home can be dealt with by limiting the option initially to those trusted and dependable employees whose work best lends itself to being performed at home—researchers and writers, data clerks, financial analysts, computer programmers, and the like—and by ensuring that these employees spend some time in the office to attend meetings and training programs and to confer with other staff personnel. Refinement of technology, managers who learn that they can trust dedicated employees, and new social values about work will eventually make this option widely used, to the mutual benefit of company and employee.

Conclusions

Companies can utilize a number of flexible work options to assist employees in dealing with child care problems and family/work conflicts. Substantial majorities of the employees believed that companies should be involved in providing these options. In fact, of all the various alternatives for dealing with child care and family/work problems, these options received the highest percentage overall of employee support. Part of the explanation is that flexible work options are a benefit that all employees can take advantage of (whereas many of the others, such as day care) focus exclusively on parents with young children and dual-career families), thus eliminating the question of equity in benefits. Yet despite the desire of many employees to utilize these options, the number of companies involved in providing them is relatively small.

The question for corporations, it seems, is simple: Will they recognize the tremendous change in family/work relationships that has occurred in the past twenty years and adopt modern employment policies to accommodate these changes? Or will they adhere rigidly to outdated practices that reduce their productivity and cut into their profits?

Perhaps the major reason corporate America has been reluctant to offer flexible work options is the old notion, rooted in the Puritan work ethic, that a person who doesn't want to work regular full-time hours is lazy or immoral—or both. Another reason is that many corporate executives believe that *good* employees are able to take care of their child care responsibilities and family/work conflicts on their own, without any help from the company. A third reason is that corporate policies are designed and implemented by males who traditionally have been able to relegate all child care and family responsibilities to their homemaker wives. They are quick to blame "the younger generation" itself—rather than the circumstances of their home and work lives—for lowered productivity.

Flexible work options are not a panacea for all family/work conflicts, but for many employees such options would ameliorate scheduling problems and greatly reduce the stress inherent in such conflicts. Further, such options can potentially benefit companies as much or more than they benefit employees. In the next chapter we will deal with a more controversial option: corporate financial assistance to employees for child care services.

9
Corporate Financial Support for Child Care Arrangements

In addition to the sheer demands of time placed on employed single parents and on women in dual-career families, the stress produced by conflicting schedules and responsibilities results in lost work time and diminished productivity for corporations. Probably chief among the many stress factors affecting such workers is the problem of finding, maintaining, and paying for quality care for their children—a problem that also contributes greatly to the difficulty of balancing dual roles.

Locating a good day care center for preschool children is fundamental to resolving the problem of finding quality child care, but day care centers are not a panacea for all of the stress-producing difficulties associated with working parenthood. Most centers do not accept sick children, nor are they staffed to accompany children to medical and dental appointments (most of which must be scheduled during normal working hours). Furthermore, as the survey's respondents so clearly demonstrated, finding suitable arrangements for older children before and after school and during vacation periods can be even more complicated than locating day care services for preschoolers. Not the least of parents' concerns in meeting all of these requirements for child care is the problem of paying for it.

The survey participants are probably a "best case" example with regard to financing child care. They are better paid, by industry standards, than most American workers, and a significant percentage of them reported little or no child care expense, either because their children were old enough to stay alone or, in the case of many male managers, wives or mothers stayed at home to care for young children. Nevertheless, the participants strongly believed that corporations have a role to play in helping employees resolve these problems. In this chapter we will look at their views of what role corporations should play in the financing of child care, along with an analysis of the pros and cons of each possible form of corporate financial assistance—not only for day care centers but also for the care of sick children, for keeping medical and dental appointments, and for before- and after-school care.

In chapter 2 we saw that corporate involvement in child care dates back almost to the first American nurseries and kindergartens. Around the turn of the century, a few progressive companies in industries such as shoe and clothing manufacturers, and canneries that employed large numbers of women, provided child care services as long as the supply of women with the requisite skills was limited. This lukewarm response on the part of corporations continued until World War II called forth all available man- and womanpower to work for victory. Impelled by the enormous demands of the war effort, both federal and state governments as well as corporations launched a massive drive to provide women with child care services and flexible work options that would lure them into the factories. This commitment, however, was short-lived: as soon as victory was assured and the men came home, government and corporate support for child care services and working women disappeared, almost overnight. For the next two decades, neither the government nor corporate America showed much interest in providing women with viable career opportunities, or—for those who had to and those who wanted to work—any type of child care assistance.

The Civil Rights Act of 1964, spurred on by the civil rights and women's movements, exerted some pressure on corporate America to see women as viable, permanent members of the work force; but significant civil rights laws have not changed many Americans' social viewpoint toward working women. Those changes that have occurred in corporate attitudes toward working women have not been readily translated into the provision either by corporations or the government of child-care assistance to working parents, especially to mothers, who carry the main responsibility for child-rearing. Of the 2,000 or so companies in 1985 that were offering their employees any form of child care assistance, only 15 percent were providing financial assistance for day care services, after-school care, or the care of sick children. Catalyst's study of 374 firms showed the difference between intention and action. It found that only 19 percent of firms were providing monetary assistance for child care, despite the fact that 54 percent said they favored this approach.[1] Following are the survey participants' opinions on these issues.

What Participants Believed Companies Should Do

In the following question, participants were asked about a variety of ways in which companies could fund child care services:

To what extent do you agree or disagree that companies should do the following things in order to assist in the child care needs of their employees?

1. Subsidize an existing community-provided child care program (either directly support the service or buy slots for company employees).

2. *Assist in off-site community or private enterprise child care facilities.*
3. *Provide for summer care and/or vacation care for school-age children.*
4. *Provide on-site child care facilities for employees only:*
   a. *Totally supported by the company*
   b. *Subsidized to some extent by the company*
   c. *Run as a profit center*

The largest percentage of employees (more than 50 percent) believed that companies should provide on-site for-profit child care centers. The lowest percentage of employees believed that corporations should completely subsidize on-site centers. Table 9–1 details the responses to the preceding question.

A significant difference emerged between women with and without children 18 and under on all questions except for the option of operating on-site programs as profit centers. For example, more than double the percentage of women with children 18 and under (40 percent), compared to women with no children under 18 (18 percent), believed that companies should provide for summer care and/or vacation care for school-age children. For men, the only significant difference was in regard to the same item: 9 percent with no children under 18, compared to 16 percent with children 18 and under, believed that companies should provide vacation and/or summer care. The table also shows that the responses of women with no children under 18 were much more similar to those of men, regardless of parenthood status, than to those of women with children under 18. This may be the case because many of the women without children under 18 were single, had never had children, and, therefore, had little

Table 9–1
Participants Who Believe Companies Should Provide Financial Support for Child Care Services
(*percentages*)

Type of Support	Women with Children 18 and under (N = 1,227)	Woman without Children 18 and under (N = 1,103)	Men with Children 18 and under (N = 1,597)	Men without Children 18 and under (N = 926)
Profitable on-site center	60	54	52	52
Some subsidy for on-site center	56	38	33	29
Provide assistance to noncompany off-site centers	57	38	29	29
Subsidize existing community centers	54	35	26	22
Provide summer and/or vacation care	40	18	16	9
Totally company-supported on-site center	20	9	9	8

sympathy with or understanding for the difficulties of rearing children while working full-time. The other possible explanation is that women who did have children but no longer had any under 18 were saying to themselves, "I did it without help; why can't they?"

There were no significant differences in the responses of single and married women on these individual issues, but men did differ except on the question about on-site child care centers run for profit. For example, 45 percent of the women, single or married, compared to 40 percent of the single men and 23 percent of the married men, agreed that companies should subsidize an existing community-provided child care program (either directly or by buying slots for company employees).

An index was formed to evaluate the strength of employees' commitment to corporate involvement in these areas, and the results are shown in tables 9–2 and 9–3, both of which indicate that a substantial majority of the employees believed that companies should be involved in some form of financial support for child care. The tables also show that men at upper levels of management were least likely to agree on the desirability of the various forms of this support; women at higher levels were generally more likely to agree than those at lower levels.

Upper-level male managers, who far surpassed upper-level female managers in terms of numbers and positions of power and authority, were much less likely than managers on other levels to believe that companies should provide financial assistance for child care, which indicates how extremely difficult it is going to be to convince them that their corporations' best interest lies in moving ahead with this support. Women at higher levels of management generally favor this kind of corporate assistance more than those at lower levels of management because their jobs involve proportionately more pressure and their family responsibilities likewise create more stress and conflict.

Table 9–2
Strength of Women's Beliefs about Companies' Financial Support for Child Care

(percentages)

	0[a]	*1*	*2*	*3*	*4*	*5*	*6*
Craftsworkers (N = 1,109)	20	17	11	14	14	15	8
Lower-level managers (N = 706)	19	35	11	11	13	7	3
Lower–middle-level managers (N = 241)	17	36	14	12	14	7	1
Middle–upper-level managers (N = 25)	9	26	9	26	13	4	13

[a]Range is from none (0) to all (6).

Table 9–3
Strength of Men's Beliefs about Companies' Financial Support for Child Care
(percentages)

	0^a	1	2	3	4	5	6
Craftsworkers (N = 678)	27	23	11	13	12	9	4
Lower-level managers (N = 949)	31	38	12	7	7	3	1
Lower–middle-level managers (N = 540)	28	45	11	7	5	2	1
Middle-level managers (N = 137)	24	42	12	3	10	9	1
Middle-upper-level managers (N = 47)	21	57	13	4	4	0	0
Upper-level managers (N = 24)	45	27	18	9	0	0	0

[a]Range is from none (0) to all (6).

Since care is more expensive for younger children than for older ones, a much higher percentage of employees with younger children agreed that companies should be involved in financing child care. For example, 73 percent of the women and 44 percent of the men with preschoolers, compared to 40 percent of the women and 17 percent of the men with children in high school, believed that corporations should provide at least three of the six forms of assistance suggested.

People of color were more likely than whites, regardless of occupational level or gender, to believe that companies should provide financial assistance for child care, and women were more likely than men of the same race to agree. The biggest discrepancy in opinion occurred between white male and female employees. The following figures by race and gender show the percentage of employees who believed that the company should offer at least three of the six financial options:

	Women	*Men*
Black	65%	60%
Other color	60%	56%
White	43%	23%

Since people of color tend to be clustered in the lower end of the corporate pay scale, they are more likely than whites to believe that corporations should be involved in these areas. Further, these groups include a higher percentage of single parents.

The open-ended responses of the survey participants provide us with more insight into their feelings and thoughts about corporate involvement in child care. A white, female lower-level manager gave a number of valid arguments which many social scientists have put forth in favor of such involvement:

> I would like to see the company put in a day care center in the headquarters building. One that takes infants from six weeks on up. Day care centers are dependable, have well-balanced meals, good play and learning activities, etc. Also it's almost unheard of for a licensed day care center such as Kindercare or any other reputable day care center to be charged with child abuse. Let's face it, private sitters in the home (even if they are licensed by the state) have no one to check up on them periodically. They're the ones who give every mother the worry. It would also be nice to spend my lunch hour with my child. I believe happy mothers and fathers make for happier and more productive workers.

Other comments were:

> I feel if we can put in fitness centers and pay for most college classes being taken, then we should be able to put in a day care center that supports itself with maybe a little subsidizing. I also feel our company should take the attitude that our children are more important than any job. Also, if done properly, it could probably be another good tax write-off for the company.
>
> —*white, female lower-middle-level manager*

> It doesn't matter how the unit is subsidized—a day care center would be wonderful. I believe the company would benefit a great deal by doing this. Also, it is very important to have the center where you work.
>
> —*Hispanic, female craftsworker*

> The only way to put a parent's mind to rest about his child is to put that child as close to him as possible. That is, at an on-site child care center.
>
> —*black, male lower-level manager*

> Companies that offer child care are making a wise investment.
>
> —*white, male craftsworker*

As the index shows, many of the employees did not support corporate involvement in all of these areas but did support it in some of them. Their comments also were insightful:

> I feel that having child care in the company would be beneficial. I don't think the company should pay for the care, but some subsidizing should be considered.
>
> —*white, female craftsworker*

I don't think it would be fair for the company to pick up the total cost for child care for employees. Maybe the company could furnish the facilities and the employees could pay for the rest.

—black, female lower-level manager

In very young children, I think a child care facility *that the parent must pay for* close to the working site would be wonderful. Parents do have lunch hours when they could visit/care for the child. Parents feel the guilt of being absent, particularly working professionals who want to do their best in every role. I disagree with total subsidization because parents would feel economically that they had no choice. But if the company offered one option, it would be very helpful and improve sometimes extremely difficult situations.

—white, female lower-level manager

Personally, I feel that company-sponsored (especially subsidized) child care is about as acceptable as company-sponsored religious training. Both are needed, but I feel that they are outside a company's jurisdiction unless done as a separate subsidiary.

—white, female craftsworker

I don't want a handout from the company. I don't feel that childless employees need to feel that they are missing a company-provided benefit. A referral program would be good. Space made available in the building or close to it for a Kindercare center (which is privately owned and profitable) would be better.

—white, female craftsworker

I don't believe that company-sponsored day care is necessary or the issue. People *choose* to have children. But a designated amount of days to use for child care would be helpful.

—white, middle-level manager

I strongly agree that the company should provide these options for its employees. I strongly *disagree,* however, that these options should be provided with the sole consideration of child care, as the question implies. It is the employee's free choice as to work when a child care situation is involved. No company resources should be expended for child care except as a profit center.

—white, middle-level manager

Employees who were totally opposed to any financial assistance for child care based their feelings largely on what might be classified as the antichild, antiwoman stance. Here are some typical comments:

Most employees are financially able to pay on their own. If not, maybe they should take a look at their economic priorities (e.g., a new car or care for my children).

—white, male middle-level manager

I feel that we handle our problems at home very well and it is very seldom, if ever, that this will affect my work or my mate's. I feel that child care is my responsibility. I decided to become a parent, and it should not be up to my employer to foot the bill, other than helping with medical expenses, which can really drain the average person.

—*white, male lower-level manager*

The "problems" will never be solved as long as we never do much of anything to discourage absenteeism, fibbing about sickness, etc. Why pay for child care and discriminate? Stockholders should have a voice in it.

—*white, female lower-level manager*

I asked you for a job—you did not pull me off the street and beg me to work for you. I *do not* expect any payment regarding my children.

—*white, female craftsworker*

Regardless of employers' pros and cons, a very clear pattern emerged among employees with children 18 and under when responses to the questions on productivity and family/work stress were correlated with employees' beliefs concerning company involvement in these areas. In all four productivity areas (absenteeism, tardiness, leaving work early, and unproductive time) there was a significant relationship between the number of times women said they had lost time on the job and their support of corporate financial assistance for child care arrangements. For example, more than two-thirds of those who had missed work, compared to about two out of five of those who had not, believed that companies should offer at least three of the six financing options. There was a significant difference in men's responses in every category except leaving work early. More than three out of ten of those men who had dealt with family issues during working hours, compared to about one out of five of those who had never done this in the previous year, supported at least three of the options.

The relationship between stress level and support of corporate financing of child care was extremely significant among only those employees with children 18 and under, as figure 9–1 illustrates. For example, women and men who reported experiencing a great deal of stress as the result of child care and family/work problems were two and three times as likely, respectively, to support corporate financial aid as those who reported no stress. One can conclude that family/work stress had a more significant impact on the opinions of parents about corporate financial support for child care than did such things as missing work and coming to work late.

Managers who were oriented to the bottom line saw in these data a clear indication that action on their companies' part with regard to some of these options would make good business sense. We will now go on to examine the pros and cons of these various types of corporate financial involvement in day care.

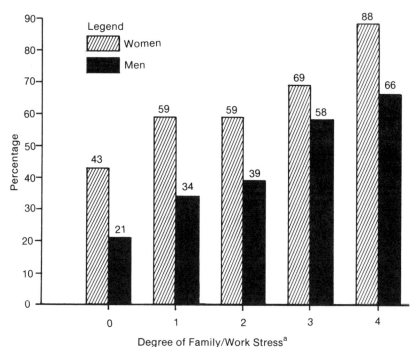

Degree of Family/Work Stress[a]

[a]Range is from no stress (0) to a great deal of stress (4).

Figure 9-1. Percentage Who Believe Company Should Offer At Least Three Out of Six Financial Assistance Options

Subsidizing Existing Off-Site Day Care

The first type of assistance we will consider is the subsidizing of existing off-site child care programs, either through direct subsidy or by purchasing slots for company employees. In most cases, if companies directly support or indirectly assist these off-site non–company-operated centers, it is with the understanding that their employees receive preferential admission treatment and/or reduced fees. In 1982, the National Employer Survey revealed that 123 companies, most of them hospitals, were participating in one or more of these subsidizing and assisting activities.[2]

The various types of assistance and subsidies that companies offer generally fall into one of these categories: outright one-time grants, ongoing grants, legal and professional help, equipment, furniture, food, transportation, space, supplies, and/or maintenance. Grants are used to expand facilities, adjust hours, improve programs, upgrade staff, provide transportation services, and so forth. An example of a successful company venture in this area is the relationship established by the Merck Pharmaceutical Company with the First Presbyterian

Church of Rahway, New Jersey, which is located one mile from Merck head-quarters. The center is private and nonprofit but is run by Merck employees. Merck provided a substantial one-time grant and also supports the center on an ongoing basis with cash grants and services, as needed; however, in the past two years, the program has been self-sustaining. Currently, sixty children attend, and 85 children (ranging in age from 3 months to kindergarten age) are on the waiting list. Fifteen percent of the children attending are from the local community. The hours of the center are 7:30 a.m. to 5:30 p.m., and fees range from $120 a week, for infants, to $75 a week for children in kindergarten.

Some companies assist or subsidize existing child care centers by using a voucher system whereby employees make a selection from among existing centers and the company reimburses them for all or part of the child care expenses, usually depending on employees' income. The reimbursement may take the form of coupons, vouchers, or an increase in pay. Polaroid is one company that does this: for its employees whose salaries are under $25,000, it subsidizes 5 to 85 percent of the cost of child care at licensed family day care homes and at day care centers.

The Ford Foundation in New York City has implemented a similar plan. The children must be under the age of 12, and eligible employees must earn less than $25,000 a year to participate. Employees have a choice of facilities and are reimbursed for 50 percent of their costs, up to a maximum based on the average New York City rate for a comparable level of care.

The Campbell Soup Company in Camden, New Jersey, has an on-site day care center operated by the for-profit corporation, Kindercare Learning Center. Kindercare rents the space from Campbell for $1 a year, and Campbell subsidizes the cost of the care to the tune of 50 percent. The fees range from $65 to $75 a week, depending on the ages of the children; the center is open between 7:00 a.m. and 6:00 p.m.

Some companies in specific neighborhoods have formed consortia. This has meant that corporations concerned about the cost of day care assistance can pool their resources and share the cost. Such firms as TRW, Hewlett-Packard, and Airtech Industries belong to the Sunnyvale Child Care Service Center Consortium in Silicon Valley, California, which has an enrollment of 200 children between 3 months and 9 years of age and operates from 6:00 a.m. to 6:00 p.m. Open to children from the community as well as from participating companies, with waiting-list priority given to employees, the $50 to $75 weekly rates are discounted to $47.50 and $71.25 for employees. The companies provide ongoing funding support and meet regularly to discuss the center's operation.

Some of the advantages of these centers are minimal start-up time and administrative involvement, lower and more controllable costs, and flexibility to adjust child care support to employees' changing needs. In addition, depending on the specific type of assistance the company provides and how it characterizes the assistance, a company can qualify for considerable tax advantages, and corporate liability is less than it is with company-operated centers. Finally, such support of existing centers is a way of helping employees and the community, which in turn enhances the company's image. For parents, the approach offers more flexibility and a wider range of choices than a company-run on-site center.

One major problem with this type of assistance is that it cannot help employees if there are not sufficient, convenient, affordable, quality child care facilities in the area. Another disadvantage is that it offers less opportunity for company control on such important issues as quality of the environment and professionalism of the staff. Among the advantages of the voucher and reimbursement system of subsidy is the fixed cost to employers and the freedom of choice for employees. More so than many other forms of assistance, though, this approach raises the question of equity between employees with children and those with no children.[3] One solution to this problem is to offer a cafeteria benefit plan that allows employees to select from a variety of benefits up to a certain dollar level. Flexible benefit plans are discussed in detail in the concluding chapter.

The advantages of all of these forms of assistance far outweigh the disadvantages. The effect of assisting employees and communities in these areas can only enhance corporate productivity, employee morale, and the corporate public image.

Company-Provided Day Care

As the reader will recall, company-operated on-site child care run as a profit center for the company was—by a factor of three—the most popular alternative in the eyes of the survey participants. (More than half the respondents [55 percent] favored this approach over the fully subsidized on-site center [13 percent].) About 37 percent of the participants supported the idea of a partially subsidized on-site center. A recent study of over 800 working parents with children under 6 revealed that 53 percent of these parents believed that on-site day care was an excellent solution to child care problems and 30 percent thought it was a good idea.[4] Very few companies have attempted to provide on- or off-site day care centers, regardless of the amount of company subsidy and tax breaks offered by local, state and federal governments.

A classic example of an on-site center is the one operated by Hoffman-La Roche in New Jersey, serving 56 children ranging in age from 2½ to 8 years. It opens at 6:45 a.m. and closes at 6:00 p.m., five days a week. The program offers not only day care but also after-school care for older children, as well as a referral and counseling service. The staff is subject to the same stringent employment requirements as other departments in the company, and the program's reputation is so outstanding that there is a continuous waiting list of some 200 children.

In Stockton, California, American Savings Bank (whose employees are 80 percent female, more than half of them mothers) renovated a run-down inner city church and turned it into a day care center for its employees. The center serves 135 children between the ages of 2 and 10 from 7:00 a.m. to 7:00 p.m. Tuition is $125 a month for five twelve-hour days. The center has a staff of eighteen, supplemented by several specialized teachers from the local public schools. Parents drive the children to the center, park their cars there, and are transported by school bus to the bank. A bus returns them to their cars and children at the end of the day.

The Zale Corporation in Texas is another company that set up a day care center near its corporate headquarters building. This center handles a maximum of seventy-four children, including eighteen infants. All of the staff members, like those at Hoffman-La Roche and American Savings, have good credentials. The fees vary, depending on the ages of the children: $40 a week for infants under eighteen months, $35 between the ages of eighteen and thirty months, and $32 for children over thirty months. The center is open from 6:30 a.m. to 6:00 p.m., Monday through Friday. The program emphasizes developmental, educational, and physical activities. Besides start-up cost, the company subsidies amount to about $2,500 a month (1982 figure).

Although corporate-operated child care can work for some companies, it should be noted that this is not a practical route for all employers. As M. F. Romaine, vice president of public relations for the Zale Corporation, has pointed out, "There are categories of businesses that simply would not realize any benefit from establishing on-site child care facilities—small companies with few employees that cannot justify the fixed costs, companies that function almost as efficiently with a high turnover, companies with downtown offices where traffic problems or licensing requirements are insurmountable, and companies where the work performed involves dangerous materials, harmful substances, or hazardous equipment."[5]

On-site child care centers make it easy for parents to visit their children during breaks and lunch hours and to deal with child care emergencies without losing travel time. Whether on- or off-site, company-operated day care centers also offer the advantage of greater operating control. Presumably, this in turn engenders better-quality centers and provides opportunities to build employee loyalty, morale and enhance the company's image, from the standpoint both of public relations and sales and as a recruitment tool for employees. Finally, the company that offers its own child care services is eligible for tax credits on capital expenditures and operating costs.

All of these advantages result in the greatest corporate benefit: increased productivity through decreases in absenteeism, tardiness, and dealing with family problems at work. In addition, the stress level of employees will be greatly lessened, and the rate of employee retention will rise.

Employer-sponsored day care centers are not, however, without their liabilities, which include their high cost relative to other alternatives, increased administrative burdens, legal liability to the corporation, and general complexity of utilization. Other disadvantages are the difficulties involved in expanding capacity and the potential hazards of an on-site center located in a congested urban area. Many parents do not want to take their children with them on a crowded subway, bus, or train to their place of work; others, however, prefer to bring their children to quality, company-operated day care centers rather than to rely on other facilities. The issue of disparate treatment of employees with and without children can also cause problems unless companies offer a cafeteria-style benefit program.[6]

The major complaint of employers regarding this approach is cost; but with tax deductions, the savings inherent in increased productivity, and the option of employees paying for the care, the cost issue is questionable at best.

Family Day Care

Family day care is the care of children in the homes of providers, usually mothers with young children of their own. Although the survey participants were not asked specifically about this option, it is the most frequently used form of child care in the United States and thus merits discussion. Very few companies support this form of child care. (In the National Employer Survey, only 5 out of 415 companies were providing family day care as a primary service, and 4 were providing it as part of their company-sponsored child care options.)[7] In the survey of 846 working parents with children under 6, 15 percent thought this form of child care was an excellent solution for working parents, and 40 percent thought it was a good idea.[8] Despite its being the most frequently used form of child care, family day care is not considered the best solution by most working parents, who prefer day care centers. Parents' main objections to family day care are that the quality varies greatly, the homes of providers are not subject to regulation in many states, and the care is not as dependable as center care because a single caretaker is in charge. Regulated homes comprise only 6 percent of the nation's 2 million family day care homes.

Companies that support the family day care option deal with these objections (most often through networks with other companies) by recruiting women who are licensed to care for a few children in their home. The companies usually provide training in child development and educational counseling to the caregiver, along with equipment, resources, toys, transportation, and/or small grants. Several companies also offer some or all employee benefits to the providers. The ultimate goal of these corporate efforts is to improve the quality and stability of family day care.

The Illinois Masonic Medical Center in Chicago has developed a network of private homes for employees with children between 3 months and 2½ years of age. The hours and number of slots vary, depending on demand from employees. The cost varies by home from $60 to $80 a week. The center not only provided start-up funds but also pays salaries and provides space and utilities for the local administrative group. In conjunction with the homes, the center offers an on-site child care program for children over 2½ years.

Advantages of family day care include low cost (compared to some of the other options), greater flexibility in location, programs tailored to specific ages of children, and the availability, in some instances, of specially designated "sick bay" homes where children can be taken even when they are ill. Scheduling is often easier because the hours can be adjusted, and capacity can be adjusted rapidly to meet the demand for service simply by enlisting additional providers.

From the company's standpoint, the disadvantages of such facilities are that the company has less control of the quality of the care provided, the dependability (or availability) of single providers can be questionable, and the possibility of legal liability increases as the number of providers increases. Further, family day care is a kind of low-profile service and offers little in the way of public relations or image-building for the company.[9]

None of these disadvantages, however, is insurmountable. Greater company involvement, particularly in the area of network-building among the providers for mutual support and resource-sharing, could make this an even more viable option.

Care for School-Age Children

Most of the previously discussed child care arrangements are not designed for school-age children. In fact, many parents find it more difficult to identify sources of before- and after-school care than all-day care for younger children. In this study, 48 percent of the women and 23 percent of the men saw care for school-age children as a problem at least to a small extent; 26 percent of the women and 10 percent of the men considered it at least somewhat of a problem.

There are more than 18 million children between the ages of 6 and 14 in this country, and a great many of them are "latch-key kids." They come home after school to an empty house and fend for themselves until the workday ends. Although in some cases this experience can be a valuable lesson in independence and responsibility, these children are in fact at risk both physically and psychologically; they are particularly vulnerable to fires, accidents, juvenile delinquency, and substance abuse. More than three out of five of the participants in the General Mills study believed it would be a good thing if schools provided more child care before and after school hours.[10]

The primary source of care for children who do not stay alone is family day care. Others attend special programs in community agencies like the YMCA and YWCA, Boys' and Girls' Clubs, park and recreation departments, and churches. Increasingly, public schools are developing early-morning and after-school programs, many of them supported by corporations and/or community funds. As of May 1984, however, only 125 of 15,000 U.S. school districts offered before- and after-hours child care programs. Some corporations (Northwestern Bell and Control Data, for example, in several Minneapolis communities) support after-school care by financing the expansion of programming and extension of hours in off-site child care centers. One such center started out with twenty infants and eighty preschoolers; it now serves an additional twenty-six school-age children up to the age of thirteen. For $7.25 a day, a child receives breakfast, is transported to school, and returns at 3:00 p.m. to the center, where he or she is picked up by a parent at the end of the day.[11]

Hawaii's Office of Children and Youth is in the process of working with interested organizations to come up with programs that would deal with care for school-age children and to assist local communities in these efforts.

As far back as 1981, the mayor's office of San Francisco was working with the local school district to reduce rental fees for community-based after-school programs. It also secured private-foundation funding to help community organizations start up their local programs.

A simple and relatively low-cost variation on after-school programs that originated in Houston is Chatters. This is an organized service through which, on a daily basis, children who stay home alone are called by a trained counselor who checks on their safety and chats with them briefly. If the child seems frightened, is lonely, or appears to be worried about something, the counselor will continue to call at intervals and, in an emergency situation, will go to the child's home. Parents pay a small monthly fee for the service.[12]

Very few companies provide on-site child care, and fewer still offer any type of care for school-age children. Hoffman-La Roche is an exception. It offers not only full- and part-time day care but also after-school, summer, and emergency care for children of employees. Another exception is Soft Sheen, an 800-employee black-owned firm whose owners found that absenteeism on the weekends dropped sharply when they instituted a program to provide care and activities on Saturdays and Sundays for workers' children up to age 16.

The responses of survey participants showed that the need for child care assistance does not end with day care centers for preschoolers. Forty percent of the women and 16 percent of the men with children 18 and under indicated that they believed companies should help with care for school-age children during the children's vacations and holidays. Although productivity problems related to child care decrease as the ages of employees' children increase, it is important to remember that the significant decrease occurs in families with children who are 11 or older. Many parents find it even more difficult to make arrangements for children who require supervision for three or four hours after school than for toddlers, who can be accommodated by all-day centers. School holidays and vacation periods are also problems for parents with children too young to care for themselves.

Despite this common difficulty, very few companies make any provision for assistance with school-age children. An exception is Fel-Pro, which for some years has offered a summer program on its own recreation grounds for about 300 of its employees' children. The program, for 7- to 15-year-olds, is operated from 7:15 a.m. to 4:00 p.m., and transportation is provided to the camp, which is 40 miles from the company. The cost is only $10 per family for each session.

Each of these initiatives has its pros and cons. Ideally, corporations will develop a variety of strategies based on the determined needs of their individual employees and on available resources.

Care for Sick Children

As noted earlier, caring for a sick child is an almost universal problem for employed parents who rely on day care centers, because the centers will not accept a child who is ill. Of the fifteen potentially troublesome areas related to child care and family/work problems, this one drew the largest percentage of positive responses: 45 percent of the women and 17 percent of the men said it was at least somewhat of a problem. Missing work, coming to work late, leaving work early, dealing with family issues during working hours, and employee stress were all highly correlated to positive responses regarding the problem of caring for sick children.

The National Employer-Supported Child Care Project reported that of 415 surveyed companies, only 5 indicated any involvement in services for sick children.[13] Hoffman-La Roche is one of 4 companies that offer care in a company-operated center; the fifth company supports a community day care program for sick children.

B. Adolf and K. Rose cited a study conducted in Minneapolis and St. Paul which found that (1) few services exist for the care of sick children, (2) care for sick children is costly for parents, since it may involve paying for the regular caregiver as well as for special services, (3) in many instances, companies treat professional and clerical employees differently, and (4) experts disagree as to whether a parent should be at home with a sick child.[14]

When the respondents were asked whether they believed that companies should pay for professional (licensed) caretakers for sick children, about one-fifth of the women (19 percent of the single women and 23 percent of the married women), and one-sixth (17 percent) of the single men said that they should. Only about one-tenth (11 percent) of the married men concurred.

Table 9–4 shows that the ages of children greatly influenced employees' responses to this question. More than double the percentage of both women and men with preschoolers than those with children over 11 or with no children believed that companies should pay for the care of sick children.

Table 9–4
Participants Who Believe Companies Should Pay for Caretaker Who Comes to Home to Care for Sick Children
(percentages)

Age of Child	Women (N = 2,353)	Men (N = 2,547)
Under 2	36	20
2 to 5	33	20
6 to 11	28	16
12 to 14	19	11
15 to 18	14	8
No children under 19	11	8

Craftswomen (26 percent) were more likely than women in management (11 percent) to believe that companies should pay for the care of sick children. Twenty-two percent of the craftsmen, compared to 2 to 8 percent of the male managers, concurred. This occupational difference is owing mainly to the fact that crafts employees are younger and are of child-bearing age. Another part of the explanation is that the inflexibility of their jobs gives craftsworkers little choice but to miss work in order to take care of a sick child.

About equal percentages of women and men of color (29 percent), compared to 17 percent of white women and 11 percent of white men, believed that companies should provide assistance for the care of sick children.

Understandably, those employees who said that caring for a sick child was at least somewhat of a problem were more likely than those who did not to support company involvement in this area; and the higher the employee's rate of absenteeism, the more likely he or she was to favor company involvement. Following are three comments from employees who responded positively to this question:

> When a child is sick and too small or otherwise unable to care for himself or is turned away from day care facilities because of a communicable disease, the employee should either get time off to care for that child or be reimbursed for professional care.
>
> *—white, female lower-level manager*

> When a child is sick, he/she needs a parent, not a professional. Give the parent time off with pay.
>
> *—white, male craftsworker*

> I am a single parent with an only child. When he became seriously ill, I lost my house and the $12,000 equity I had in it. If the company had been willing to

help me, I could have saved my house. What I should have done was go to a psychiatrist and have him declare me incompetent to work due to my child's illness. Then the company would have had to pay me.

—white, female lower-level manager

Some employees, however, maintained that this was not the company's responsibility. One white, female lower-level manager said she believed that "unless the illness is serious, parents should take vacation time to stay home with sick children"; she didn't think the company should pay anyone to stay home with a child. "If you choose to work," she said, "you should have child care available—and I have a 3-year-old!"

Despite that comment, the data show on the whole that corporations could benefit greatly by assisting their employees with the care of sick children. There are other options besides providing professional in-home care or paid leave to parents. Companies can also support day care centers established specifically for this purpose or sections of existing centers that are equipped to take children with minor illnesses into a special sick bay area. And companies can support or stimulate the development of community programs for the care of sick children—such as special day care homes established specifically for this purpose or health services with trained health aides who can care for the children in the children's own homes.

Employer support of such services is rare. In the Minneapolis-St. Paul area, 3M and other companies have assisted employees with the care of sick children through Children's Hospital in St. Paul. The hospital sends health care workers to the employees' homes to care for children, and 3M pays up to half the $4-an-hour wage plus the hospital's administrative costs, which amount to an additional $2.25 an hour. But this is an exceptional approach; Texas Commerce Bank in Houston uses a different one. The company has recognized that most employees do not admit the real reason for their absence when they are staying home to care for a sick child, and therefore, it simply accepts the use of sick leave for this purpose.

Of all the child care benefits a company could provide, care for a sick child probably would offer some of the greatest savings in terms of reduced absenteeism and employee stress.

Paid Time Off for Doctor and Dentist Appointments

The second most commonly cited child care problem in this survey was that of arranging for children's doctor and dentist appointments. Most doctors see patients only during normal working hours, and employees whose children are too young to go alone to an appointment are faced with having to use entire "leave" days (sick or vacation) in order to take their children to an appointment that may take only one hour to complete. Those who try to squeeze such appointments into a lunch hour may be adding more stress to an already stressful existence. "I work two hours every morning just getting us ready for the sitter and work," wrote a white craftswoman who was the single parent of a 4-year-old. "My lunch hours are consumed with doctors' appointments and running errands. There are days when I work—at home and at the plant—nineteen out of twenty-four hours."

She is not alone in her frustration. Forty-two percent of the women and 17 percent of the men said that keeping doctor and dentist appointments was a problem, and those employees who said this was a problem were much more likely than those who did not to put in unproductive time at work. One solution is for companies to provide paid leave time that would allow parents to take their children to doctors and dentists. By providing two hours' leave time, the company might well avoid a full day's absence. Further, by encouraging preventive health care, companies might reduce absenteeism due to illness either of employees or their children.

Survey participants were also asked whether companies should provide support by paying for working time missed due to children's doctor and dentist appointments. As might be expected, one of the factors influencing their responses was the ages of their children. Table 9–5 clearly illustrates this relationship.

Race and occupational level had significant impacts on employees' response to this question, as on the question of company support for the care of sick children. Those employees who had had to deal with child care issues during working hours were more likely than those who had not to believe that companies should pay for the time needed to take children to health care appointments.

As with other issues, some employees insisted that this was not the company's responsibility. For example, a white craftsman said, "Paid time off for

Table 9–5
Participants Who Believe Companies Should Provide Paid Leave for Children's Dentist and Doctor Appointments
(percentages)

Age of Child	Women (N = 2,353)	Men (N = 2,547)
Under 2	41	37
2 to 5	40	34
6 to 11	39	28
12 to 14	29	22
15 to 18	25	19
No children under 19	15	20

children's doctor appointments would be abused, as is the time now granted for employees' own appointments."

That comment and similar ones notwithstanding, there was a high correlation between the incidence of unproductive work time and the acknowledgment that handling children's health appointments was a problem, which suggests that corporations should become more flexible in their approach to this difficulty, either granting paid leave time or offering flexible work options and the opportunity to make up lost time at the mutual convenience of company and employee. That such flexibility on the part of supervisors has a positive impact on employee productivity was documented in chapter 6.

Conclusions

It is obvious that a broad range of options exists for company support of child care.[15] Each option has its advantages and disadvantages, including cost factors and appropriateness or the lack thereof for a variety of individual needs. The bottom line is that potential cost must be viewed in terms of potential return on investment: increased productivity, reduced stress, and improved morale for employees, and enhanced image for corporations.

While a significant majority of the survey participants were not in favor of such assistance as totally subsidized on-site company day care, a large majority was in favor of day care centers run for profit. Parental status, ages of children, amount of lost work time and the degree of family/work stress greatly affected employees' responses to questions. Employees with children—especially younger children—were much more likely than those with older children or with no children to believe that companies should provide assistance with child care. Those with a great deal of family/work stress and lost work time were much more likely than those who experienced no family/work stress or lost work time to believe in corporate financial assistance.

This having been said, it is important to understand the overall message conveyed by a substantial number of the 5,000 employees in this survey, who felt strongly that companies should become involved in financial assistance for child care. Unfortunately, the conviction was less strongly expressed by employees at the top levels of management—those who are in the best position to effect change.

The objections to corporate involvement in financing child care are many: it is too costly; it is unfair to those employees who have no children; it is impractical; it is not "the company's business." In most cases, these arguments are not valid. Cost must be viewed in terms of productivity gains and potential tax savings, not as a give-away to families who cannot handle their personal lives. Equity issues can be resolved through cafeteria benefit plans. Corporations that do not offer such plans should view the equity issue not in the light of individual feelings of unfairness but with the understanding that corporate financial support of child care is an investment in corporate resources—its working parents—which will positively affect profits and ensure jobs for *all* employees. Careful needs assessment and planning can identify practical solutions, which abound because the employee body is so diversified.

The real reason that few companies have been active in providing child care assistance has little relationship to such objections. It is based on the belief that child care is just a woman's problem. To the top-level managers, most of whom are men whose wives are traditional, full-time homemakers, child care is not a *personal* problem. If these managers would take the time, however, to look closely at the nature of their work force and at the toll child care problems are taking on their employees' productivity, they would realize that child care is a *personnel* problem, and one that must be dealt with.

10
Corporate Provision of Child Care Resources and Training

The comments of the survey participants, as well as the vast majority of professional commentary in the field, suggest that American society is not adequately prepared to deal with the inevitable role of women as permanent, integral members of the work force or with the impact of that change on family roles. Mixed messages have been sent out to both women and men about their "new" roles.

Society has told women, through the law, that they are entitled to equal employment opportunities, but in countless subtle and not so subtle ways, it also tells them that they are not good mothers if they leave their children to go to work, and they are not good wives if they do not work full-time on the job *and* full-time at home. Men are told that they must get used to the idea of women holding full-time jobs and pursuing careers; yet, at the same time, it is suggested that men who are unable to support their families by themselves are not real men, and society impugns the masculinity of those who seriously undertake an egalitarian role at home by sharing in household tasks. Then the rope is tightened even more with the insistence that men spend sufficient time with their children in order to inculcate in them proper moral values and discipline.

Although many have recognized that working parents are often inadequately prepared to deal with family/work conflicts and child care problems, few social scientists or corporate executives have acknowledged the inadequate preparation of most supervisors to understand and constructively assist employees confronted with these problems.

This chapter will explore the various types of child care resources that companies can provide for employees and the degree of interest expressed by employees in such resources as in-house consultants, referral systems, and training programs. These forms of assistance are presented as supplements to, rather than substitutes for, the flexible work options and financial aid outlined in chapters 8 and 9.

Child Care Resources

There are a number of ways in which corporations can assist employees in dealing with conflicting signals about their proper roles regarding child care and family/work problems. One of them is to provide employees with the information and skills they need to resolve such problems on their own. In their responses to the following question, the survey participants strongly supported the need for such an initiative:

> *To what extent do you agree or disagree that companies should do the following in order to assist in the child care needs of its employees:*
>
> 1. *Develop and provide brochures on child care*
> 2. *Conduct seminars on parenting issues*
> 3. *Establish a staff resource person to help employees with family-related issues*
> 4. *Provide a child care referral service*

Well over half of the employees responded positively to all four options, and three-fourths of the women supported the idea of a company-sponsored referral service. Almost as many women (72 percent) said the company should hire a staff resource person to help with family-related issues. Men's responses to these two suggestions were 58 and 59 percent in favor, respectively. Fewer—but still a majority—of both men and women thought the brochures and seminars were a good idea. (Fifty-seven percent of the women and 54 percent of the men favored brochures; 61 and 51 percent, respectively, supported the idea of company seminars on parenting.)

Responses to the four suggestions were formed into an index in order to determine the strength of employees' desire for corporate involvement in these areas. The results of the tabulation are illustrated in figure 10–1.

As one might expect, a much higher percentage of women and men with young children than those with older children were in favor of these provisions. Fifty-six percent of the women and 38 percent of the men with preschool children believed that companies should offer all options, compared to favorable responses from 49 percent of the women and 27 percent of the men with children over 11 but not over 15. When controls were established for race, substantial differences emerged, partly because more people of color were employed in crafts and were women, who are more prone to favor company involvement in child care issues. On this issue, unlike previous ones, the strongest support came from the top level of management, from both men and women—a hopeful sign that the companies involved in the study may begin to implement these strategies.

The availability of corporate child care resources can greatly affect the amount of unproductive work time spent by employees. The more frequently employees lost time at work through absenteeism, tardiness, and so forth, the more likely they were to agree that child care resources were needed. For

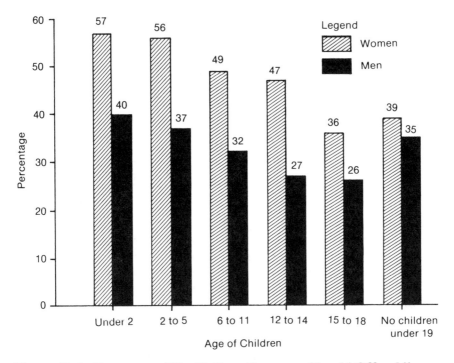

Figure 10-1. Percentage Who Believe Company Should Offer All Four Child Care Resource Provisions

example, 52 percent of the women and 43 percent of the men who had never dealt with family issues on the job, compared to 65 percent of the women and 53 percent of the men who had done so at least once, believed that companies should offer three of the four child care resource options.

Employees with children 18 and under who were experiencing a great deal of stress were much more likely than those who reported no stress to believe that the company should provide these resources. Table 10-1 illustrates the strong relationship, regardless of gender, between degree of stress and belief that companies should make these resources available. Virtually all of the men and nine out of ten of the women who were under great stress supported company provision of at least three of the four resources; the numbers dropped to 52 and 42 percent, respectively, for women and men who reported no stress.

A more detailed look at each of these options and a discussion of the ways in which companies can implement them follows.

Informational Activities

A very useful tool for working parents and one that is relatively inexpensive to develop is a series of informational brochures addressing the various problems

Table 10-1

Stress in Participants Who Want Three or Four of the Child Care Resource Options

(percentages)

Degree of Stress[a]	Women (N = 1,236)	Men (N = 1,584)
0	52	42
1	66	53
2	66	56
3	76	60
4	91	100

[a]Range is from no stress (0) to a great deal of stress (4).

discussed in this book. Northwestern Bell, for example, has developed a brochure to inform employees about various internal and external resources that assist working parents. Although useful in itself, this approach is much more effective when tied into an information referral system. Approximately 900 companies now offer various forms of informational services.

Of the 415 companies surveyed by the National Employer-Supported Child Care Project, 36 indicated that their primary child care program consisted of referral services, and 6 others said that referral services were a part of their overall child care assistance to employees.[1] IBM and Gillette are companies that use external referral services. Northwestern Bell, among several other companies, supports an external referral agency; however, Bell also has a part-time internal child care consultant to assist employees.

One of the main purposes of an information referral service, internal or external, is to provide information about available types of child care and the characteristics of each (that is, quality, hours, location, and cost). Having this information available and current for employees who have newly become parents, new employees (or transferees) who may not be familiar with the community, and employees who need to alter their child care arrangements is invaluable and greatly reduces parental stress, especially because the various resources have been prescreened and evaluated by the referral agency.

Referral agencies serve to keep a systematic tab on supply and demand as an aid to employees and also to corporations in determining their strategies for child care assistance. (Where there is a shortage of available day care slots, for example, a company may want to consider establishing an on-site center or supporting the expansion of an existing off-site center in the community.) Some referral services also offer extensive counseling to parents on a wide variety of child care issues, such as children's separation anxiety on their first day at the center, and the guilt their anxiety commonly provokes in parents.

IBM is one corporation that has gone into the child care referral business in a big way. It has hired "Family/Work Directions" to establish a nationwide network of 150 local referral agencies that provide information on available forms of child care suitable to employees' needs. IBM does not, however, guarantee quality or recommend specific providers.

Child Care Systems, near Philadelphia, is an excellent example of an independent referral agency. A Child Care Kit for Working Parents, provided by the company, gives new parents and parents new to the area a means of selecting appropriate child care. The guide includes a four-page questionnaire designed to assess employees' needs. Within one week after the questionnaire is returned, the organization matches up the employee's requirements with child care facilities available in Delaware Valley and Philadelphia, and parents receive ten to twenty pages of such listings near their home and/or job. Three to six months later, Child Care Systems supplies the corporation with a detailed summary of the data collected from its employees, and management uses the data to further refine its approach to providing child care assistance for employees. Bell of Pennsylvania is among the companies utilizing the service.

E. Galinsky has stressed the point that companies should expand their concept of information and referral to resources and referral. The latter does all of what the former does, in addition to counseling employees with regard to child care choices and providing resources to improve the quality and quantity of child care services.

Information and referral services are not expensive, they are easy to establish, and they are of great value to employees. They should *not* constitute a company's only effort to address its employees' child care problems because, in most cases, they do not address two of the survey participants' principal concerns: supply of available services, which is a crucial issue, and the provision of assistance in locating a caretaker for a sick child.

On-Staff Resource Consultants

An in-house resource consultant's responsibilities are much broader than those of a referral service. An effective resource person is a trained family/work counselor who is available to assist employees with any family/work and child care problems. In 1984, 3M created a position for a full-time child care coordinator, and Northwestern Bell now has a part-time child care resource person on its payroll. Both companies indicate that employees are utilizing the service and are pleased with it.

The following comments by survey participants about one of the companies involved in the study which established a part-time resource person illustrate the positive impact child care resource personnel could have:

> We have appreciated the role _____ has played in our understanding of parenting, especially in dispelling myths of guilt for me as a working mother. Thank you for her availability as a consultant.

Some years ago [the] company had a pretty good in-house child care referral service. It seemed like a good way to help employees help themselves. I visited one of the homes and was impressed with the program. [The] company also provided training aids to those persons who cared for children in their own homes, and visited homes to evaluate them prior to referral.

_____ has been wonderful in advising our small group of working parents about our problems.

The addition of a full- or part-time resource person to the company payroll may appear costly, but the benefits to supervisors in helping them to resolve their subordinates' child care and family/work problems would be invaluable. In-house resource personnel are more effective in some cases than external counselors because they are more familiar with a given company's expectations of employees and its perceptions of child care issues. In short, an on-staff child care resource person, despite the cost, can be a valuable part of an overall effort to deal with the issues this book is addressing.

Training Seminars

Training seminars on child care problems and family/work conflict resolution, like resource consultants and referral services, are not the whole answer to employees' child care problems, but they can greatly assist corporations in reducing the productivity loss that results from these problems. The effectiveness of the training programs will depend on corporate recognition of their value to *all* employees: to parents because they will acquire new skills in dealing with their problems, to supervisors because they will gain a clearer understanding of their subordinates' problems and develop skills to deal more effectively with work group conflict, and to childless employees because they will become more sensitive to the problems and conflicts their colleagues are facing.

Table 10–2 shows employees' responses by gender and parenthood status to the question of company support for training seminars. Those who were most interested in training opportunities were women with children 18 and under. Far behind them were men with children 18 and under followed by women with no children 18 and under and, lastly, men with no children 18 and under. The table also shows that the type of training that most interested employees with children under 18 was building self-esteem in children. This may be partly because of the guilt parents often feel when both are working, owing to the common belief that this situation has a negative effect on a child's self-esteem. In a broader sense, it confirms the research findings of Dr. Jerome Taylor, social psychologist at the University of Pittsburgh, who has identified self-esteem as one of six values that parents consistently seek to instill in their children. The second most popular area of training among both men and

Table 10–2
Participants Interested in Training for Working Parents At Least to Some Extent
(percentages)

Type of Training	Women with Children 18 and under (N = 1,225)	Woman without Children 18 and under (N = 1,110)	Men with Children 18 and under (N = 1,547)	Men without Children 18 and under (N = 928)
Building self-esteem in children	80	34	58	28
Moderating influence of children's peer groups	74	30	50	22
Dealing with stress	72	37	42	30
Balancing family and work responsibilities	71	35	37	24
Preventing burnout in working parents	70	26	34	19
Setting limits/discipline	69	29	44	21
Handling children's bad behavior	62	23	35	14
Information on available child care	50	28	28	21
Helping children adjust to separation	50	24	29	19
Guidelines for selecting quality child care	49	27	27	20
Proper selection of child care	48	25	25	18

women with young children was that of moderating the influence of children's peer groups. One of the most popular across both gender and parenthood lines was training to deal with the stress of job-related and family problems.

Overall, craftsmen and women were more likely than their management counterparts to be interested in the various available training options, partly because of the higher percentage of craftsworkers than managers who were at child-bearing ages, and also because craftsmen were more likely than male managers to have wives who worked full-time.

Another finding is that people of color were much more likely than their white counterparts to desire such training. This was not surprising, considering that people of color in the sample were younger and represented a higher percentage of single parents than did their white counterparts. Some of the participants' comments follow:

My immediate supervisor does not have children. It's very difficult for childless individuals to really understand what parents are faced with. I know that I would have a difficult time if I did not have children and supervised someone who did. Perhaps we need an awareness session to deal with this issue.

—white, female middle-level supervisor

This is such a new dilemma. I feel all parents could and would want to be a part of this education. I *never* felt that these would be problems I'd be faced with. They are things my parents or school never educated me on.

—Hispanic, female lower-level manager

One Hispanic craftswoman stated the position of many managers who weren't interested in training:

I don't feel child-rearing is the company's business. Eventually, the company and the government will want to take the parents' role. It should stay with the parent.

A closer examination of the various types of training follows, along with the overall strength of the employees' interest in each. Before doing this, a note of caution. This training is not to put the company in the role of changing parents' philosophy and style, but to give the parents information and resources to help them deal with child care issues.

Training for Dual Family/Work Roles

Productivity is lowered not only as result of lost time (through absenteeism, lateness, and so forth) but because stress makes employees less efficient and less productive when they are on the job. Family/work stress can have a serious negative impact on family life if the issue of balancing dual roles is not effectively dealt with by dual-career families and single parents. Family stress and work stress feed on one another and can ultimately affect employees' mental and physical health.

The survey participants were asked the following question regarding stress and seminars to address it:

How interested would you be in participating in any of the following training seminars?

1. Preventing working parent burnout

2. Balancing working family responsibilities

3. Dealing with the stress job-related problems impose on family care

Employees were more likely to be interested in training that deals with stress imposed on family care by job-related problems (56 percent of the women and 38 percent of the men answered affirmatively). Employees showed the least interest in seminars on the prevention of working family burnout (50 percent of the women and 29 percent of the men indicated interest in this area of training).

Figure 10-2 shows that the presence of children under 18 in employees' families had a strong impact on the responses, particularly children under 12. Nevertheless, 33 percent of the women and 24 percent of the men with no children under 19 said they were interested in at least two of the three stress-related training seminars. (All working employees must balance dual roles to some extent.)

Considering the fact that the lower a male employee is in the corporate hierarchy, the more likely his wife is to work full-time, it would be logical for such an employee to see a greater need for training than a male employee in the upper levels of the corporate hierarchy—which, in fact, proved to be the case. A higher percentage of female managers at the middle level or above, on the other hand, saw more of a need for training than did lower-level female managers, because, as we have seen, their jobs tend to be more demanding of their time and involve higher levels of stress.

What *was* surprising was the extremely high percentage of men and women who reported very little stress but were still interested in the training seminars.

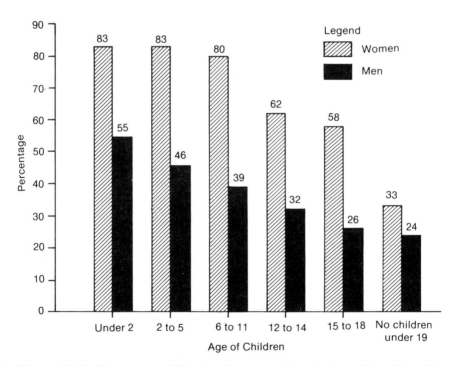

Figure 10-2. Percentage Who Are Interested in At Least Two Out of Three Family/Work Stress Seminars

Table 10-3 shows that at least four out of five women and one out of two men who experienced *any* degree of family/work stress were interested. The consistently strong support for such training shows that there is a real need for corporations to offer appropriate seminars and workshops related to family/work stress, not only for employees with children 18 and under but also for those without children under 19.

Training on Child Development

Comments referring to the quality of child care and to the impact of day care services on children reflected an overwhelming concern on the part of many parents about the ways in which their children's development was being affected by child care arrangements. The participants expressed guilt about leaving their children in alternative care or, in the case of latch-key children, leaving them alone, along with concerns about their children picking up bad habits from other children in day care services and being exposed to an environment that might not be conducive to their well-being. Another question on a set of training options was posed to employees as follows:

How interested would you be in participating in any of the following training seminars?

1. *Helping children adjust to being separated from their parents*

2. *Handling "bad day" behavior in children*

3. *Setting limits and discipline*

4. *Building self-esteem in children*

5. *Affecting the influence of a child's peer group*

Table 10–3
Stress in Participants Who Want Two or Three of the Stress Training Seminars
(*percentages*)

Degree of Stress[a]	Women (N = 1,231)	Men (N = 1,585)
0	57	29
1	80	50
2	82	59
3	93	82
4	96	100

[a]Range is from no stress (0) to a great deal of stress (4).

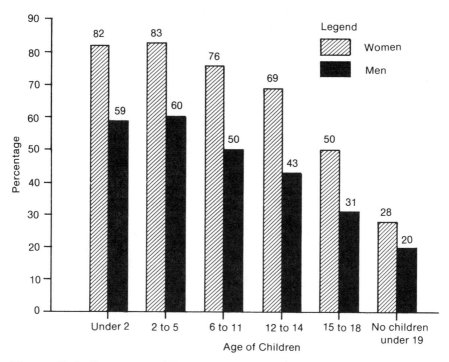

Figure 10-3. Percentage Who Are Interested in At Least Three Out of Five Child Development Seminars

Expected paterns in responses emerged, based on the ages of employees' children. Notice in figure 10–3 that 28 percent of the women and 20 percent of the men with no children 18 and younger expressed an interest in this type of training. Some of these employees were interested because, as supervisors, they saw the potential of this type of training to help them deal with the problems of their subordinates and thus to exert a positive impact on corporate profits. A little counsel from the supervisor might prevent a day's absence, as the following information suggests.

Parents lose work time in order to deal with children who are having adjustment problems. Thus, there should be a significant relationship between child development training and lost work time. For example, the greater the rate of absenteeism, the more likely employees were to be interested in this type of training. This is the case with our data.

Phoenix Mutual Life Insurance Company of Hartford is one of a number of companies that have attempted to address the issue of guilt about leaving children alone to care for themselves. It has developed seminars enabling employees to teach their children how to survive as latch-key children—how to deal with strangers, how to answer the door and phone, and so forth. The seminars also teach parents how to have siblings watch and assist one another.[2]

Parents who are concerned that their working adversely affects the development of their children could be expected to experience greater stress and increased difficulty in balancing family/work conflicts, and an extremely strong relationship was demonstrated between employees' desire for child development training and the degree of stress they were experiencing. There is a very serious need for employers to take some positive steps in this area.

Training on Selection of Child Care Services

In light of widespread concern about abuse in child care centers, one would expect a stronger expression of interest on the part of employees for training in selection of quality child care facilities. In reality, child care centers figure in only about 2 percent of the cases of child abuse, most of which occur in the home of a relative. Probably because of the ages of the survey participants and the high proportion of them who had no children, the level of interest in this area of training was lower than that in any other.

> *How interested would you be in participating in any of the following training seminars?*
>
> *1. The working parent and the selection of proper child care*
>
> *2. Providing information on available child care facilities*
>
> *3. Providing guidelines for selecting quality child care arrangements*

The range of responses on these questions is small: a one-point variation for women (38 to 39 percent) and a four-point variation for men (22 to 26 percent) who would be interested in each one. When employees' desire for training and the ages of their children were correlated, the usual large difference in responses of parents with younger children and those with older children was apparent. Although the percentage of the overall survey population interested in two out of three of these options was not large compared to the percentage interested in other types of training, interest was extremely high among employees with young children. Table 10–4 illustrates these points.

As with stress training and child development training, there was a correlation between how bad an employee's record was regarding unproductive time and how likely he or she was to want this kind of training. Similarly, a strong correlation existed between workers who missed work, arrived at work late, left work, and dealt with family issues on the job and those who saw a value in child care selection training.

Table 10–4
Participants Interested in Two Out of Three
Seminars on Child Care Selection
(percentages)

Age of Child	Women (N = 2,353)	Men (N = 2,547)
Under 2	80	45
2 to 5	71	41
6 to 11	52	27
12 to 14	34	19
15 to 18	25	15
No children under 19	26	20

There was also a predictably strong relationship between employees' perception of child care selection needs and the amount of stress they were experiencing on the job. For example, more than twice the percentage of women with a great deal of stress (80 percent) than women with no stress (38 percent) were interested in two out of three forms of child care selection training. For men, the discrepancy was even more dramatic: only about one-fifth (21 percent) of those with *no* stress problems, compared to a large majority of those with a great deal of stress (83 percent), were in favor of child care selection training.

Is Training Effective?

Interest in the various types of training ran high among the survey participants, but implementation would not be problem-free, as the following comments indicate:

> Training seminars on these subjects would be difficult. The one-hour (or less) videotape presentation would fit better into my busy work schedule.
>
> *—white craftsworker*

> Training seminars are out of the question unless they are on company time. As a parent, my time is already overburdened, and I am very tired. Who will watch the children while I go off for training? Who will pay the sitter?
>
> *—female lower-level manager*

> My only concern is having the *time* to attend all these seminars. I, like many working mothers and maybe some fathers, need more than another demand on my time.
>
> *—female lower-level manager*

Just one important problem. Where do you fit courses in parenting/time management in a working parent's already cramped schedule?

—*white, male craftsworker*

But time is not the only barrier to instituting such training seminars:

If the company involves itself in the training of children, they better be prepared. Do you take the Christian view—or follow "new age" thinking?

—*white, male lower-level manager*

We should leave such training to the family and the church.

—*white, male lower-level manager*

I have gone to a number of informative meetings on many of these subjects through my church and my children's school. I think it is really very important to be a "good parent" and to make this effort. If others haven't done so on their own, I don't think they ever will.

—*white, male craftsworker*

Other responses, however, were more positive:

I could use all the above training. I am finding it very difficult to balance all the balls in the air.

—*white, female middle-level manager*

I believe that some type of training like this would help me and my family.

—*black, female lower-level manager*

Any type of training on these issues will be welcomed.

—*black, male middle-level manager*

Finally, a black female manager put forth an interesting suggestion: "As long as you're involving the child up to 18, how about a program dealing with the growing teenager? If a parent needs to be 100 percent on the job, and if you're going to deal with the little ones, it is important to remember that the big ones cause just as much misery in the teenage years, from 13 to 18."

Some corporations fear that bringing parents together for such training programs would encourage them to pressure their companies to provide on-site child care. In practice, however, this has not occurred. In fact, the outcome of training programs is more often the formation of parent-support groups that serve to expand the learning and stress reduction of the formal programs.

Many corporations object to instituting training programs during work hours because they are reluctant to take valuable employees off the job for even one or two hours a week to attend seminars on issues that they consider personal family matters. These employers are ignoring the increased productivity that would result as workers became better equipped to deal with family problems, as well as the possibility of scheduling seminars during nonworking time, such as lunch hours.

Training—properly focused and professionally handled—could help many parents as well as workers without children to deal with changing societal trends and the family conflicts and stress that result from them. Training programs can be relatively inexpensive and offer employees the flexiblility to adapt to emerging issues. But isolated training programs are much less effective than training which is one component of an overall corporate strategy for dealing with family/work conflicts and child care problems.

Conclusions

To executives who oppose corporate involvement in flexible work options and financial support of child care because of cost and equity issues, information and referral systems and training seminars should be more palatable as first steps toward dealing with employees' child care and family/work problems. The cost of these options can be relatively low, and with regard to seminars, there need not be an equity issue, since all employees could benefit from a better understanding of child care and family/work problems.

The participants' response to the questions on training options, regardless of parenthood status and age of children, demonstrate the strong support for companies to become actively involved in disseminating information and offering training to employees. Of great interest were topics related to family/work conflicts and stress. Child development was also of interest to the majority of the survey participants, and a significant number of them indicated a need for information and guidance regarding the selection of child care providers. Despite the lesser degree of interest in this last category of training options, they are of particular value to employees with young children and therefore should not be summarily dismissed. About 25 percent of employees with no children under 19 were interested in all the training options, which supports the hypothesis that some employees do recognize they could be more effective in assisting their work group, especially parents, in dealing with child care problems if they had such training.

Training and information services in themselves cannot resolve employees' problems. However, as part of a total corporate strategy to deal with family and child care issues that impinge on company profits, such services could go a long way toward improving employee morale and productivity.

11
Conclusion

Corporate America Must Face Up to Child Care Issues

As this country progresses toward the 1990s, it is inevitable that the number of working women, dual-career families, and single heads of household will increase dramatically. For example, social scientists and government officials are projecting that by the year 1990, 60 percent of all families will be dual-career families. Furthermore, two out of three mothers with children under 13 will be working, and 55 percent of these mothers will have at least one child under the age of 6. Population trends indicate that by 1990 there will be about a 25 percent increase in the number of children under age 6. Overall, by the next decade, 80 percent of all working mothers will rear children during some portion of their working careers.[1] This situation will heighten the tension caused by the conflict between work and family life, and ultimately this stress—if it is not dealt with by corporations, government, and parents themselves—will have a negative impact on this nation's capacity to be a productive and competitive society in the new world economy.

Precedents exist for a systematic approach to family/work conflicts and child care issues. Many European countries have developed much more concrete national policies than has the United States regarding working parents and their child care needs. Countries like Sweden, France, West Germany, and Hungary have developed such programs for a combination of historical, social, and economic reasons. For example, Sweden's societal philosophy is historically socialistic, based on the concept of providing citizens with tools to be productive citizens. The French and West Germans, though their mentality differs from the Swedes', were pushed into a more aggressive and comprehensive approach to child care because a shortage of manpower made it essential for women to become permanent members of the work force; they chose to help women work rather than import large numbers of foreigners to keep their economies going. As a Communist country, Hungary embraces a more enlightened policy toward full employment and, as a result, has made some progress toward developing a comprehensive policy.

Although these countries have not totally solved the problems of child care and of family/work stress, they are committed to some form of national policy. The United States has no such policy but, as S.B. Kamerman and A.J. Kahn have noted, it is "beginning to notice the issue." In detailing the progress of other nations, Kamerman and Kahn reported that "West Germany is expanding benefits steadily and expanding services somewhat slowly but steadily; Hungary is expanding services, albeit at a moderate pace; France is expanding benefits for low-income women and services for all; and Sweden is expanding services as rapidly as it can and discussing new benefits.[2]

H.H. Bohen wrote about these national policies which support European families:

> The major European policies that Americans are fond of citing as more supportive of families than U.S. policies revolve around four sets of national laws: (1) mandated paid and unpaid work leaves of various lengths for mothers in connection with childbirth (and for fathers in Sweden, although men rarely take leave); (2) direct cash child or family allowances paid to families to help cover extra costs of raising children; (3) free universal health coverage for most citizens; and (4) public child care for young children, especially the French crèches and kindergartens.[3]

Bohen cited data indicating that 48 percent of all French women, 52 percent of all West German women, 69 percent of all Swedish women, and 56 percent of all American women between the ages of 15 and 64 were employed. French women (85 percent) had the highest full-time participation rate and Swedish women (50 percent) had the lowest. Sixty percent of West German women and 67 percent of U.S. women worked full-time. Because of its child care system and flexible work options, especially part-time work, Swedish women had the highest participation rate (58 to 78 percent) of mothers with preschoolers and school-age children. In the United States the figures for women in this category were 35 to 56 percent. France, which had the highest overall full-time participation rate for women, had the next highest participation rate for women with young children (44 percent for those with preschoolers and 48 percent with school-age children). Germany had the lowest overall rates (32 to 41 percent).[4]

G. Erler et al. noted in their survey of maternity leave, parental leave, and home care measures in Finland, Sweden, Hungary, Austria, and West Germany that only in West Germany do large numbers reject the idea of working mothers.[5]

What explains the comparable participation rates of American women and their European counterparts despite the lack of a national child care policy? Probably the biggest reason is that the United States has stronger equal employment laws than do European nations. Thus, if the United States were to develop a national family policy in partnership with industry, the employment of women on a permanent basis would increase at a much more accelerated rate, and child care problems and family/work conflicts would decrease.

The United States *is* taking notice of these issues and has made some minimal efforts to move ahead. The last 1984 Congress discussed a wide range of options which if adopted, would move the country ahead in dealing with child care and family/work problems. Some of the items under review are:

Establishment of a matching fund program to encourage communites to develop and expand informational and referral services

Development of tax incentives to encourage employers to move beyond the stage of rhetoric in providing or supporting child care services such as those we have described

Establishment of funds to help states and communities develop before- and after-school programs for latch-key children

Improvement of the tax deductions employees receive for child care expenses

Regardless of these incentives and programs, corporations dominated by older male managers will not move forward as expeditiously as they should unless they understand and believe that child care problems and family/work conflicts cost their corporations a great deal of money in unproductive time and also that their own involvement is part of the solution. They need to recognize that this nation can ill afford, in the competitive world economy of the 1980s and 1990s, to run its companies in less than the most efficient, cost-effective manner. It is a given that if any significant part of a corporate human resource is not fully and productively utilized, it will become a liability to the company that, in the long run, cannot be ignored. The same executives need to recognize that the change in women's work status will increasingly affect their male work force.

Needs Assessment and Multiple Approaches

This book has suggested a wide variety of ways in which corporations can deal with the child care and family/work problems of their employees. Some of the solutions are costly and some are not, but even the most costly solutions promise benefits that far outweigh the expense of providing them.

Two of the most important options involve very little cost to the company. Training supervisors to be responsive, sensitive, and flexible in handling their subordinates' problems pays enormous dividends. Flexible work options (flextime, permanent part-time positions, job-sharing, and opportunities to work at home) similarly increase productivity, reduce stress, and cost companies very little.

The price tag does go up when it comes to providing or supporting various forms of day care, but even here, the cost varies significantly. Most costly is a company-operated center, fully subsidized on- or off-site. A less costly alternative is supporting a network of family day care homes or existing community child care centers. Nevertheless, the growing number of tax incentives for employers to become involved in the provision of day care services, coupled with increased productivity, make even the more costly options cost-effective in the long run.

Another way to reduce the cost of providing additional benefits while simultaneously avoiding the equity problem among childless employees is to establish a cafeteria benefit plan whereby employees can choose from among an array of benefits of comparable value. Support for cafeteria plans came from some of the participants:

> I totally disagree with company support of child care at the expense of all employees. Employees should choose their own benefits, of which child care could be one, but those who choose this option should give up one of equivalent cost.
>
> —*white, male middle-level manager*

> Child care provisions should be considered as an optional or variable benefit. I am tired, as a single person, of compensating continuously for *choices* made by other women.
>
> —*single, Hispanic, female craftsworker*

> Some of us, like me, don't have children, but we have parents or, as in my case, grandparents who need (it seems to me) more care than most children. Children grow up, and become more independent, but grandparents get older, sicker, develop more problems. You can't look away; these problems must be dealt with.
>
> —*white, female middle-level manager*

Cafeteria plans vary, but there are three common approaches. Under one, employees are "given" a specified dollar amount and a list of benefits with their respective costs, from which they may "purchase" to the extent of their allowance. Another form establishes a basic set of benefits provided to all employees along with a set of options of comparable cost from which the employee may select a specified number. Finally, some companies offer a choice of employee-selected benefits up to a given dollar amount, or a comparable amount in cash with which the employee may purchase, from some outside source, benefits not offered by the company.

Flexible benefit plans deal with the issues of cost and equity and also offer tax advantages under the Dependent Care Assistance Act, which states that child care benefits provided under this act are not taxable income. An employee who chooses child care as a benefit, in other words, also shelters that portion of her/his income from taxation. Comerica is a large Detroit bank holding company that started a cafeteria-style benefit plan in 1982. Ninety-five percent of its 5,500 employees selected plans that differed from the traditional standard plan, a clear indication that the usual packages being offered by companies are not meeting the needs of their employees. Child care reimbursement is one of the options in the Comerica plan. Employees who select this option specify a certain amount of taxable salary to be deducted in order to pay for child care expenses. From the standard package, which includes medical, life, and disability insurance, the employees are allowed to waive any amount they wish and apply the value of the waived benefits to other benefits. In addition, employees can assign pretax income to purchase additional benefits, such as participation in the company savings plan, additional vacation time, and disability insurance.

While cafeteria plans offer a great many benefits to corporations and their employees, only 8 percent of the 374 firms in a Catalyst study said they had such plans, although 62 percent of these same companies said they favored such an approach.[6] If a cafeteria benefit plan were instituted, would there be a significant number of "takers" for day care subsidy over standard benefits like insurance and savings plans? The participants in this study were asked to name the existing benefit they would sacrifice in order to have substantial child care assistance. Table 11-1 shows their responses.

The area most employees were willing to sacrifice for child care assistance was coverage for eye care, followed by vacation leave and savings plans. They were least willing to give up dental, medical, and life insurance, in that order. Notice the much higher percentage of men than women who selected the "other" category. This is the area, apart from vision care, in which responses differed markedly between the sexes. Some of those who selected "other" indicated that they were uncertain which of the suggested benefits to eliminate or that they would prefer to reduce the level of several benefits rather than completely eliminate any of them. Others said they did not want to sacrifice any benefits but would like to add child care services to the benefit plan.

Table 11-1
Participants Who Would Substitute Other Benefits for Child Care Benefits
(*percentages*)

	Single Women (N = 275)	Married Women (N = 958)	Single Men (N = 46)	Married Men (N = 1,564)
Vacation time	16	17	19	19
Medical coverage	2	3	8	5
Dental coverage	2	2	0	0
Vision coverage	28	32	22	17
Life insurance	5	5	3	4
Savings plan	18	11	5	11
Other	28	29	43	45

Women with younger children were more likely than those with older children to want to substitute child care assistance for vision care and the company's savings plan, and women with older children were more willing to substitute other types of benefits. For example, 39 percent of women with children 5 and under, compared to only 22 percent of women with children over 11, would substitute vision care for one or more of the standard benefits. For men, the findings were similar.

When responses were analyzed by race for benefits employees would sacrifice for child care, some differences emerged among the women. For example, 18 percent of the other women of color, 25 percent of the black women, and 33 percent of the white women were willing to sacrifice vision care for child care assistance. Twenty percent of the other women of color, 23 percent of the black women, and 11 percent of the white women were willing to substitute their company's savings plan for child care assistance. Among the men's responses there were no significant differences.

Employees' attitudes are clear in these responses.

The way things are set up for my family right now, I would not change my child's care. If you had a day care [center] available to me, I would use it on a limited basis.

—white, female middle-level manager

The question is easy. Of course I would give up vision coverage, but I would even go so far as to give up the savings plan, life and dental insurance if necessary.

—white, female craftsworker

Take medical, dental, vision coverage; just give me the option of nonpaid time for child care. I *need* my vacation.

—white, female craftsworker

I don't care to give up any of these. Add child care *to* these.

—white, female craftsworker

None. Put my child care money in the savings plan.

—white, male middle-level manager

People with child care problems that could be solved by company subsidy should be given the option of substituting that for another benefit. But if benefits are going to be flexible, then individuals with other problems should also have the privilege.

—white, male lower-level manager

Make child care another company profit center.

—white, male upper-level manager

Good child care is a must for the working parent and the child. I would like to see our company initiate child care funding as a benefit. However, let's ask the parents what would help them and try to follow their direction.

—*white, female middle-level manager*

A white, female lower-level manager brought up the question of equity in a different context. "My medical coverage is already waived because my spouse also works here. So I've always felt that I haven't gotten the same benefits as others. I'd gladly take child care benefits in place of the medical coverage I'm not getting anyway." Her point is valid not only for spouses working for the same company but also for employees who have spouses working for other companies. Many employers provide family coverage as a standard benefit for all employees, regardless of whether the spouse is employed. In cases where both spouses are employed, employees either waive the coverage from one employer (and often feel short-changed by doing so) or maintain needless duplicate coverage at the expense of the employers. Instances like this strengthen the case for cafeteria benefit plans.

On the whole, the responses showed that the cost factor is not a crucial one. There are ways of providing child care assistance without adding cost to the benefit plan, either through substitution or by establishing a profit-making service that will pay for itself. A more crucial issue for corporations is choosing the form or forms of child care best suited to their employees' needs and most appropriate in light of available care in the community. The pros and cons of the various forms of child care were discussed in detail in chapter 9.

Less costly alternatives to the direct provision or financing of child care are flexible work options and the various counseling and guidance approaches discussed in chapters 8 and 10: employment of a staff resource person, referral programs, and training seminars. These alternatives provide a positive initial step for employers who are not ready to offer direct child care services as well as invaluable support for employers who provide more tangible benefits.

What is most crucial for effective corporate intervention in family/work conflicts and child care problems is an initial needs assessment and consideration of multiple approaches. No single approach is without its benefits and its disadvantages, and no single approach will resolve *all* problems faced by *all* employees. Day care centers may, for example, meet many of the needs of parents with preschool children, but unless they include before- and after-school programs, they offer little assistance to those employees with older children and no assistance to parents who are wrestling with the stresses of their children's adolescence. Unless the centers make provision for sick children, they have little impact on the absenteeism caused by the need to care for a youngster who is ill. By the same token, referral and counseling services are helpful only to the extent that the community's supply of child care centers is adequate to meet the needs of working parents.

Any program, therefore, must take into consideration the varied needs of its employee population, and even such indirect services as referral and training should address the special concerns of employees with children at various ages, along with the variety of sources of tension that stem from balancing dual family/work roles, even in households where there are no children. Only a well-conceived and carefully planned, multifaceted approach will have a significant impact on the problems delineated in the first part of this book.

Merck is a company which recognizes that its employees have various and different child care needs. In addition to assisting with child care facilities, the company offers flextime and, for some maternity cases, the option of working at home. It is studying a permanent part-time program and an employee counseling service to help families deal with child care and family/work problems.

One final caveat: no amount of corporate child care or family/work conflict assistance will relieve the stress of the balancing act without a fundamental change in the sexist role patterns that have been perpetuated through the years in this country.

The Bureau of National Affairs surveyed 691 employees whose children attended company-operated or company-sponsored child care, with the following findings:

Thirty-eight percent selected their company because of child care assistance.

Sixty-nine percent were encouraged to stay with their company because of child care assistance.

Sixty-three percent had a more positive attitude about their company because of child care assistance.

Fifty percent recommended their company to others because of child care assistance.[7]

Among the survey participants, a significant minority of the women but a much smaller percentage of the men said they would consider leaving their companies, all else being equal, if another company offered better child care benefits. Table 11–2 shows the responses of the participants. Notice that over 53 percent of the women with children 2 and under, and 20 percent of the men in this category, said they would consider doing this, compared to less than 20 percent of the women and less than 5 percent of the men with children over 11 who concurred.

Any loss of highly skilled employees, who cost a minimum average each of $50,000 to train, is a significant drain on corporate profits. It also gives the competition—if it has a progressive child care policy—an edge because its training costs will be much lower as the result of reduced turnover.

Child care assistance and effective training can do much to help employees change their attitudes and organize their personal lives to reduce overloads, but much of the responsibility for lowering stress levels rests with employees themselves. M. Fox and S. Hesse-Biber wrote an excellent review of the dual-career

Table 11–2
Employees Who Would Consider Leaving Their Jobs for Better Child Care Benefits
(percentages)

Age of Child	Women (N = 1,228)		Men (N = 1,558)	
	Would Leave[a]	Would Not Leave	Would Leave[a]	Would Not Leave
Under 2	53	30	20	64
2 to 5	43	38	15	73
6 to 11	29	56	8	84
12 to 14	19	71	4	93
15 to 18	12	80	3	95

[a]"Would leave" means those who would consider leaving at least to some extent. It does not include those who responded "to a small extent."

family. They pointed out that families *can* change, and husbands and wives *can* learn to compromise on the issues of household tasks, child-rearing responsibilities, and individual career goals. Work and child care can be shared; houses need not be immaculate; and career goals can be modified to satisfy the demands of family life.[8] Often parents can help each other come up with various solutions, with or without company support, by forming networks to exchange services and share concerns and ideas. Such an internal support system can in itself relieve stress, as one white craftswoman in the survey sample pointed out:

> We have been working overtime a great deal for the last eight months. However, among our staff, we occasionally sit together and talk about the stresses we are experiencing. That relieves a lot of the tension because I really don't have anyone to talk to about home life.

A white, female lower-level manager said, "We have formed our own support group. We try helping each other with child care problems. A few weeks ago, my baby and the child of a coworker both came down with the flu. She stayed home one day, and I, the next."

Despite the best efforts of political conservatives, and now the Reagan Administration, it seems, to turn back the clock and to relegate women to the home, the reality is that mothers—in increasing numbers—are going to be a part of this nation's work force. The problems so clearly articulated by the survey participants will continue to threaten family stability and drain valuable productivity from corporate America until employers, with government support, acknowledge the reality of these problems and deal with child care issues and family/work conflicts in a systematic fashion.

The time for debating whether mothers *should* work and whether real men *should* share household tasks is long past. Tax incentives for women to remain at home, such as those proposed recently by President Reagan, will have no effect on whether the vast majority of working mothers remain in the work force—mothers who are single, whose husbands' earnings cannot support a household, and who have career ambitions of their own. Work disincentives (such as lowering the deduction for child care expenses and reducing the exemption for working couples) will only exacerbate the problems now facing working parents, particularly those who are in lower-income brackets.

The time has come to deal in a practical manner with the fact that most children are not going to have mothers at home to take care of them full-time and that both family stability and corporate productivity are diminished by the enormous stresses and demands of living with family/work conflicts. This book has set forth a wide range of options that can be utilized by those whose top management has the foresight and business acumen to invest in their companies' most important asset—their work force. It has also provided the hard data, both from the survey on which it is based and from other research in the field, on which social planners and legislators can base efforts to develop a sound national child care policy. And, finally, it has shown the need for society as a whole to rethink its sexist attitudes toward men and women.

The problems of finding and financing quality child care and of resolving family/work conflicts are not solely problems of the poor, of minorities, of women, or of single parents. They are problems of American society and, therefore, of government and the corporate structure, and they will be resolved only by a collective effort on the part of all concerned.

This book is a call for corporate action based on sound business principles and enlightened self-interest. But it is also a call for an ongoing partnership between business and government, with impetus from the more than 200 million people that government represents, to deal with issues that are of prime concern to the nation's security—social as well as economic.

To do otherwise is, quite simply, to ignore reality.

Notes

Chapter 1
Overview

1. H.B. Lewis, *Psychic War In Men and Women* (New York: New York University Press, 1976), 123-24.

2. E. Janeway, *Man's World, Woman's Place* (New York: Dell, 1971), 163-67.

3. B. Ehrenreich and D. English, *Complaints and Disorders* (New York: Faculty Press, 1973), 16.

4. U. Sinclair, *The Jungle* (New York: New American Library, 1906).

5. S.M. Rothman, *Woman's Proper Place: A History of Changing Ideals and Practices, 1870 to the Present* (New York: Basic Books, 1978), 42.

6. Ibid., 221-22.

7. Ibid., 224.

8. Ibid., 229.

9. S.L. Burud, R.C. Collins, P.D. Hawkins "Employer Supported Child Care: Everybody Benefits," *Children Today* 12, no. 3 (May-June 1983), 3.

10. U.S. Bureau of Census, "1980 Current Population Reports Series," no. 125 (Washington D.C.: U.S. Government Printing Office), 60. Also "Children of Working Mothers," U.S. Department of Labor Bulletin 215T (March 1983), 1-2.

11. *The General Mills American Family Report at Work: 1980-81—Families Strengths and Strains,* (Minneapolis: General Mills, 1981), 11.

12. R.A. Rosenfeld, "Women's Intergenerational Occupational Mobility," *American Sociological Review* 43 (February 1978): 36-46.

13. J.P. Fernandez, *Racism and Sexism in Corporate Life: Changing Values in American Business* (Lexington, Mass.: D.C. Heath, 1981), 70.

14. S.S. Scarr, *Mother Care: Other Care* (New York: Basic Books, 1984), 50-54.

15. H. Hayghe, "Dual-Earner Families," in ed. J. Aldous *Two Paychecks: Life in Dual-Earner Families,* (Beverly Hills, Calif.: Sage Publications, 1982), 33.

Chapter 2
Child Care Arrangements

1. R.F. Baxandall, "Who Shall Care for Our Children? The History and Development of Day Care in the United States," in *Women: A Feminist Perspective,* ed. Jo Freeman, (Palo Alto, Calif.: Mayfield Publishing Co., 1979), 135–36.

2. Ibid.

3. E.F. Zigler and E.W. Gordon, eds., *Day Care: Scientific and Social Policy Issues* (Boston: Auburn House, 1982), 459.

4. Baxandall, "Who Shall Care for Our Children?," 137.

5. Ibid., 138.

6. Ibid., 139.

7. E.F. Zigler and J. Goodman, "The Battle for Day Care in America: A View from the Trenches," in *Day Care,* ed. E.F. Zigler and E.W. Gordon (Boston: Auburn House, 1982), 338–49.

8. Scarr, *Mother Care: Other Care,* 44.

9. A.J. Brenner and D.S. Iskowe, "Taxpayers with Dependents and Their Employers Both Have Tax Planning Opportunities," *Accounting 30* (March 1983): 160–64.

10. L. Bennetts, "Parents Find a Wide Variety of Day Care Quality in U.S.," *New York Times,* September 3, 1984, 7.

11. I. McMillan, "Pa. Asked to Spend $94 Million More on Women's Issues," *Philadelphia Inquirer,* March 9, 1985, 3.

12. BNA Report, *Employers and Child Care: Development of a New Employee Benefit* (Washington, D.C.: Bureau of National Affairs, 1984), 18.

13. A. Burtman, "Who's Minding the Children?," *Working Women* (April 1984): 86.

14. D.A. Williams, et al.; "What Price Day Care?", *Newsweek* (September 10, 1984), 14.

15. Burtman, "Who's Minding the Children?," 86.

16. P. Jones, N.J. Brown and L.M. McCurdy, *Child Care Profile for Pittsburgh and Allegheny Counties* (Pittsburgh: Pittsburgh Child Care Network, 1984) xiv–xv.

17. D. Friedman, "Corporate Financial Assistance for Child Care" New York: The Conference Board, 1985, 6–7.

18. Jones et al., *Child Care Profile for Pittsburgh and Allegheny Counties,* xiv–xv.

19. K. McCartney et al., "Environmental Differences Among Day Care Centers and Their Effects on Children's Development," in *Day Care,* ed. E.F. Zigler and E.W. Gordon (Boston: Auburn House, 1982), 147–48.

Chapter 3
Child Care Problems: Impact on Employee Productivity

1. S. L. Burud, P.R. Aschbacher, and J. McCroskey, *Employer-Supported Child Care: Investing In Human Resources* (Dover, Mass.: Auburn House, 1984), 31.

2. T.I. Miller, "The Effects of Employer-Sponsored Child Care on Employee Absenteeism, Turnover, Productivity, Recruitment or Job Satisfaction: What Is Claimed and What Is Known," *Personnel Psychology* 37 (1984): 277.

3. BNA Report, *Employers and Child Care*, 3.

4. S.A. Youngblood and K. Chambers-Cook, "Child Care Assistance Can Improve Employee Attitudes and Behaviors," *Personnel Administrator* (February 1984): 44–45.

5. Burud et al., *Employer-Supported Child Care*, 21–48.

6. R.Y. Magid, *Childcare Initiatives For Working Parents: Why Employers Get Involved* (New York: American Management Association, 1983), 39.

7. Burud et al., *Employer-Supported Child Care*, 162–63.

8. C. Hymonitz, "Women on Fast Track Try to Keep Their Careers and Children Separate," *Wall Street Journal* (September 19, 1984), 35.

9. A. C. Emlen and P.E. Koren, *Hard to Find and Difficult to Manage: The Effects of Childcare on the Workplace* (Portland, Oreg.: The Workplace Partnership, 1984), 6.

10. U.S. Census Bureau data, *USA Today*, May 21, 1984: Children of Working Mothers, U.S. Department of Labor, March 1983, Bulletin 2158, 1–13. Also T. Schreiner, "We're Staying Single Longer," *USA Today*, May 21, 1984, 1.

11. Unpublished report used according to instructions not to mention company's name, 5.

12. H. Rogers, "Executive Women Find It Difficult to Balance Demands of Job and Home," *Wall Street Journal*, October 30, 1984, 33.

13. M.F. Fox and S. Hesse-Biber, *Women at Work* (Palo Alto, Calif.: Mayfield Publishing Co., 1984), 196.

14. A. Trafford et al., "She's Come a Long Way—Or Has She?," *U.S. News and World Report*, August 1984, 50.

15. Unpublished report used according to instructions not to mention company's name, 6.

16. Ibid.

17. G.L. Greif, *Single Fathers* (Lexington, Mass.: Lexington Books, 1985), 63.

Chapter 4
Family/Work Conflicts and Stress: Impact on Employee Productivity

1. See K.E. Walker and M.E. Woods, *Time Use: A Measure of Household Production of Family Goods and Services* (Washington, D.C.: American Home Economics Association, 1976).

2. J.J. Vanek, "Time Spent on Housework," *Scientific American* (November 1974): 118.

3. S.F. Berk, *The Gender Factory: The Appointment of Work in American Households* (New York: Plenum Press, 1985), 7–8.

4. Ibid., 65–66.

5. J.T. Mortimer and J. London, "The Varying Linkage of Work and Family," in *Work and Family*, ed. P. Voydanoff (Palo Alto, Calif.: Mayfield Publishing Co., 1976), 20–35.

6. E. Goodman, "Observations on Parenting and the Women's Movement," in National Institute of Education, *Parenthood in a Changing Society* (Urbana, Ill.: ERIC Clearing House on Elementary and Early Childhood Education, University of Illinois, 1980), 5–6.

7. J.H. Pleck, "Men's Family Work: Three Perspectives and Some New Data," *The Family Coordinator* 28 (October 1979): 487.

8. J. Grimaldi and B.P. Schnapper, "Managing Stress: Reducing the Costs and Increasing the Benefits," *Management Review* (August 1981): 24.

9. R. Rapoport and R.N. Rapoport, *Dual-Career Families Re-Examined* (New York: Harper & Row, 1976), 302–5.

10. Scarr, *Mother Care: Other Care*, 132.

11. Emlen, *Hard to Find and Difficult to Manage*, 5.

12. D.A. Skinner, "Dual Career Family Stress and Coping: A Literature Review," in *Work and Family*, ed. P. Voydanoff (Palo Alto, Calif.: Mayfield Publishing Co., 1984), 267.

13. J.G. Hunt and L.L. Hunt, "Dual Career Families: Vanguard of the Future or Residue of the Past?" in ed. J. Aldous *Two Paychecks: Life in Dual-Earner Families*, ed. J. Aldous (Beverly Hills, Calif.: Sage Publications, 1982), 45.

14. J.H. Pleck, "The Work-Family Role System," *Social Problems* 24 (April 1977): 417–27. Also Fox and Biber, *Women at Work*, 179–97.

15. K. Keating, "How Is Work Affecting American Families?," *Better Homes and Gardens* (February 1982): 21.

16. Skinner, "Dual Career Family Stress and Coping," 268.

17. G. Ritzer, *Working: Conflict and Change* (Englewood Cliffs, N.J.: Prentice-Hall, 1977), 114.

18. Greif, *Single Fathers*, 3.

Chapter 5
Child Care and Scheduling Problems: Impact on Employee Productivity

1. R.P. Quinn and G.L. Staines, *The 1977 Quality of Employment Survey* (Ann Arbor, Mich.: Survey Research Center, 1979), 265.

2. *General Mills American Family Report: 1980–81*, 19.

3. E. Galinsky, "Stress and Supports on Families in the 80's," in *Family Life and Corporate Policies*, ed. M. Yogman and T.B. Brazelton (Boston: Harvard University Press), forthcoming.

4. Keating, "How Is Work Affecting American Families?," 22.

5. *General Mills American Family Report: 1980–81*, 43–48.

6. Mortimer et al., "The Varying Linkages of Work and Family," 27–28.

7. Fox and Hesse-Biber, *Women at Work*, 182.

8. Quinn and Staines, *1977 Quality of Employment Survey*, 256.

9. R.M. Kanter, "Jobs and Families: Impact of Working Roles on Family Life," *Children Today* (March/April 1978): 14.

Chapter 6
Other Evidence That Child Care and Family/Work Problems Affect Productivity

1. Greif, *Single Fathers*, 3.
2. Ibid.
3. K.A. Moore and I.V. Sawhill, "Implications of Women's Employment for Home and Family Life," in *Women Working: Theories and Facts in Perspective*, ed. A. H. Stromberg and S. Harkness (Palo Alto, Calif.: Mayfield Publishing Co., 1978), 210.
4. Catalyst, "Corporations and Two-Career Families: Directions for the Future," (New York: Catalyst, 1984), 5.
5. Greif, *Single Fathers*, 61.

Chapter 7
What Should Corporations Do About Child Care and Family/Work Problems?

1. J. Immerwahr, "Building a Consensus on the Child Care Problem," *Personnel Administrator* (February 1984): 32.
2. Quinn and Staines, *1977 Quality of Employment Survey*, 250.
3. Immerwahr, "Building a Consensus on the Child Care Problem," 32.
4. Ibid., 35.
5. Scarr, *Mother Care: Other Care*, 85.
6. L.W. Hoffman, *The Study of Employed Mothers Over Half a Century*, paper presented at the annual meeting of the American Psychological Association, Los Angeles, 1983.
7. M. Rutter, "Social-Emotional Consequences of Day Care for Preschool Children," in *Day Care: Scientific and Social Policy Issues*, ed. E.F. Zigler and E.W. Gordon (Boston: Auburn House, 1982), 3.
8. L.W. Hoffman, "Maternal Employment: 1979." *American Psychologist* 34, no. 10 (1979): 859.
9. L.W. Hoffman and F.I. Nye, *Working Mothers* (San Francisco: Jossey-Bass, 1975), 164.
10. *General Mills American Family Report: 1980–81*, 9.
11. Ibid.
12. Keating, "How Is Work Affecting American Families?," 21.

Chapter 8
Flexible Work Options

1. Unnamed survey done by Parents in the Workplace, St. Paul, Minn., 1981, 1–2.
2. *General Mills American Family Report: 1980–81*, 43–58.

3. "Employee Counseling Programs of New York, Study Effects of Parenting on Corporate Women," *Employee Benefit Plan Review*, (September, 1982), 42.

4. BNA Report, *Employers and Child Care: Development of a New Employee Benefit*, 43.

5. "Corporations and Two-Career Families: Directions for the Future," 15.

6. N. Barko, "The Part-Time Path," *Working Women* (April 1985): 40.

7. See Burud et al., *Employer-Supported Child Care*, 105–10. Also Feinstein, *Working Women and Families* (Beverly Hills, Calif.: Sage Publications, 1979), 159–75.

8. BNA Report, *Employers and Child Care: Development of a New Employee Benefit*, 43–44.

9. S.B. Garland, "New Strategies Balance Demands of Work, Family," *Star Ledger*, (April 28, 1985), 1.

10. H.H. Bohen and A.V. Long, "Balancing Job and Family Life," in *Work and Family*, ed. P. Voydanoff (Palo Alto, Calif.: Mayfield Publishing Co., 1984), 325.

11. Burud et al., *Employer-Supported Child Care*, 107.

12. New York State Council on Children and Families, "Part-time Employment Implications for Families and the Workplace 1983," 7–9.

13. Ibid., 7–9.

14. Unpublished study done by a high-technology firm in 1982 on flexible work options.

15. H. Alex, *Corporations and Families Changing Practices and Perspectives*, (New York: The Conference Board, 1985), 29.

16. Interview conducted January 18, 1985.

Chapter 9
Corporate Financial Support for Child Care Arrangements

1. Catalyst, "Corporations and Two-Career Families: Directions for the Future," 15.

2. Burud et al., *Employer-Supported Child Care*, 31.

3. Ibid., 139–45.

4. Immerwahr, "Building a Consensus on the Child Care Problem," 36.

5. M.F. Romaine, "Zale's Corporate Child Care Program," *The Texas Business Executive* (Spring/Summer 1982): 25.

6. See Zigler and Gordon, *Day Care*, and Burud et al., *Employer-Supported Child Care*.

7. Burud et al., *Employer-Supported Child Care*, 31.

8. Immerwahr, "Building a Consensus on the Child Care Problem," 36.

9. See Zigler and Gordon, *Day Care*, and Burud et al., *Employer-Supported Child Care*.

10. *General Mills American Family Report: 1980–81*, 30.

11. Burud et al., *Employer-Supported Child Care*, 194.

12. Ibid., 193.

13. Ibid., 31.

14. B. Adolf and K. Rose, *The Employer's Guide to Child Care* (New York: Praeger, 1985), 60.

15. For an excellent review of corporate financial assistance for child care, see Dana Friedman's book, *Corporate Financial Assistance for Child Care* (New York, The Conference Board, 1985).

Chapter 10
Corporate Provision of Child Care Resources and Training

1. Burud et al., *Employer-Supported Child Care*, 31.

2. Garland, "New Strategies Balance Demands of Work Family," 1.

Chapter 11
Conclusion

1. "Business and Parent Workforce: Profit and Productivity" (Chicago: Family Resource Coalition, 1985), 1–16.

2. S.B. Kamerman and A.J. Kahn, "Societal Learning," *Work and Family* ed. P. Voydanoff, 333.

3. H.H. Bohen, *Corporate Employment Policies Affecting Families and Children: The United States and Europe*, (New York: Aspen Institute for Humanistic Studies, 1983), 4.

4. Ibid.

5. G. Erler, M. Jaeckel, and J. Sass, *Results of the European Study Concerning Maternity Leave/Parental Leave/Home Care Support in Finland, Sweden, Hungary, Austria, and German Federal Republic* (Munich, Germany: Deutsches Jugerdenstitut, October, 1982), 24.

6. Catalyst, "Corporations and Two-Career Families: Directions for the Future," 15.

7. BNA Report, *Employers and Child Care*, 6–7.

8. Fox et al., *Women at Work*, 179–97.

Bibliography

Abbott, S. "Full-Time Fathers and Weekend Wives: An Analysis of Altering Conjugal Rules." *Journal of Marriage and the Family* 36 (1976): 165–73.

Adam, C.T., and K.T. Winston. *Mothers at Work: Policies in the United States, Sweden, and China.* New York: Longman, 1980.

Adolf, B., and K. Rose. *Employer's Guide to Childcare: Developing Programs for Working Parents.* New York: Praeger Publisher, 1985.

_____ . *Childcare and the Working Parent: First Steps Toward Employer Involvement in Childcare.* New York: Child at Work, 1982.

Aldous, J. "From Dual-Earner to Dual-Career Families and Back Again." *Journal of Family Issues* 2 (1981): 115–25.

_____ . "Occupational Characteristics and Males' Role Performance in the Family." *Journal of Marriage and the Family* 31 (1969): 707–12.

_____ . *Two Paychecks: Life in Dual-Earner Families.* Beverly Hills, Calif.: Saga Publications, 1982.

Aldous, J., R.W. Osmond, and M.W. Hicks. "Men's Work and Men's Families." In *Contemporary Theories About the Family, Volume I,* edited by W.R. Burr et al. New York: Macmillan, 1980.

Anderson, C. "Attachment in Daily Separations: Reconceptualizing Day Care and Maternal Employment Issues." *Child Development* 51 (1980): 242–45.

Anderson, K. *Exploring Corporate Initiatives for Working Parents: An Industry by Industry Review.* New York: Center for Public Advocacy Research, 1983.

_____ . *Wartime Women: Sex Roles, Family Relations, and the Status of Women During World War II.* Westport, Conn.: Greenwood Press, 1981.

Arkin, W., and L.R. Dobrofsky. "Job Sharing." In *Working Couples,* edited by R. Rapoport and R.N. Rapoport. New York: Harper & Row, 1978.

Ashery, R., and M.M. Byusen. *The Parents With Careers Workbook.* Washington, D.C.: Acropolis Books, 1983.

Axelson, L.J. "The Working Wife: Differences in Perception Among Negro and White Males." *Journal of Marriage and the Family* 32 (1970): 457–64.

_____ . "Marital Adjustment and Marital Role Definitions of Husbands of Working and Nonworking Wives." *Marriage and Family Living* 25 (May 1963): 189–95.

Baden, R.K., A. Genser, J.A. Levine, and M. Seltzer. *School-Age Child Care: An Action Manual.* Boston: Auburn House, 1982.

Bailyn, L. "Career and Family Orientations of Husbands and Wives in Relation to Marital Happiness." *Human Relations* 23, no. 2 (1970): 97–113.

Baxandall, R.F. "Who Shall Care for Our Children? The History and Development of Day Care in the United States." In *Women: A Feminist Perspective*, edited by Jo Freeman, Palo Alto, Calif.: Mayfield Publishing Company, 1979.

Baxandall, R., L. Gordon, and S. Reverby. *America's Working Women*. New York: Random House, 1976.

Bean, F.D., R.L. Curtis, Jr., and J.P. Marcum. "Familism and Marital Satisfaction Among Mexican Americans: The Effects of Family Size, Wife's Labor Force Participation, and Conjugal Power." *Journal of Marriage and the Family* 39 (1977): 759–67.

Beck, R. "Beyond the Stalemate in Child Care Public Policy." In *Day Care: Scientific and Social Policy Issues*, edited by E.G. Zigler and E.W. Gordon. Boston: Auburn House, 1982.

Beck, S.F. *The Gender Factory: The Apportionment of Work in American Households*. New York: Plenum Press, 1985.

Beckett, J.O. "Working Wives: A Racial Comparison." *Social Work* 2 (1976): 463–71.

Belsky, J. "Two Waves of Day Care Research: Developmental Effects and Conditions of Quality." In *The Child and the Day Care Setting*, edited by R. Ainslie. New York: Praeger, 1984.

————. "The Interrelation of Parental and Spousal Behavior During Infancy in Traditional Nuclear Families: An Exploratory Analysis." *Journal of Marriage and the Family*, 41, (1979): 62–68.

Belsky, J., R.M. Lerner, and G.B. Spanier. *The Child in the Family*. Reading, Mass.: Addison-Wesley, 1984.

Bennetts, L. "Parents Find a Wide Variety of Day Care Quality in U.S." *New York Times* (September 3, 1984): 1, 7.

Berk, R.A. "The New Home Economics: An Agenda for Sociological Research." In *Women and Household Labor*, edited by S.F. Berk. Beverly Hills, Calif.: Sage Publications, 1980.

Berk, R.A., and S.F. Berk. "Supply-Side Sociology of the Family: The Challenge of the New Home Economics." *Annual Review of Sociology* 9 (1983): 375–95.

Berk, S.F. *The Gender Factors: The Apportionment of Work in American Households*. New York: Plenum Press, 1985.

Berk, S.F., and A. Shih. "Contributions to Household Labor: Comparing Wives' and Husbands' Reports." In *Women and Household Labor*, edited by S.F. Berk. Beverly Hills, Calif.: Sage Publications, 1980.

Bernard, J. "The Good-Provider Role: Its Rise and Fall." *American Psychologist* 36 (1981): 1–12.

————. *Women, Wives, Mothers*. Chicago: Aldine, 1975.

————. *The Future of Motherhood*. New York: Penguin, 1974.

Bird, C. *The Two-Paycheck Marriage*. New York: Rawson, Wade, 1979.

Blake, J. "The Changing Status of Women in Developed Countries." *Scientific American* (September 1974): 137–47.

Bohen, H.H. *Corporate Employment Policies Affecting Families and Children: The United States and Europe*. New York: Aspen Institute for Humanistic Studies, 1983.

Bohen, H.H., and A. Viveros-Long. *Balancing Jobs and Family Life*. Philadelphia: Temple University Press, 1981.

Booth A. "Does Wives' Employment Cause Stress for Husbands?" *Family Coordinator* 28 (1979): 445–49.

_____. "Wife's Employment and Husband's Stress: A Replication and Refutation." *Journal of Marriage and the Family* 39 (1977): 645–50.

Boulding, E. "Familial Constraints on Women's Work Roles." *Signs* 1 (1976): 95–118.

Brenner, A.J., and D.J. Iskowe. "Taxpayers with Dependents and Their Employers Both Have Tax Planning Opportunities." *Taxation for Accountants* 30 (March 1983): 160–64.

Brown, C.V. "Home Production for Use in a Market Economy." In *Rethinking the Family*, edited by M. Yalom. New York: Longman, 1982.

Bryson, J.B., and R. Bryson. *Dual Career Couples*. New York: Human Sciences, 1978.

Bureau of National Affairs, Inc. *Employers and Child Care: Development of a New Employee Benefit*. Washington, D.C., 1984.

Burud, S.L., P.R. Aschbacher, and J. McCroskey. *Employer-Supported Child Care: Investing in Human Resources*. Boston, Mass.: Auburn House, 1984.

Burke, R.J., and I. Wen. "Relationship of Wives' Employment Status to Husband, Wife and Pair Satisfaction and Performance." *Journal of Marriage and the Family* 38 (1976): 279–87.

Cain, G. *Married Women in the Labor Force: An Economic Analysis*. Chicago: University of Chicago Press, 1966.

Caldwell, B.M., C.M. Wright, A.S. Honig, and J. Tannenbaum. "Infant Care and Attachment." *American Journal of Orthopsychiatry* 40 (1970): 397–412.

Campbell, J.D. "The Child in the Sick Role: Contributions of Age, Sex, Parental Status and Parental Values." *Journal of Health and Social Behavior* 19 (1978): 35–51.

Card, J.J., L. Steel, and R.P. Abeles. "Sex Differences in Realization of Individual Potential for Achievement." *Journal of Vocational Behavior* 17 (1980): 1–21.

Cawsey, T., and W. Wedley. "Labor Turnover Costs: Measurement and Control." *Personnel Journal* (February 1979): 90–92.

Cazenave, N.A. "Middle-Income Black Fathers." *Family Coordinator* 28 (1979): 583–93.

Chiswick, C.U. "The Value of a Housewife's Time." *Journal of Human Resources* 17 (1982): 413–25.

Chodorow, N. *The Reproduction of Mothering*. Berkeley, Calif.: University of California Press, 1978.

Chodorow, N., and S. Contratta. "The Fantasy of the Perfect Mother." In *Rethinking the Family: Some Feminist Views*, edited by B. Thorne. New York: Longman, 1981.

Clark, R.A., F.I. Nye, and V. Gecas. "Work Involvement and Marital Role Performance." *Journal of Marriage and the Family* 40 (1978): 9–22.

Clarke-Stewart, A. *Daycare*. Cambridge, Mass.: Harvard University Press, 1982.

Collins, N.M. *Business and Child Care Handbook*. Minneapolis: Greater Minneapolis Day Care Association, 1982.

Condran, J.G., and J.G. Bode. "Rashomon, Working Wives, and Family Division of Labor: Middletown, 1980." *Journal of Marriage and the Family* 44 (1982): 421–26.

Cowan, R.S. *More Work for Mother*. New York: Basic Books, 1983.

Crosby, F. *Relative Deprivation and Working Women*. New York: Oxford University Press, 1982.

Cummings, E. "Caregiver Stability and Day Care." *Developmental Psychology* 16 (1980): 31–37.

Davidson, L., and L.K. Gordon. *The Sociology of Gender*. Chicago: Rand McNally, 1979.

Degler, C.N. *At Odds: Women and the Family in America from the Revolution to the Present*. New York: Oxford University Press, 1980.

Demos, J. "The American Family in Past Time." *American Scholar* 43 (1974): 422–46.

Dilks, C. "Employers Who Help with the Kids: Providing Child-Care Benefits Can Benefit the Company Too." *Nation's Business* (February 1984): 59–60.

Douglas, J. *Dollars and Sense: Employer-Supported Child Care*. Washington, D.C.: Office of Child Development, 1976.

Duncan, R.P., and C. Perrucci. "Dual Occupation Families and Migration." *American Sociological Review* 41 (1978): 252–61.

Dyer, W. "The Interlocking of Work and Family Social Systems Among Lower Occupational Families." *Social Forces* 34 (1956): 230–33.

Ehrenreich, B. "Life Without Father: Reconsidering Socialist-Feminist Theory." *Socialist Review* 14 (1984): 48–57.

Ehrenreich, B., and D. English. *Complaints and Disorders*. New York: Faculty Press, 1973.

Emlen, A.C., and P.E. Koren. *Hard to Find and Difficult to Manage: The Effects of Childcare on the Workplace*. Portland, Oreg.: The Workplace Partnership, 1984.

Epstein, C.F. "Law Partners and Marital Partners: Strains and Solutions in the Dual-Career Family Enterprise." *Human Relations* 24 (1971): 549–63.

———. *Women's Place: Options and Limits in Professional Careers*. Berkeley, Calif.: University of California Press, 1970.

Erlanger, H.S. "Social Class and Corporal Punishment in Childrearing: A Reassessment." *American Sociological Review* 39 (1974): 68–85.

Erler, G., M. Jaeckel, and J. Sass. *Results of the European Study Concerning Maternity Leave/Parental Leave/Home Care Support in Finland, Sweden, Hungary, Austria, and German Federal Republic*. Munich, Germany: Deutsches Jugerdenstitut, October 1982.

Etaugh, C. "Effects of Nonmaternal Care on Children: Research Evidence and Popular Views." *American Psychologist* 35 (1980): 309–19.

Farrell, M.P., and S. Rosenberg. *Men at Midlife*. Boston: Auburn House, 1981.

Farrell, W. *The Liberated Man*. New York: Random House, 1974.

Farris, A. "Commuting." In *Working Couples*, edited by R. Rapoport and R.N. Rapoport. New York: Harper & Row, 1978.

Feinstein, K.W. *Working Women and Families*. Beverly Hills, Calif.: Sage Publications, 1979.

Fernandez, J.P. *Racism and Sexism in Corporate Life: Changing Values in American Business*. Lexington, Mass.: D.C. Heath, 1981.

———. *Black Managers in White Corporations*. New York: Wiley & Sons, 1975.

Ford, G. "Childcare Is for Everybody." *Parade Magazine* (October 23, 1983): 15–16.

Freeman R.B. "The Work Force in the Future: An Overview." In *Work in America: The Decade Ahead*, edited by C. Kerr and J.M. Rosow. New York: Van Nostrand Reinhold, 1979.

Friedman, D.E. *State and Local Strategies Promoting Employer Supported Child Care.* New York: Center for Public Advocacy Research, 1983.

Fox, M.F., and S. Hesse-Biber. *Women at Work.* Palo Alto, Calif.: Mayfield Publishing Co., 1984.

Galinsky, E. "Business and the Parent Workforce: Profit and Productivity." *Family Resource Coalition* 3, no. 3 (1984): 1–16.

The General Mills American Family Report, 1980–81. Families at Work: Strengths and Strains. Minneapolis: General Mills, Inc., 1981.

Giele, J. "Changing Sex Roles and the Future of Marriage." In *Contemporary Marriage: Structure, Dynamics and Therapy*, edited by H. Grunebaum and J. Christs. Boston: Little, Brown, 1976.

Giele, J., and A. Smock. *Women: Roles and Status in Eight Countries.* New York: John Wiley & Sons, 1977.

Gilbreth, L. *The Homemaker and Her Jobs.* New York: D. Appleton & Company, 1929.

Glenn, N.D., and C.N. Weaver. "A Multivariate, Multisurvey Study of Marital Happiness." *Journal of Marriage and the Family* 40 (1978): 269–82.

Gold, D., and D. Andres. "Developmental Comparisons Between 10-Year-Old Children with Employed and Non-Employed Mothers." *Child Development* 49 (1978): 75–84.

————. "Relations Between Maternal Employment and Development of Nursery School Children." *Canadian Journal of Behavior Science* 10 (1978): 116–29.

Goldberg, H. *The Hazards of Being Male.* New York: New American Library, 1976.

Goode, W.J. "Why Men Resist." In *Rethinking the Family*, edited by B. Thorne and M. Yalom. New York: Longman, 1982.

Goodman, E. "Observations on Parenting and the Women's Movement." In The National Institute of Education, *Parenthood in a Changing Society*, Urbana, Ill.: ERIC Clearing House on Elementary and Early Childhood Education, University of Illinois (1980): 4–7.

Gove, W.R., and M.R. Geerken. "The Effect of Children and Employment on the Mental Health of Married Men and Women." *Social Forces* 58 (1977): 66–76.

Greenblatt, B. *Responsibility for Child Care.* San Francisco: Jossey-Bass, 1978.

Greif, G.L. *Single Fathers.* Lexington, Mass.: Lexington Books, 1985.

Greywolf, E. *The Single Mother's Handbook.* New York: Quill, 1984.

Gronau, R. "The Effect of Children on the Housewife's Value of Time." *Journal of Political Economy Supplement* 81 (1973): 168–99.

Gronseth, E. "The Breadwinner Trap." In *The Future of the Family*, edited by L.K. Howe. New York: Simon & Schuster, 1972.

Hagen, E. "Child Care and Women's Liberation." In *Child Care—Who Cares?* edited by P. Roby. New York: Basic Books, 1975.

Hall, F.S., and D.T. Hall. *The Two-Career Couple.* Reading, Mass.: Addison-Wesley, 1979.

Hamner, T.J., and P.H. Turner. *Parenting in Contemporary Society.* Englewood Cliffs, N.J.: Prentice-Hall, 1985.

Handy, C. "The Family: Help or Hindrance?" In *Stress at Work*, edited by C.L. Cooper and R. Payne. New York: John Wiley & Sons, 1978.

———. "Going Against the Grain: Working Couples and Greedy Occupations." In *Working Couples*, edited by R. Rapoport and R.N. Rapoport. New York: Harper & Row, 1978.

Hannan, M.T. "Families, Markets, and Social Structures: An Essay on Becker's *A Treatise on the Family*." *Journal of Economic Literature* 20 (1982): 65–72.

Hansen, D.A., and V.A. Johnson. "Rethinking Family Stress Theory." In *Contemporary Theories About the Family, Volume 1*, edited by W. Burr, R. Hill, I. Reiss, and F.I. Nye. New York: Free Press, 1979.

Hayghe, H. "Dual-Earner Families." In *Two Paychecks: Life in Dual Earner Families*, edited by J. Aldous. Beverly Hills, Calif.: Sage Publications, 1982.

———. "Families and the Rise of Working Wives: An Overview." *Monthly Labor Review* 99, no. 5 (1976): 12–19.

Henze, D.L. *Equity in Family Work Role Among Dual Career Couples: The Relationship of Demographic Socioeconomic, Attitudinal and Personality Factors.* Minneapolis: University of Minnesota Press, 1984.

Hofferth, S.L. "Day Care in the Next Decade: 1980–1990." *Journal of Marriage and the Family* 41 (1979): 649–58.

Hoffman, L.W. *The Study of Employed Mothers Over Half a Century.* Paper presented at the Annual Meeting of the American Psychological Association, Los Angeles, 1983.

———. "Effects of Maternal Employment on the Child: A Review of Research." *Developmental Psychology* (1974): 204–28.

———. "Effects on Child." In *Working Mothers*, edited by L.W. Hoffman and F.I. Nye. San Francisco: Jossey-Bass, 1974.

Hoffman, L.W., and F.I. Nye, eds. *Working Mothers.* San Francisco: Jossey-Bass, 1975.

Hoffman, W. "Maternal Employment: 1979." *American Psychologist* 34, no. 10 (October 1979): 859–65.

Holahan, C.K., and L.A. Gilbert. "Conflict Between Major Life Roles: Women and Men in Dual Career Couples." *Human Relations* 32, no. 6 (1979): 451–67.

Holmstrom, L.L. *The Two-Career Family.* Cambridge, Mass.: Schenkman, 1972.

Hopkins, J., and P. White. "The Dual-Career Couple: Constraints and Supports." *Family Coordinator* 27 (1978): 253–59.

———. "Dilemmas and Contradictions of Status: The Case of the Dual-Career Family." *Social Problems*, 24, (1977): 407–16.

Hunt, J.G., and L.L. Hunt. "Dual-Career Families: Vanguard of the Future or Residue of the Past?" In *Two Paychecks: Life in Dual-Earner Families*, edited by J. Aldous. Beverly Hills, Calif.: Sage Publications, 1982.

Immerwahr. J. "Building a Consensus on the Child Care Problem." *Personnel Administrator* (February 1984): 31–37.

Janeway, E. *Man's World, Woman's Place.* New York: Dell, 1971.

Johnson, C.L., and F.A. Johnson. "Parenthood, Marriage and Careers: Situational Constraints and Role Strain." In *Dual-Career Couples*, edited by Fran Pepitone-Rockwell. Beverly Hills, Calif.: Sage Publications, 1980.

———. "Attitudes Toward Parenting in Dual-Career Families." *American Journal of Psychiatry* 134 (1977): 391–95.

_____ . "Role Strain in High-Commitment Career Women." *Journal of American Academy of Psychoanalysis* 4 (1976): 13–36.

Jorgensen, S. "Socioeconomic Rewards and Perceived Marital Quality: A Re-Examination." *Journal of Marriage and the Family* 41 (November 1979): 825–35.

Kamerman, S.B., and A.J. Kahn. *Child Care, Family Benefits and Working Parents: A Study in Comparative Policy.* New York: Columbia University Press, 1981.

Kamerman, S.B., and C.D. Hayes, eds. *Families That Work: Children in a Changing World.* Washington, D.C.: National Academy Press, 1982.

Kamerman, S.B., and A.J. Kahn, eds. *Family Policy: Government and Families in Fourteen Countries.* New York: Columbia University Press, 1978.

Kanter, R.M. "Jobs and Families: Impact of Working Roles on Family Life." *Children Today* (March/April 1978): 11–16.

_____ . *Men and Women of the Corporation.* New York: Basic Books, 1977.

_____ . *Work and Family in the United States: A Critical Review and Agenda for Research and Policy.* New York: Russell Sage, 1977.

Kember, T.D., and M.L. Reichler. "Work Integration, Marital Satisfaction and Conjugal Power." *Human Relations* 29 (October 1976): 929–44.

Kerr, V. One Step Forward—Two Steps Back: Child Care's Long American History." In *Child Care—Who Cares?*, edited by P. Roby. New York: Basic Books, 1975.

Lacey, D. "Exploring the Potential of Decentralized Work Settings." *Personnel Administrator* 29 (1984): 48–52.

Lakein, A. *How to Get Control of Your Time and Work Life.* New York: Signet Books, 1973.

Lamb, M.E. *The Role of the Father in Child Development.* New York: John Wiley & Sons, 1975.

Lamb, M.E., A.M. Frodi, C.P. Hwang, and M. Frodi. "Varying Degrees of Paternal Involvement in Infant Care: Attitudinal and Behavioral Correlates" and "The Perception of the Role of the Father." In *The Role of the Father in Child Development.* New York: John Wiley & Sons, 1982.

Lane, N.M., R.H. Todd, J. Roberts, and G. Miller. *Study of Employer Cost Benefit.* Raleigh, N.C.: Work Place Options, August 1983.

Leggon, C.B. "Black Female Professionals: Dilemmas and Contradictions of Status." In *The Black Woman*, edited by La Frances Rodgers-Rose. Beverly Hills, Calif.: Sage Publications, 1980.

Lerman, S. *Parent Awareness: Positive Parenting in the 1980s.* Minneapolis: Winston Press, 1980.

Levine, J. *Day Care and the Public Schools.* Newton, Mass.: Educational Development Corporation, 1978.

_____ . *Who Will Raise the Children?* New York: Bantam Books, 1976.

Lewis, H.B. *Psychic War in Men and Women.* New York: University Press, 1976.

Locksley, A. "On the Effects of Wives' Employment on Marital Adjustment and Companionship." *Journal of Marriage and the Family* 42 (1980): 337–46.

Long, L. *On My Own: The Kids' Self Care Book.* Washington, D.C.: Acropolis Books, 1984.

Long, L., and T. Long. *The Handbook For Latchkey Children and Their Parents.* New York: Arbor House, 1983.

Lorber, J. "Beyond Equality of the Sexes: The Question of Children." In *Marriage and Family in a Changing Society*, edited by J. Henslin. New York: Free Press, 1980.

Magid, R.Y. *Child Care Initiatives for Working Parents: Why Employers Get Involved.* New York: AMA Membership Publications Division, American Management Associations, 1983.

Manser, M., and M. Brown. "Marriage and Household Decision-Making: A Bargaining Analysis." *International Economic Review* 21 (1980): 31–44.

Martin, T.W., K.W. Berry, and R.B. Jacobsen. "The Impact of Dual-Career Marriages on Female Professional Careers." *Journal of Marriage and Family* 37 (1975): 734–42.

Masnick, G., and M.J. Bane. *The Nation's Families 1960–1990*. Cambridge, Mass.: Joint Center for Urban Studies of M.I.T. and Harvard University, 1980.

McCartney, K. et al. "Environmental Differences Among Day Care Centers and Their Effects on Children's Development." In *Day Care*, edited by E.F. Zigler and E.W. Gordon. Boston: Auburn House, 1982.

McCroskey, J. "Work and Families: What Is the Employer's Responsibility?" *Personnel Journal* (January 1982): 30–38.

McMillan, I. "Pennsylvania Asked to Spend $94 Million More on Women's Issues." *Philadelphia Inquirer* (March 9, 1985): 3.

Merrill, J., and D.W. Gross. *Monday through Friday: Day Care Alternatives*. New York: Teachers College Press, 1982.

Miller, S.M. "The Making of a Confused, Middle-Aged Husband." In *Toward a Sociology of Women*, edited by C. Safilios-Rothschild. Lexington, Mass.: Xerox College Publishing, 1972.

Miller, T.I. "The Effects of Employer-Sponsored Child Care on Employee Absenteeism, Turnover, Productivity, Recruitment or Job Satisfaction: What Is Claimed and What Is Known." *Personnel Psychology* 37 (1984): 277–89.

Mitchell, J. *Woman's Estate*. New York: Pantheon Books, 1971.

Molnar, J.M. *The Differential Effects of Group and Family Day Care: An Observational Study in Home and Day Care Settings*. Ithaca, N.Y.: Cornell University Press, 1984.

Moore, K.A., and I.V. Sawhill. "Implications of Women's Employment for Home and Family Life." In *Women Working: Theories and Facts in Perspective*, edited by A.H. Stanley and S. Harkness. Palo Alto, Calif.: Mayfield Publishing Co., 1978.

Mortimer, J.T. "Dual Career Families—A Sociological Perspective." In *The Two Career Family: Issues and Alternatives*, edited by S.S. Peterson, J.M. Richardson, and G.V. Kreuter. Washington, D.C.: University Press of America, 1978.

Mortimer, J.T., and J. London. "The Varying Linkages of Work and Family." In *Work, and Family*, edited by P. Voydanoff. Palo Alto, Calif.: Mayfield Publishing Co., 1976.

Nadelson, C.C., and T. Nadelson. "Dual-Career Marriages: Benefits and Costs." In *Dual-Career Couples*, edited by Fran Pepitone-Rockwell. Beverly Hills, Calif.: Sage Publications, 1980.

Nollen, S.D., and V.H. Martin. *Alternative Work Schedules. Part 1: Flextime, an AMA Survey Report*. New York: American Management Association, 1978.

Norris, G., and J. Miller. *The Working Mother's Complete Handbook*. New York: New American Library, 1984.

Olson, J.T. "The Impact of Housework on Child Care in the Home." *Family Relations* 30 (1981): 75–81.

Orden, S.R., and N.M. Bradburn. "Working Wives and Marriage Happiness." *American Journal of Sociology* 74 (1969): 391–407.

Papanek, H. "Family Status Production: The 'Work' and 'Non-Work' of Women." *Signs* 4 (1979): 775–81.

Pepitone-Rockwell, F., ed. *Dual-Career Couples*. Beverly Hills, Calif.: Sage Publications, 1980.

Peterson, S.S., J.M. Richardson, and G.V. Kreuter. *The Two-Career Family: Issues and Alternatives*. Washington, D.C.: University Press of America, 1978.

Pleck, J.H. "The Work-Family Problem: Overloading the System." In *Outsiders on the Inside: Women and Organizations*, edited by B.L. Forisha and B.H. Goldman. Englewood Cliffs, N.J.: Prentice-Hall, 1981.

————. "Men's Family Work: Three Perspectives and Some New Data." *The Family Coordinator* 28 (1979): 481-88.

————. "The Work-Family Role System." *Social Problems* 24 (1977): 417-27.

Pleck, J.H., and G.L. Staines. "Work Schedules and Work-Family Conflict in Two-Earner Couples." In *Two Paychecks: Life in Dual-Earner Families*, edited by J. Aldous. Beverly Hills, Calif.: Sage Publications, 1982.

Poloma, M.M., and T.N. Garland. "The Married Professional Woman: A Study of the Tolerance of Domestication." *Journal of Marriage and the Family* 33 (1971): 531-40.

Poloma, M.M., B.F. Pendleton, and T.N. Garland. "Reconsidering the Dual Career Marriage." *Journal of Family Issues* 2 (1981): 205-24.

Provence, S. "Infant Day Care: Relationships Between Theory and Practice." In *Day Care: Scientific and Social Policy Issues*, edited by E.F. Zigler and E.W. Gordon. Boston: Auburn House, 1982.

Provence, S., A. Naylor, and J. Patterson. *The Challenge of Day Care*. New Haven: Yale University Press, 1977.

Quinn, R.P., and G.L. Staines. *The 1977 Quality of Employment Survey*. Ann Arbor, Mich.: Inter-University Consortium for Political and Social Research, 1979.

Rapoport, R., and R.N. Rapoport. "Three Generations of Dual-Career Family Research." In *Dual Career Couples*, edited by F. Pepitone-Rockwell. Beverly Hills, Calif.: Sage Publications, 1980.

————. *Dual-Career Families Re-Examined*. New York: Harper & Row, 1976.

————. "The Dual Career Family: A Variant Pattern and Social Change." In *Toward a Sociology of Women*, edited by C. Safilios-Rothschild. Lexington, Mass.: Xerox, 1972.

————. *Dual-Career Families*. New York: Penguin, 1971.

————. "The Dual-Career Family: A Variant Pattern and Social Change." *Human Relations* 22 (1969): 2-30.

————. "Work and Family in Modern Society." *American Sociological Review* 30 (1965): 381-94.

Rapoport, R., R.N. Rapoport, and V. Thiessen. "Couple Symmetry and Enjoyment." *Journal of Marriage and the Family* 36 (1974): 588-91.

Rice, D. *Dual-Career Marriage: Conflict and Treatment*. New York: Free Press, 1979.

Richardson, J.G. "Wife Occupational Superiority and Marital Troubles: An Examination of the Hypothesis." *Journal of Marriage and the Family* 41 (1979): 63–72.

Ridley, C.A. "Exploring the Impact of Work Satisfaction and Involvement on Marital Interaction When Both Partners Are Employed." *Journal of Marriage and the Family* 35 (1973): 229–37.

Ritzer, G. *Working: Conflict and Change*. Englewood Cliffs, N.J.: Prentice-Hall, 1977.

Roby, P. "What Other Nations Are Doing." In *Child Care—Who Cares?* edited by P. Roby. New York: Basic Books, 1975.

Rodman, H. "How Children Take Care of Themselves." *Working Mother* (July 1980): 61–63.

Romaine, M.F. "Zale's Corporate Child Care Problems." *The Texas Business Executive* (Spring/Summer 1982): 20–25

Rosenfeld, R.A. "Women's Intergenerational Occupational Mobility." *American Sociological Review* 43 (1978): 36–46.

Rothman, S.M. *Woman's Proper Place: A History of Changing Ideals and Practices, 1870 to the Present*. New York: Basic Books, 1978.

Rubenstein, J.L., and C. Howes. "Caregiving and Infant Behavior in Day Care and in Homes." *Developmental Psychology* 15 (1979): 1–24.

Rubin, R.S. "Flextime: Its Implementation in the Public Sector." *Public Administrative Review* 39 (1979): 277–82.

Ruopp, R.R., and J. Travers. "Janus Faces Day Care: Perspectives on Quality and Cost." In *Day Care: Scientific and Social Policy Issues*, edited by E.F. Zigler and E.W. Gordon. Boston: Auburn House, 1982.

Russell, G. "Shared-Caregiving Families: An Australian Study." In *Nontraditional Families: Parenting and Child Development*, edited by M. Lamb. Hillsdale, N.J.: Erlbaum, 1982.

Rutter, M. "Social-Emotional Consequences of Day Care for Preschool Children." In *Day Care: Scientific and Social Policy Issues*, edited by E.F. Zigler and E.W. Gordon. Boston: Auburn House, 1982.

Ryan, M.P. *Womanhood in America: From Colonial Times to the Present*. New York: New Viewpoints, 1975.

Scarr, S.S. *Mother Care: Other Care*. New York: Basic Books, 1984.

Siegel-Gorelick, B. *The Working Parents' Guide to Child Care*. Boston: Little, Brown, 1983.

Simpson, I.H., and E. Mutran. "Women's Social Consciousness: Sex or Worker Identity." In *Research on the Sociology of Work, Volume I*, edited by R.L. Simpson and I.H. Simpson. Greenwich, Conn.: JAL, 1981.

Sinclair, U. *The Jungle*. New York: New American Library, 1906.

Skinner, D.A. "Dual Career Family, Stress and Coping: A Literature Review." In *Work and Family*, edited by P. Voyandoff. Palo Alto, Calif.: Mayfield Publishing Co., 1984.

Slocum, W., and F. Nye. "Provider and Housekeeper Roles." In *Role Structure and Analysis of the Family*, edited by F. Nye. Beverly Hills, Calif.: Sage Publications, 1976.

Snyder, D.K. "Multidimensional Assessment of Marital Satisfaction." *Journal of Marriage and the Family* 41 (1979): 813–23.

Stafford, F.P. "Women's Use of Time Converging With Men's." *Monthly Labor Review* 103 (1980): 57–79.

Stein, S. "The Company Cares for Children." In *Child Care—Who Cares?* edited by P. Roby. New York: Basic Books, 1973.

Steinfels, M.O. *Who's Minding the Children? The History and Politics of Day Care in America.* New York: Simon & Schuster, 1973.

Tavris, C., and C. Wade. *The Longest War: Sex Differences in Perspective,* (2d ed.). New York: Harcourt Brace Jovanovich, 1984.

Taylor, M.G., and S. Hartley. "The Two-Person Career: A Classic Example." *Sociology of Work and Occupations* 2 (1975): 354–72.

Terman, L.M. *Psychological Factors in Marital Happiness.* New York: McGraw-Hill, 1938.

Timmins, W.M. "Day Care Programs and Public Employees: A New Initiative and Direction for Public Personnel Systems." *Public Personnel Management* 11 (Fall 1982): 256–67.

Travers, J.R. *Research Results of the National Day Care Study: Final Report of the National Day Care Study.* Cambridge, Mass.: Abbott Books, 1980.

Turner, C. "Dual Work Households and Marital Dissolution." *Human Relations* 24 (1971): 535–48.

U.S. Comptroller General. "Benefits From Flexible Work Schedules—Legal Limitations Remain." In *Report to the Congress: EPCD-78-62.* Washington, D.C.: General Accounting Office, 1977.

Vanek, J.J. "Household Work, Wage Work and Sexual Equality." In *Women and Household Labor,* edited by S.F. Berk. Beverly Hills, Calif.: Sage Publications, 1977.

———. "Housewives as Workers." In *Women Working,* edited by A.H. Stromberg and S. Karkess. Palo Alto, Calif.: Mayfield Publishing Co., 1977.

———. "Time Spent in Housework." *Scientific American* (November 1974): 116–20.

Voydanoff, P., ed. *Work and Family.* Palo Alto, Calif.: Mayfield Publishing Co., 1984.

Wachs, T.D., and G.E. Gruen. *Early Experience and Human Development.* New York: Plenum Press, 1982.

Wade, M. *Flexible Working Hours in Practice.* East Kilbride, Scotland: Gower, 1973.

Waite, L.J. "Working Wives and Family Life Cycle." *American Journal of Sociology* 85 (1980): 272–94.

Waldholz, M. "Cafeteria Plans Let Employees Fill Their Plates, Then Pay with Tax-Free Dollars." *Wall Street Journal* (May 9, 1983): 58.

Walker, K.E. "Time Spent in Household Work by Homemakers." *Family Economics Review* 3 (1979): 5–6.

———. "Time Spent by Husbands in Household Work." *Family Economic Review* 4 (1970): 8–11.

Walker, K.E., and M.E. Woods. *Time Use: A Measure of Household Production of Family Goods and Services.* Washington, D.C.: American Home Economics Association, 1976.

Walker, K.E., and W. Gauger. "Time and Its Dollar Value in Household Work." *Family Economics Review* 7 (1973): 8–13.

Wallace, P. *Black Women in the Labor Force.* Cambridge, Mass. M.I.T. Press, 1980.

Watson, J. *Psychological Care of Infant and Child.* New York: Norton, 1928.

Webb, N.B. *Preschool Children With Working Parents: An Analysis of Attachment Relationships.* Lanham: University Press of America, 1984.

White, M.S. "Women in the Professions: Psychological and Social Barriers to Women in Science." In *Women: A Feminist Perspective*, edited by J. Freeman. Palo Alto, Calif.: Mayfield Publishing Co., 1979.

Wines, L. "Company Day Care and the Bottom Line." *Working Mother* (October 1981): 149–54.

Wright, J.D. "Are Working Women Really More Satisfied: Evidence from Several National Surveys." *Journal of Marriage and the Family* 40 (1978): 301–14.

Youngblood, S.A., and D.C. Cook. "Child Care Assistance Can Improve Employee Attitudes and Behaviors." *Personnel Administrator* (February 1984): 45–46, 93–95.

Zigler, E.F., and J. Goodman. "The Battle For Day Care in America: A View From the Trenches." In E.F. Zigler and E.W. Gordon, ed., *Day Care*. Boston: Auburn House, 1982.

Zigler, E.F., and E.W. Gordon, eds. *Day Care: Scientific and Social Policy Issues.* Boston: Auburn House, 1982.

Zigler, M.E. *Assessing Parents' and Children's Time Together.* Paper presented at the Annual Meeting of The Society for Research in Child Development. Detroit, 1983.

Index

About the Author

John P. Fernandez is division manager of Personnel Services, AT&T Communications Headquarters Region. In addition, he is president of Advance Research Management Consultants, and he teaches part-time at the University of Pennsylvania. He was previously a manager of education and development at AT&T and an assistant professor of sociology at Yale University. Dr. Fernandez has also served as operations manager for a large, multidepartment division of Bell of Pennsylvania. He received his A.B. magna cum laude from Harvard University and his Ph.D. from the University of California, Berkeley. He has written two previous books, *Black Manager in White Corporations* and *Racism and Sexism in Corporate Life: Changing Values in American Business.*